Miss Le Vane has been unduly flattering about myself and my collection. I can only hope that since the Ranch Museum is now open to the public, those who visit it will enjoy seeing the works of art as much as I have enjoyed acquiring them

J. Paul Getty.

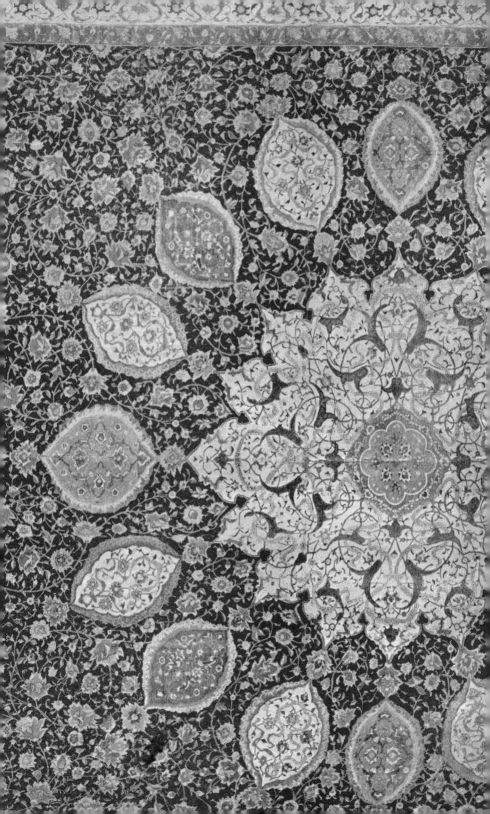

Collector's Choice

ETHEL Le VANE

J. PAUL GETTY

Collector's Choice

THE CHRONICLE OF AN ARTISTIC ODYSSEY

THROUGH EUROPE

W. H. ALLEN

LONDON

First published September 1955
Reprinted January 1956

Printed and bound in England by The Camelot Press Limited, Southampton
for the publishers, W. H. Allen
Essex Street, London, W.C.2

Contents

We would like to express our thanks to Mr. Bernard Berenson for graciously permitting the description of a first visit to his unique *I Tatti*.

THE AUTHORS.

List of Illustrations

7

List of Illustrations

The front endpaper shows a section of the famed Ardabil carpet in the Getty Collection

· I ·

The Marten Looten

T HE boat-train from Southampton was over an hour late arriving at Waterloo Station. One of London's famed November fogs blanketed the city and its environs. A tall, loose-limbed American peered out of his compartment window. "A traditional British welcome," he observed. Swiftly and decisively he secured a porter, and tipped the man generously.

"Taxi, sir?" the porter beamed and, helping the traveller and his two suitcases into a creaking automobile asked: "Where to, sir?"

"Dorchester 'Otel?" the taxi-driver queried. "You mean Dorchester 'Ouse."

"No, I don't want Dorchester House. I want the Dorchester Hotel," the American replied firmly. The middle-aged Cockney taxi-driver pressed down the accelerator and his taxicab responded with a jerk which caused its passenger to sit squarely back in his seat. Soon, however, traffic slowed down to a crawl, and the driver peered enquiringly at his fare. "An interestin' lookin' gent," he thought. "Soberly dressed, too, for a Yank. No dazzlin' bright necktie like so many of them wear—real shockers. Could almost be mistaken for an Englishman, 'e could, except for 'is twang. But then any English gentleman would 'ave known that Dorchester 'Ouse and the Dorchester 'Otel was one and the same place."

As traffic moved forward at snail's pace the taxi-driver became garrulous.

"When I was a nipper, Dorchester 'Ouse was one of

London's great town 'ouses," he said. "A beauty, too, she was! I just 'ated to see 'er bein' pulled down to make way for that luxury 'otel. Every time one of them ancestral 'omes goes it seems to me that another bit of old England's gone. Me and the missus—we like to stroll round the old squares, and see them lovely big 'ouses and watch the gentry come and go. At the rate London's movin' everything'll soon be flats, or office buildin's, or 'otels."

His emphasis of the latter caused the American to smile and think: "This guy seems to have a down on 'otels." The loquacious taxi-driver continued:

"I'm afraid old England's in for a bad time—I don't 'old with Chamberlain and that Munich Pact. 'Itler's a bad egg. 'E needs puttin' in 'is place *now*, I says."

Traffic lights, changing from red to green, pierced the sooty fog and absorbed the driver's attention. Thankfully, his passenger relaxed. Accustomed to American taxi-drivers and their spontaneous and uninvited conversation, this was the first time he had encountered a talkative cabbie in England: always polite, they were generally more taciturn than friendly.

With a feeling of relief that they had reached their destination without mishap the American entered London's Dorchester Hotel. Its warm, brightly lit interior, scented with mingled perfumes from the florist's stand, gay with magazines on the newstand, made a luxurious contrast to the misty exterior.

He checked in, and was shown to an attractive suite of rooms on the fourth floor, overlooking Hyde Park. Several messages and telegrams awaited him. He unpacked, took a warm shower, changed his clothes; refreshed, he was leisurely reading his correspondence when the Dutchman arrived. The two men greeted each other cordially.

"It's a pleasure to see you again, sir. You look well—as fit as ever."

"So do you, Mueller."

His visitor had changed little in appearance during their many years of acquaintanceship, thought the American. Short and corpulent, his round face and frank grey eyes blinking owlishly from behind frameless spectacles, belied his shrewd 'art dealer and critic' reputation. Only his hair was noticeably different, it had thinned almost to baldness.

"One can't cheat time," Mueller observed with a philosophical nod. "I'm losing my hair and adding to my girth; typically Dutch."

The American suppressed a smile: Mueller so obviously epitomized the universal idea of a typical Dutchman—blond, bland, pot-bellied and serene.

In turn the art dealer mentally appraised his client. Of similar age—both were in their middle forties—he contrasted the other man's athletic five feet eleven with his own stocky five feet six, and decided that Nature had not endowed him as generously as she might have done.

The American's hair was still plentiful, but a sprinkling of grey was now evident among the light-brown. Strong facial bone-structure accentuated his features into a lean, clean-cut profile. Of almost mask-like coldness, his face bore a preoccupied and serious expression until he smiled.

Mueller wondered why his client's smile was so infrequent. Transforming that first impression of a stern and even forbidding character, a boyish quality revealed itself. The light blue eyes widened and took on all the keenness of their native Mid-West. Undoubtedly the American was a complex individual, sensitive though of inflexible purpose.

"So we got it, Mueller!"

"Yes, sir. The 'Marten Looten' is now yours for the sum of one hundred and two thousand guilders—exactly sixty-five thousand dollars."

"How much did Mensing pay for it at the Holford sale?"

13

"Three hundred and thirty thousand guilders."

"Ummm-m," the American mused. "I authorized you to bid higher—if necessary—because the experts believed it would sell for at least a hundred thousand dollars. I wonder why it didn't fetch more? Was the bidding brisk?"

"Just the reverse, sir. Godesberg has been a severe scare; war seemed imminent. Frankly, if the 'Night Watch' itself had been up for auction I doubt whether that masterpiece would have brought fifty per cent. of its true value."

His companion smiled wryly. "Yet they'll probably yell long and loud when they discover that another 'Rembrandt' has gone to America. People usually wake up after their horse has quit its stable! Mensing—with the best of intentions couldn't persuade your Government to acquire this treasure."

The Dutch art dealer shrugged his shoulders with resignation. "Anton Mensing owned the Looten portrait for ten years; his lifelong ambition was to restore Holland's treasures to Holland. He, personally, tried to buy back many important paintings which had left the Netherlands. According to rumour he succeeded only in this one instance. Incidentally this hotel was formerly the Holford town house. During Sir George Lindsay Holford's lifetime this was the home of your Rembrandt."

"Dorchester House, of course! How stupid of me not to realize it." The American related his experience of the voluble cabbie, and then asked: "Wasn't the 'Marten Looten' exhibited in London, also?"

"Yes. After Mensing bought it in '28 it was displayed at an 'Exhibition of Dutch Art' at the Royal Academy. If I recall correctly, that was early in '29."

"Three hundred and thirty thousand guilders ten years ago— today one hundred and two thousand," the American ruminated. "It hardly seems equitable. Yet, who am I—to question? It was an honest sale; you were the highest bidder; and I now own my first Rembrandt. It's an exciting purchase, Mueller.

By the way, did anyone know for whom you were bidding?"

In reply, the Dutchman drew a sheet of newspaper out of his sombre tweed jacket pocket and, translating from Dutch into English, he read aloud:

"That which we are afraid of has become grim reality. Rembrandt's famous portrait of Marten Looten, brought back to this country in 1928 by Anton Mensing, has been purchased, it is said, on behalf of an unnamed American. Must this old Amsterdam figure be doomed to continue its nomadic existence?"

"May I keep this newspaper?"

"Certainly," replied Mueller. "It's true that the Looten has been a wanderer. Where did you first see it, sir?"

"At Boymann's Museum in Rotterdam. Remember the 'Rembrandt Exposition' there? In all, about forty works were displayed. After seeing most of them, I was shown into a smaller, semi-private room where only four paintings hung. These, according to my informant, were outstanding works of art—the choice of the collection. They were very fine, as you can doubtless recall. Of those four, one impressed me forcibly—the Marten Looten portrait. I hadn't followed the history of this canvas, in fact, I was actually seeing it for the first time. For some indefinable reason, that painting haunted me; it has the same magnetic quality of the 'Night Watch'. Once seen, one cannot forget it.

"It's many years since I saw the Looten portrait, yet I remember every detail of it vividly. I've often wondered just why this painting fascinated me, Mueller. Was it Rembrandt's superb artistry? Or was it some unique characteristic of his subject?

"No one seems to be very familiar with Marten Looten or his ancestry. Now that I own the painting, I'd like to investigate its background. I know some of the chronological history of the canvas. It first left Holland over a century ago, was acquired by Napoleon Bonaparte's uncle, Cardinal Fesch—while he was French Ambassador to the Vatican—and when he died in 1845, it was sold with his other possessions.

"In those days it fetched what was considered to be a mighty high price—about four thousand, five hundred dollars. In 1849 the Looten appeared in the Coningham Collection, somewhere near London. One year later the Holfords bought it for the low figure of eight hundred pounds. That family made a handsome profit! Anton Mensing paid twenty-six thousand guineas for the portrait at Christie's auction in 1928. The pendulum of art-values certainly swings to extremes!"

"I was delighted when you cabled me to represent you," the art dealer told his client. "But the war scare which recently swept Europe played havoc with the art-world markets. Most works realized only half of what we expected. All your purchases were good—those seventeenth-century Dutch paintings—Kalf's 'Still Life' and Pickenoy's 'Portrait of an Unknown Lady'. Of course there's only one 'Marten Looten'. Whenever you decide to undertake its investigation, sir, I'd like to offer you my help."

"And I'll gladly accept it, Mueller. Meanwhile, how about joining me for dinner."

The hotel restaurant was filled for the most part with immaculately groomed diners. Observing that the newcomers were not wearing formal evening clothes, the *maître d'hôtel* discreetly seated them at an unobtrusive corner table.

The American commented upon this die-hard British custom of formal dress for dining. He liked it, yet preferred less formality in his own everyday living. Mueller admired the cream-and-gold *décor* of the room, its attractive chandeliers, its conservative *ambience*.

"The Dorchester is a fine hotel," his client concurred. "It's the first time I've stayed here. I'm usually at the Ritz. This is

PORTRAIT OF MARTEN LOOTEN BY REMBRANDT

(Chapter "*The Marten Looten*")

"PORTRAIT OF AN UNKNOWN LADY" BY PICKENOY

(Chapters "Marten Looten" and "The Ranch")

to be a quick trip and I don't particularly want it known that I'm in town; hence my change of address."

He went on to say that he intended loaning his Rembrandt and other paintings from his varied art collection to the World's Fair in New York, an event scheduled to take place early in 1939. The pictures would be displayed at the Arts Pavilion in the section, "Works of Great Masters".

"I understand, sir, you have a superb collection of eighteenth-century French furniture."

"Well, I have a few important pieces, and some beautiful Savonnerie carpets—rare ones. My tapestry collection is, I believe, considered really fine. It includes some of the best Beauvais Bouchers in the world."

"Are you adding to your collection?"

"To some part of it. I've got a few ancient marbles—Greek and early Roman—and some day I'd like to build a small but choice sculpture gallery."

"Any silver?" queried the art dealer with sharpening interest.

"A little—Georgian, mostly. I'm not what you'd call an avid or extensive collector, Mueller. I like to concentrate on choice items of museum quality."

"Will your collection ever be open to the public?"

The American thought before replying. Then he said slowly, "I have loaned some of my treasures to museums and art exhibitions from time to time. The public has seen them on those occasions. Frankly, I've not given much thought to inviting public viewing of my own collection. But maybe—later."

Conversation veered to the controversial topic of how and why art collectors are "born".

"An inherent love of beauty and all things beautiful," the American suggested without hesitation.

The Dutchman smiled and benevolently shrugged his shoulders. "A dealer discovers many reasons, sir. To some, collecting works of art is purely an investment—a business. To others, it means surrounding themselves with rare and

B   17 lovely objects of which they have an intrinsic appreciation yet no classical knowledge whatsoever. Then there's the group who collect only works of great value, irrespective of whether they're beautiful or not. It flatters their ego to possess famous art-objects, and enhances their own importance in the eyes of their friends and associates."

"In my opinion," said the American, "many collectors belong in the category of frustrated artists. They themselves lack creative ability, yet appreciate beauty of symmetry and line—blending of colour. They have a certain sensitivity—an imaginative gift—but no talent for artistic self-expression."

His evaluation was shrewd and deep; he was not—as Mueller had sometimes suspected—merely an individual with acquisitive habits and enough money to indulge his whims. Sincerely appreciative of the arts, he commanded the art dealer's respect.

While they talked the Dutchman's opinion of his client increased in respect. The latter, he now discovered, had recently written a book entitled *Europe in the Eighteenth Century*. And the vast amount of research this subject entailed had added to both his knowledge and understanding of art in general. He could speak several languages and had used his linguistic talent in the study of old, obscure books, often available only in a foreign tongue. In this manner he gained much rare information, beyond the knowledge of even the widely experienced art dealer.

"Where did you learn so many languages?" the Dutchman enquired with mounting interest. "In my experience, Americans attach little importance to foreign languages. Most Europeans are familiar with one other than their native tongue; it's more or less a necessity. But you, sir, I must confess, surprise me."

A fleeting smile brightened his client's face. "I was carried away by the subject, Mueller I'm not usually this talkative. I studied languages at school, and have spent a good deal of time in Europe. My love of artistic expression is, I suppose, inherited from my father. He had an intelligent appreciation of the arts even though he never had much time for collecting. And as you of all people must know, serious collecting takes up one's time."

Conversation returned to the American's recent journey across the Atlantic.

"It was a fair crossing for November—only one rough day. When you cabled me that you'd completed the Rembrandt purchase and would be in London, I had by good fortune to do some business here. A happy coincidence! Now, I'd like nothing better than to extend my visit and go on to Holland where I could explore the Looten background. But it's impossible, this trip.

"All that seems to be known about this painting is that it was Rembrandt's second commissioned portrait. His first, of Nicholaes Ruts, is—as you know—in the Pierpont Morgan collection. There's a lot of data available on Ruts, but scarcely anything on Marten Looten."

"When do you expect to visit Holland, sir?"

"Oh, some time during next year. Possibly in the fall of '39."

The autumn of 1939, however, did not find the art-loving American in Holland. As the Cockney taxi-driver had so grimly prophesied, Old England was in for a bad time. And so was most of Europe. For Prime Minister Neville Chamberlain's much-hoped-for Munich Pact proved a fiasco. World War Two was declared. . . .

It was late August of 1949 when the American arrived in Holland. By arrangement, the Dutchman was on hand to greet his client at Rotterdam. After complying with the necessary Customs and Immigration formalities they drove in Mueller's newly imported Buick car to Amsterdam.

The intervening years had not drastically changed the

physical appearance of either man. The American was still lean of frame and keen of eye, though his hair was greyer at the temples. The Dutchman, rotund as ever, was now almost bald, yet his face was still youthfully untroubled and unlined. The only visible change was an acute nervous blink of his eyes behind their frameless spectacles.

After the American had checked in at the Amstel Hotel, they both sat out of doors on its terrace overlooking the Amstel River, which was alive with tug-boats and all manner of small and medium-sized craft, conveying varied cargo across the city by river and through canals.

"A delightful old city, Amsterdam—Venice of the north! Tell me something about life over here during these past years, Mueller. How was the Occupation?"

The Dutchman shrugged his shoulders. "It was hard, very hard. But it's past history, nowadays. Naturally, it wasn't easy to take. We endured much. For some, the hardships were less bearable than for others. I was one of the lucky ones. An old bachelor is spared the more serious responsibilities of a family man."

He changed the subject so abruptly that his companion did not pursue the matter. The German occupation of his native Holland was obviously a phase of living which Mueller preferred to forget—if he could. So they began to discuss ways and means of investigating the "Marten Looten".

"As you once observed, sir, our Dutch people woke up after their horse had left its stable. Interest in Rembrandt's 'Marten Looten' was revived after the canvas was shipped to the United States. There was, in fact, strong criticism of both the Netherlands' Government and the Rijksmuseum for permitting an 'unnamed American' to acquire this national treasure. It caused much public resentment. In some quarters there's ill-concealed animosity against today's dollar power."

There was a pregnant silence before his companion said quietly:

"I can understand the resentment. Nations like to keep their national treasures. But what a short-sighted policy! Spreading Dutch culture across the world surely enhances Dutch prestige? If the 'Marten Looten' had stayed in Holland, relatively few people would have known it. As it is, hundreds of thousands now have an opportunity of seeing it. The painting has been shown at the New York World's Fair, the Metropolitan Museum in New York City, the Chicago Art Institute in Chicago, and now it's at the Los Angeles Museum in Southern California. I wonder when Europeans will stop thinking of Americans as Red Indians or Wild West cowboys; as an uncultured, uncultivated people? We're young; but we're learning, Mueller. And fast! Art, like music, is universal. It's meant to be shared, not hoarded."

It was the first time the art dealer had seen his client angry or on the defensive. "I'm sorry," he apologized. "I thought it better to inform you of the facts."

"It's a natural reaction, I suppose. Let's go over to the Rijksmuseum before it closes." The American was still smarting and abrupt.

The Rijksmuseum buzzed with the chatter of people of many nationalities. American and English, however, appeared to dominate this tourist invasion. In the large gallery, where Rembrandt's famed "Night Watch" was displayed, a party of schoolchildren giggled. They were reprimanded by a teacher accompanying them.

"It's magnificent, simply magnificent!" the American exclaimed. "Whenever I see this painting I feel that I'd trade my entire collection just to own this single masterpiece."

"One of the Netherlands' greatest treasures," the Dutchman said proudly.

They walked through and around some of the other

21

galleries, admiring "Syndics of the Cloth Hall," which symbolized Rembrandt's third period (having been acclaimed as its most successful contribution), and the sombre but beautiful "Jewish Bride" before returning to again look at the "Night Watch," which was painted in Rembrandt's middle, or second period.

This picture had recently been cleaned, and a new angle of lighting showed it to the best advantage. The giggling schoolchildren had left, and there were now only three or four people in the gallery. They, too, gazed reverently upon the master work.

Art dealer and client both agreed that this portrait and the "Marten Looten" held the same "magic". Although painted in different periods of Rembrandt's career—the "Looten" helped him to fame, the "Night Watch" marked his decline—the mystery of that unsurpassed genius of light and shade was evident in both. All the unique quality was there—Rembrandt's profound knowledge of human nature, the blend of tragic power, humour and poetry. His insight into the character of his sitter was unrivalled: fused idealism and realism, drama in action.

Mueller proclaimed that Marten Looten could assuredly have been one of the many figures depicted in the "Night Watch", so similar were their characteristics. . . . The "Night Watch"—a painting of the City Company of Amsterdam—failed to satisfy Rembrandt's clients and they refused to pay him for it. Controversy raged. When it was finished, most of the sitters declared that their faces were bad likenesses, out of focus or distorted, and not recognizable.

One and all they refused to accept this treatment of light and shade, this painting which was destined to be proclaimed a masterpiece—one of Rembrandt's two greatest contributions to the world, and to the cultural grandeur of Holland. . . .

The American could hardly tear himself away from the canvas. Still drinking in its beauty, he said: "And to think that

Rembrandt died here, at the age of sixty-three, in the Amsterdam which now honours him—bankrupt, suffering privation, and forgotten."

The Dutchman was discreetly silent.

Next day they drove to The Hague, the Dutch capital, and at the Mauritshuis, Holland's National Museum, saw another of Rembrandt's great paintings, "The Anatomy Lesson of Professor Nicholas Tulp". Like his first commissioned portrait of an important Amsterdam merchant, Nicholaes Ruts, and, later, Marten Looten, this portrait of eight persons grouped around a corpse was painted in Rembrandt's first or early manner. And the same year that he painted Marten Looten.

"No wonder they call him the Shakespeare of Holland," said the American.

. . . Rembrandt Harmensz Lugdunensis—known as Rembrandt Van Rijn—was only twenty-six years old when, in 1632, he painted the "Anatomy Lesson" which made his name as an outstanding portrait painter. He was acclaimed as one of the great discoveries of the period, extolled as poet as well as painter. Critics and public alike praised the power and skill of the young artist. From then onwards Rembrandt's career was spectacular. Commissions poured in. He began to teach, and later had as many as seventy pupils, among whom were Gerard Dou, Ferdinand Bol, Hermann Flinck, and Nicholas Maes. Rembrandt's work excelled in every branch, and as an etcher his technique and power of suggestion have never been equalled. . . .

Critics unanimously praised the "Anatomy Lesson". It was young, full of vigour, exciting, original. Later, some maintained that the "Night Watch" (painted ten years afterwards—in 1642) more than equalled it. The tragic truth, however, was that during the second phase of Rembrandt's career (1640-50) public taste had changed; the artist was no longer fashionable.

Some of his pupils, in fact, became popular at the expense of their former teacher.

The Dutch people then—as now—preferred Rembrandt's first manner of solid and realistic painting, somewhat like Van Dyck, but with greater power and insight. In his second period, Rembrandt painted with a broader brush and more emphasis on light and shade. His contemporaries were puzzled and disconcerted.

His third period or phase—1650 until his death in 1669—was marked by a still greater departure. His painting became a study in light and shade, colour and contrasting colour.

Today most critics prefer his third manner because it is farthest removed from the photographic—that *bête noir* of the modern painter and critic.

Rembrandt's contemporaries, however, liked his third manner even less than his second. Complaining that the faces of his subjects were unrecognizable, they denounced him for having abandoned the solid ground of Renaissance painting (which he had so enriched and glorified in his first manner) for the quicksands of the experimental and the unrealistic.

"Would it interest you to see another phase of the Netherlands—our new dykes?" the art dealer asked his client.

"It certainly would. I'm told that your great Sea Barrier is a remarkable feat of engineering."

"Fantastic!" the American exclaimed when they got out of the car. "What a sight! On my left, as far as the eye can reach, the cold expanse of the North Sea. On my right, the old Zuyder Zee—and Holland patiently reclaiming her land from the water, inch by inch. It's quite fantastic! I've always believed that the United States was the land of engineering genius. But this must equal anything we've got. It's a great achievement. You can rightly be proud of it."

The two men stood in awed silence watching man—the pygmy—subdue and even conquer Nature, the giant. Mueller explained the presence of what appeared to be a series of wire-pegged cages.

"They're eel-nets. Smoked eel is one of Holland's national delicacies. You must taste some."

. . . Leiden, they decided, would be their next stop—Leiden the birthplace of Rembrandt van Rijn, and where the Looten family once resided.

Leiden was far from being the sleepy little market town the American had envisaged. "It's sure changed in these past three hundred years," he declared. "All the pictures I've ever seen show it to be little more than a village. I guess in those days a trip to the big city, Amsteldam—as it was called then—was a major event in any Dutchman's life, Rembrandt's included."

Leiden was now a modern, thriving little town, its main street dotted with shops of every description, including department stores and even a branch of an American multiple five-and-ten-cent store.

"The march of time," said the Dutchman, proud that even the villages of his country were keeping up with the times. He found his companion to be an energetic and indefatigable sightseer; it was an effort to keep pace with him. Mueller also discovered that the American possessed a unique faculty of recapturing the past and reconstructing life as he imagined it to be in other days. Visitors to Holland—Americans in particular—focused the average Dutchman's attention upon monuments and places of historical and national interest so casually accepted as part of the everyday horizon, commented the art dealer.

"We're a naturally inquisitive breed, Mueller: always curious to find out what's on the other side of the mountain. It's part of our pioneer inheritance."

Leiden produced several important links in the chain they were trying to assemble.

Rembrandt's father, a prosperous miller, had evidently been acquainted with the wealthy Looten family; he may, indeed, have been on friendly terms with them. The son Marten, some twenty years Rembrandt van Rijn's senior, had moved to Amsterdam when still a youth; thus, they conjectured that the artist's association must have been with the Looten family rather than with Marten as an individual. It was probable, they thought, that when Rembrandt's father died in the latter part of 1631 and Rembrandt himself moved to Amsterdam, he had called upon their former neighbours. Nor was it unlikely that Marten Looten—by then a man in his middle forties—had taken an interest in the energetic, ambitious young painter from his former home town. He might even have helped him financially, as well as socially, was their final summing up.

Neither man considered this visit to Leiden a wasted effort as they drove back to Amsterdam. . . .

Mueller had made arrangements for both of them to visit the city's Municipal Archives on the following Monday. With much tact he had enlisted the aid of Charles van Hoboken—Chief of Research there who promised to supply whatever information he could. Van Hoboken was naturally curious as to why the art dealer should suddenly want to investigate the "Marten Looten". Not wishing to digress too far from the truth and aware of existing resentment against the "unnamed American", Mueller discreetly intimated that his client was compiling background material preparatory to writing yet another article on Rembrandt, for eventual publication in the United States of America.

It was Sunday, the sun shone and the late August day was as balmy as June.

Arriving at the Amstel Hotel around mid-morning, Mueller telephoned to his client from the lobby and suggested that they meet on the terrace. The American joined him within a matter of minutes.

"Another glorious day," he began. "Amsterdam is surely giving us lovely weather. The river seems sort of quiet, though: there's hardly any water traffic as compared with weekdays. But your houseboats make a picturesque scene. It's all so neat and tidy-looking, just clean as a whistle. I like your city, Mueller."

The latter beamed. "It's not difficult to fall in love with Amsterdam. And talking of the picturesque, sir, have you seen Volendam, or Marken?"

"No, I haven't."

The Dutchman consulted a large, old-fashioned silver watch, perhaps a family heirloom, which he took from his blue serge waistcoat pocket. His companion again had occasion to hide a smile. Mueller always dressed as one expected a typical Dutchman to dress—in sombre grey most of the time, blue serge on Sunday.

"We can visit both places today, if you'd like to, providing we leave here immediately."

"Swell! That's fine with me. There's not much else we can do today, anyway."

Volendam, with its residents wearing their traditional centuries-old costumes, the women's bonnets snow-white and stiffly starched for "Sunday best", fascinated the American. It was turning over a page into the past. And comparisons were even more incongruous when he recalled how modern and streamlined the ancient village of Leiden had now become.

The streets were thronged with people, for Volendam's Catholic populace were just coming out of church. The Dutchman stopped his car and simultaneously two young boys jumped on to the running board, one on either side. They volunteered to show the strangers around town.

"Sunday or no Sunday," Mueller said, "they're always

27

on the look-out for a few guilders. I don't think their priest would approve."

"What the heck! Kids are kids the world over." The American dug into his pocket. "Here." He handed each youngster a silver coin and like well-trained soldiers they jumped to the ground, opened the doors and stood at attention, waiting for both men to step down on to the sidewalk.

The boys proved excellent guides, and after a couple of hours the American concluded that he had seen everything of interest there was to be seen in ancient Volendam, including its starkly simple though inspiring church.

The Dutch art dealer admitted that although he had visited this unique thirteenth-century village on previous occasions, this was the first time he had been inside a house, typifying Volendam's family life.

It was a tiny house. Its owner—a tiny hunch-backed elderly woman—appeared delighted to have an opportunity of showing the visitors its quaint furnishings and explaining their traditional significance and usage.

As they emerged into the street from out of its narrow doorway, the American exclaimed:

"You're right, Mueller. This *is* picturesque! I'm indebted to you for bringing me here."

"The compliment should be reversed, sir. Without you, I would never have explored Volendam so thoroughly. Now we'll have to drive back to Monnikendam in order to get a boat for the island of Marken with its fifteen hundred people in twelfth-century costumes."

The tourist season was virtually over, and the art dealer and his client were the only paying passengers on the boat. Its skipper was accompanied by his wife and two young children. The woman wore Marken's traditional coiffure, a fashion which has remained unchanged throughout the centuries. Her flaxen hair was clipped short at the back, the two sides left as long as the hair would grow and braided into two plaits, one hanging over each shoulder, while short straight bangs—or a fringe—adorned her broad forehead.

The boat trip was smooth, the Gouw-Zee calm, and in twenty minutes they anchored at the wharf in Marken's picturesque harbour.

Here, as at Volendam, the American felt the thrill of the past.

With the skipper and his family, they explored this quaint twelfth-century fishing village, where, but for the addition of electricity and running water, almost everything had remained stationary for hundreds of years.

All the island children were dressed alike until they were six years of age. None had their hair cut; all wore skirts; and the only way one could distinguish a girl from a boy was that the latter had a red circle of cloth sewn on to the back of his small, round cap.

They went into one of the tiny houses—just as they had done at Volendam—and discovered that such visits were a regular "tourist procedure". On this occasion their hostess was a cheerful old character. Gaily, she produced photographs of herself taken with some of the illustrious personalities who had visited the island during its summer season.

"*I* am the Mae West of Marken," she proudly declared, showing them letters addressed simply to "Mae West, Island of Marken, Holland". In this house the typical cupboard bed was so high that a Beddebankje stood by its side to enable one to climb in. At the foot a cradle was built-in—"for the baby", Mae West explained "I am fifty. My husband is a fisherman. We have ten children." And to the visitors' astonishment, a door opened and children came tumbling out of what appeared to be a large closet, but was in reality another small living-room. It seemed incredible that so many humans could live in such a confined space.

"Boys!" Mae West proudly indicated the red circles on their caps. "Girls!" She spun the children around, one by one, for the visitors' inspection. All were rosy-cheeked and flaxen-haired as dolls, with wide china-blue eyes staring solemnly out at the world.

Always avid for information, the American chatted with their hostess, whose English was a mixture of American idioms and polyglot phrases picked up, parrot-fashion, from the tourists. She informed him that a generation's old semi-feud existed between the residents of Marken and Volendam. Marken's all-Protestant people had little sympathy or understanding with Volendam's wholly Catholic community. On the rare occasions when there was intermarriage and the bride or groom—as the case might be—had been converted to Catholicism, the "offenders" were ostracized by the Islanders; even disdained and disowned by their families. However, the people of Marken, like those of Volendam, generally intermarried, thus most of the islanders were related and had become one enormous family.

Twilight was casting its silver shadows upon the rippling water when the two passengers finally re-embarked for the mainland. The American was laden with small packages.

"Always the collector," Mueller teased. His companion smiled wryly. "I'm a pushover for souvenirs. They're cute ashtrays, though. And the woodcuts are amusing. They'll be fine for a Lanaii, or a Rumpus Room."

. . . On the following Monday morning the American set out for Amsterdam's Municipal Archives. It was only a short walk from the Amstel Hotel along a pleasant, tree-lined street beside a canal. A feeling of suppressed excitement pervaded him. He had thoroughly enjoyed visiting the museums including the "Six House" with its world-famous family treasures, exploring Amsterdam, and sightseeing in its environs. Now a prime purpose of his visit to Holland was getting under way. For a moment the face of Marten Looten flashed before him—those soft yet penetrating eyes seemed those of a friend. And just as this portrait had haunted him from the time he had first seen it at the Boymann Exposition in Rotterdam, so its intangible appeal still beckoned. He was impelled to find out more about this painting and its subject.

Mueller and Charles van Hoboken—Chief of Research at the Municipal Archives—greeted him on his arrival. Van Hoboken understood and spoke but little English, so Mueller acted as interpreter. It was a pleasure, he relayed, to provide whatever material was available. True, many books in many languages had already been written about Rembrandt. Yet there was always room for another, even if only one hitherto unknown fact concerning the Master and his work could be unearthed and given to the world.

Van Hoboken had already assembled some old files and excerpts from files for the author to investigate. He offered the visitors access to his private office where they could delve into this material at their leisure. His courtesy and consideration were typical of the treatment accorded the American by all the Dutch people he had met. He was impressed and appreciative.

The art dealer translated, his client made notes, and at the end of three hours they returned to the Amstel Hotel, where the latter typed his memoranda on the "Baby Hermes" portable typewriter which accompanied his travels.

That evening, dining in the hotel suite, both men chronologically reconstructed the data acquired.

First, they convinced themselves that writer Fritz Lugt's summing-up was correct. Despite all dispute and controversy Marten Looten had been a successful and important merchant, and as such was not entitled to the prefix of Professor, as was so often claimed. Fritz Lugt had also discovered a descendant of the Looten family—one P. van Eaghen, and he in turn had re-created a family tree, a copy of which van Hoboken made available. Its contents disproved another long-accepted theory—namely that the Marten Looten, whose marriage to

Christine Rutgers in 1652, inspired the famous Dutch poet, Joost van den Vondel, to compose a poem dedicated to this occasion was the subject of Rembrandt's portrait.

Carefully, adroitly, the material was shaped by Mueller's ideas and his companion's quick perception into the skeleton of their story. Like the pieces of a puzzle, fact and fiction were fitted together; the latter was eliminated, and the tangible was substituted for the imaginary.

It was the American who suggested, "Let's call it a day. I believe we've broken the back of our story, and I'm more than grateful for your help. Shall we meet at the Archives at, say, ten in the morning?"

The art dealer needed no persuading, for he too seemed tired. After he left, his client again re-read:

"The Looten family originally came from Aardenburg. They were staunch Reformists, fanatical in their beliefs, and when threatened by religious persecution the entire family moved to Houndschoote in French Flanders. At that time— around 1550—Houndschoote was famous for its prosperous textile industry, especially silk-weaving and blanket-making. It was there, in 1553, that Dirck Looten, father of the Marten Looten immortalized by Rembrandt, was born.

"By all accounts, Houndschoote proved to be a prosperous haven for the Looten family, and outstandingly so for Dirck and his brother Jacob. In 1582, however, Spanish troops invaded the city and set it on fire. Jacob was killed and Dirck, placing his brother's infant son in a blanket, fled from the burning town, which old chronicles described as a "blazing inferno". Familiar with the city of Brugge, Dirck went there and settled down once more to prosper in business and raise a family. It was in Brugge that Marten, youngest of the seven Looten children, was born.

"All went well for some years, until religious persecution flared up again. The Lootens fled from city, town, and village until they finally sought refuge at the home of their ancestors.

STILL LIFE BY KALF

(*Chapters "The Marten Looten" and "The Ranch"*)

PORTRAIT OF KING LOUIS XIV—"SHOWING
A LEG" BY HYACINTHE RIGAUD

(Chapters "The Ranch" and "A Tapestry of Paris")

Aardenburg welcomed them back. Dirck became a brewer, Official Receiver, and eventually Mayor—a position once occupied by his grandfather. It seemed that wherever they settled the Looten family were destined to do well in business and achieve financial success. Unfortunately, their deep religious convictions still proved a barrier to permanent security. Fleeing, as did their ancestors before them, from Aardenburg, they chose Aachen—only speedily to change residences again. This time they chose Leiden.

"Leiden was fast becoming the textile, blanket and silk-weaving centre in Holland. With Dirck's thorough knowledge of this industry, it was therefore a logical choice. Before long he was established and writing another chapter of his phenomenal success story. In this small town, free from religious prejudice, the Looten family eventually came into their own both in a business and social sense. When Dirck Looten died in 1623, it was rumoured that he had bequeathed to each of his seven children an inheritance of one ton of gold."

The American chuckled to himself as he re-read this statement. "A ton of gold each—seven tons of gold. Imagine what it would have meant in that day and age." His own mental reservation was that Dirck Looten's fortune had become something of a fable, and was grossly exaggerated.

He stood up and stretched himself. It had been a long day and he was tired. A pleasant tiredness, though. Passing thoughts flitted across his mind. "How many art-lovers or collectors ever took the time or trouble to investigate the inner precincts of their treasures? Acquiring an important work of art provided an undeniable thrill. But exploring its creation enriched and imbued the treasure with life." Stimulated by his thoughts, he decided to take a short walk before retiring.

Some of the Amstel Hotel staff speculated upon the identity of the tall, serious-looking individual who so seldom smiled, "Something of a mystery" was the general opinion. Most of the time they saw him with Mueller the art dealer, whom many knew by name and reputation. And it was observed that on the rare occasions when he was in the hotel lounge or lobby alone, the American was absorbed in a copy of Baedeker.

Tuesday was a facsimile of Monday. The art dealer, his client and van Hoboken met at the Municipal Archives. Van Hoboken was delighted that his files had provided such useful and valuable information, and he now produced copies of many articles which had been published over a period of years. Some dealt with the portrait itself, others argued the interpretation of a letter which Marten Looten held in his hand. The Chief of Research was sparing no effort. And once again the American had justifiable cause to reflect upon this good-neighbour policy of the Dutch people. Afterwards, back at the Amstel Hotel, he confided:

"One thing I'd surely like to do—and that is to convince my critics here that all Americans are not ignorant or unappreciative of your centuries-old culture. I'd also like to dispel their animosity toward 'An unnamed American'."

His companion smiled understandingly. "Don't let Professor van Dillen's article distress you, sir. It's somewhat critical, I admit. But then he's an intensely patriotic Dutchman."

It was well past midnight by the time the art dealer left, and his client re-read that day's additions to the Looten saga:

"Some of the Looten children, including Marten, left Leiden and took up residence in Amsterdam, then known as Amsteldam. Marten, with two or three of his sisters and brothers, were converted to the Baptist faith. In the year 1608 they purchased citizenship of the city of Amsteldam. In October of the year 1617, Marten Looten, then thirty-one years old, married Cecilia Lups, aged twenty-one, who came from Dalen." The American noted with special interest that although thirty-one years of age it was still necessary for

Marten Looten to obtain his father's consent to his marriage. And although Dirck—his father—was not in Leiden for his son's wedding, but delivered his consent in writing, this signature had to be legally verified by Marten's older brother, Charles.

At this point he was confronted by a mental facsimile of the Rembrandt portrait. As always, he felt the impact of Marten Looten's personality. Knowledge of the man's family background was throwing light on a character hitherto inexplicable.

Despite a handsome and serious face, soft, penetrating and intelligent eyes, an air of self-assurance, Marten Looten was profoundly insecure. The youngest of seven children he was in constant competition with the older members of his family. Especially was he overshadowed by Charles, whose life he emulated to a marked degree. Like him, he became commercially interested in grain, and traded successfully with both the Baltic and Mediterranean as an active member of Amsterdam's Stock Exchange. But he never succeeded in gaining the eminence of his brother Charles, who served on the City Council, was a Burgomaster, and whose fortune pyramided as his business expanded with clockwork regularity. In consequence, Marten developed a sensitivity which bordered upon an inferiority complex.

In spite of his fashionable clothes, his poise, his carefully trimmed beard, there was an underlying inner conflict—an "over-anxiety to please"—which only now showed itself to the American. This combination of strength and weakness attracted him and at the same time aroused his compassion.

He continued to read: "As a member of the Baptist community, Marten Looten took a serious view of religion and preferred undogmatic piety and a sober attitude towards life. Yet, not being devoid of worldly desires, he fitted well into that milieu of Amsterdam Mennonites.

"Following the example of another prosperous Amsterdam merchant Nicolaes Ruts, Marten Looten commissioned the young and much-discussed artist, Rembrandt, to paint his portrait, and by so doing momentarily stood in the limelight. After this event, he purchased a large house and grounds on the western side of the Keizergracht, in Amsterdam, for four thousand six hundred guilders from the heirs of Harmen Harmensz—the baker.

"Old chronicles listing this purchase and its limits, read: 'Marten Looten on the northern side and the same passageway on the southern side, stretching from the street back to the hall of Looten.'"

... The American imagined that this "hall of Looten" must have been the salon in which Marten hung his treasured portrait. Understanding something of the sitter's character, he now wondered what significance could be attached to the letter held in his hand. Was it another attempt to establish himself as a personality—to raise his prestige—this flaunting declaration of his personal friendship with an artist so rapidly gaining fame? He decided to piece together the interesting theory of this letter on the following day. ...

The two men continued to reconstruct the "Looten Story" in the hotel suite rather than in van Hoboken's office at the Municipal Archives. There, they had made copious notes from the many files; they had ample material to work on. After a while Mueller said:

"I suppose you can accept whichever interpretation you prefer. For myself, I've never had any confidence in Dr. Kat's diagnosis of the mysterious handwriting. I've always felt, somewhat like Dr. Bredius, that the 'Looten letter' as interpreted by Dr. Kat's supposedly infallible chemical-optical method, drew attention to Dr. Kat, but did little to decipher what has long puzzled the experts."

The American's light blue eyes widened with interest. "This is an angle of the portrait that we in the States know little about. I believed the letter to be part of the *décor*—like a chair.

This is an unexpected twist—the dispute of its text. And what a mass of opinions! Dr. Kat, Dr. Bredius, Dr. Sterck, Professor van Dillen, Dr. Schmidt-Degener. It seems that Kat really started something. It might be a good idea to quote his conclusions in full and then give some of the reactions, in brief."

The art dealer nodded approval and his client read aloud: "With regard to the letter which Marten Looten holds in his hand, Dr. J. W. Kat has made a startling announcement. He maintains that he has been able to decipher these scribblings, which have always been regarded as being illegible. Rembrandt, he said, wrote to Marten Looten as follows:

> *"Marten Looten.*   *XVII January 1632.*
> *Lonely was for me Amsterdam, your company, friendship, just gave me unforgettable peace created from an endless respect.*
>   *(Signed) R.H.L."*

"This opinion started a violent controversy, which, in turn, revived interest in the portrait. Article after article appeared in newspapers and magazines, agreeing with, disagreeing with, applauding and condemning Dr. Kat's findings. Suddenly it became important to know whether the letter was the expression of a warm friendship, presumably shared by Looten and Rembrandt, or merely a business communication, perhaps confirming an appointment for a sitting; or even discussing the price to be paid for this portrait. Investigation of its text had always been difficult since the letter was folded. Also the letters of the words, being painted in perspective, grew steadily smaller, and to decipher some of them was regarded as well-nigh impossible. Only the monogram R.H.L. was comparatively large and could not be disputed.

"When first interviewed, Dr. Kat refused to furnish any details concerning his chemical-optical process, which had supposedly achieved this amazing result. Later, in a published article, he dealt with his interpretation word for word, doing his utmost to uphold and defend his arguments against the barrage of criticism. 'A linking up of improbabilities and wild hypotheses,' wrote Professor van Dillen.

"None of the expert graphologists confirmed any part of Dr. Kat's findings; only Professor Brugmans showed any inclination to endorse his discipherings. Others strongly repudiated its value, calling it 'pure fiction': 'not seventeenth-century language': 'entirely contrary to the general conception of how Rembrandt felt'. For during that period of time he was a strong young man, full of the joy of life, happy to be living in Amsterdam and thrilled with his early taste of success. There was no reason for this melancholia or sentimentality, as suggested by Dr. Kat. Yet it could not be denied that Marten Looten did spend his earlier years in Leiden, and in all pro-bability knew Rembrandt, who was some twenty years his junior, from those days."

"And why," demanded the American, as he finished read-ing, "could it not be assumed that the normally exuberant and optimistic Rembrandt would not have had some quiet, retro-spective, and even sad moments? Most people do. An artist is privileged to indulge in a variety of moods."

"It's a reasonable supposition. Somehow, though, Dr. Kat's interpretation sounded too smooth. It didn't seem possible that where all the experts had failed he should succeed."

"Are you sure there wasn't any personal animosity toward Dr. Kat because he was a medical man and not an art expert? The sort of feeling that he was invading your holy territory?"

His companion made no comment, and he went on:

"Frankly, the text is still an unsolved riddle. And since no one else has offered any explanation which makes sense, let's give Marten Looten the benefit of the doubt. Let's assume that he *did* become a close friend of Rembrandt. Maybe Looten *did* help Rembrandt in his early days here. It's not too far-fetched that, despite the painter's artistic success, he was lonely—deep down inside. An acquaintance from home often inspires a warm feeling of 'belonging' where newer friends fail.

"Personally, I'm amazed that so much time and importance has been given to the letter and its text. I wonder what prompted this interest?" He indicated a desk under the window, piled high with books of reference and the miscellaneous notes they had assembled at the Archives. "At least a dozen articles were published dealing with its interpretation—arguing for and against."

"It all started after Dr. Kat visited the Rijksmuseum's 'Rembrandt Exhibition' late in 1929," Mueller explained. "From all accounts, Dr. Kat was much impressed by the Looten portrait's magnetism. Also about that time the Dutch Press was loudly applauding Mensing, who, they wrote, had rendered our nation a great service by bringing 'this old Amsterdam figure back to the city where he had lived and worked'. As you will doubtless recall, until that time no one in Holland had seen this painting."

Mueller continued: "According to reports—and, of course, I can't vouch for their accuracy—Dr. Kat went on a business trip to Middelburg shortly thereafter. He stayed at an old inn, the Verseput, and was intrigued by the proprietor's name— A. Looten.

"That night, after his business was concluded, Dr. Kat talked with the proprietor, who showed him some old family pictures. He said his family had once owned an ancestral portrait painted by Rembrandt. His grandfather—unaware that this work was a Rembrandt—had sold it for the paltry sum of thirty-six guilders.

"Then, to Dr. Kat's surprise, the innkeeper produced postcard reproductions of the 'Marten Looten'. The man had read in the Press how this canvas brought three hundred and thirty thousand guilders at an auction in London. He was firmly convinced that the painting his grandfather had sold for thirty-six guilders and this portrait were one and the same.

"Dr. Kat pointed out that there was undisputable evidence of this canvas leaving the Netherlands at least a century earlier. So, concluding that A. Looten's ancestral Rembrandt was in all probability a copy of the original, he dismissed it from his mind."

The attentive listener interrupted: "But that doesn't explain Dr. Kat's interest in the letter."

The art dealer hesitated before continuing: "I presume this incident aroused Dr. Kat's curiosity. Upon his return to Amsterdam from Middelburg he evidently examined the painting in greater detail. It's said he referred to the subject's pose as being sheer genius."

Reading an excerpt from one of the several articles, he quoted:

"'Marten Looten is turning toward the right yet looking at the viewer, so that his features and expression are fully exposed. Drama is added to the pose by his wide-brimmed hat and sweeping black cloak. He holds the right hand to his breast, and a letter in his left hand.'

"Perhaps the letter assumed such importance because so very few of Rembrandt's writings are known to the world?"

"It's a logical reason, no doubt."

"Chances are if these learned doctors and professors had given more time and thought to investigating Marten Looten as a human being, they might have discovered a more direct clue to the text," the American remarked with feeling.

Mueller picked up another of the articles under discussion and commented:

"Dr. Sterck was the first authority to disagree with Dr. Kat's version. In his article entitled 'The Real Meaning' he writes: 'A touching romantic meaning has been read into these four lines, which was to have proved a revelation of Rembrandt's inner life during his early stay in Amsterdam. A Medicus has furnished a really professional diagnosis. And without a moment's doubt—something which incidentally one might

THE RANCH HOUSE WITH ITS ADDITION OF THE RANCH MUSEUM, WHICH IS ON THE RIGHT

(Chapter "The Ranch")

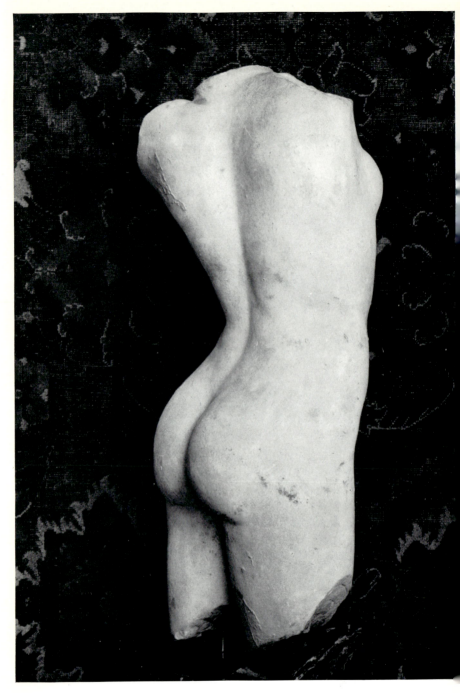

TORSO OF VENUS (SIDE VIEW)

(Chapters "*A Stroll along Minerva Street*" and "*The Ranch*")

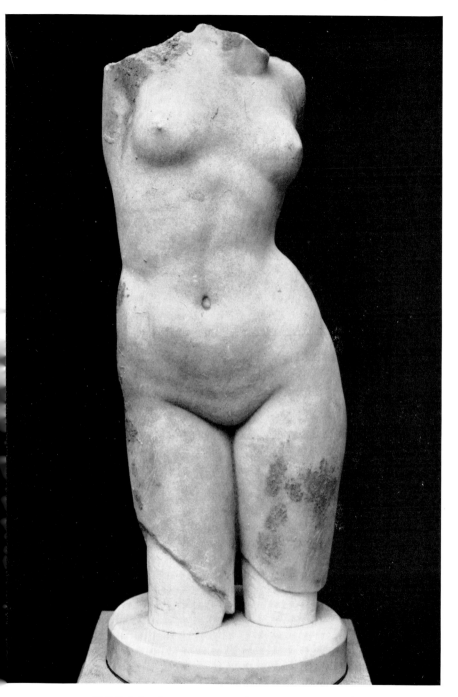

TORSO OF VENUS (FRONT VIEW)

GALLERY WITH PERSIAN RUGS, SCULPTURES AND
OBJETS D'ART IN THE RANCH MUSEUM

expect of a Medicus—he concludes that Rembrandt made this declaration. It is a great pity that Dr. Kat kept his chemical-optical method a secret; it creates mistrust.' "

He continued to read aloud: " 'Rembrandt at that time was living in the home of Hendrick Uijlenburgh, a wealthy man who was later to become his brother-in-law. Jacob van Zweiten, who reported that on July 26th, 1632, he sent a representative to discuss some legal business with Rembrandt, was assured that the artist was active, in good health, and greatly invigorated by his work. Quite contrary to any sentimental melancholia such as Dr. Kat would have us believe.' "

"In another article, Dr. van Rickevorsel offers his learned dissertation, and confirms that Rembrandt was always invigorated by his work," the American remarked. "In his opinion the artist gave Marten Looten this letter to hold in order to please him, and—as a sitter—to put him in a good frame of mind. An attitude which Rembrandt always sought to reflect. Dr. van Rickevorsel maintains this document was simply an accessory to make Looten's pose more natural and expressive. He believes that Rembrandt might have wanted to make the letter appear genuine by painting a few words on it, here and there. Like its opening—'Honourable or Esteemed Sir'—which was an accepted seventeenth-century greeting; its ending, and, of course, the monogram. I gather that no one disputes its authenticity. Sterck is certainly rabid about Dr. Kat's 'quasi-scientific findings' as he calls them. He really digs into him."

"Dr. Sterck also specializes in deciphering seventeenth-century handwritings. He acquired considerable experience when studying the Vondel documents, which he deciphered," the Dutch art dealer added.

His client, engrossed in this subject, quoted an excerpt from one of the printed articles he picked up at random.

"I see Dr. Sterck's condemnation, 'This is nothing but the

fantasy of Dr. Kat', brought a quick response through the Press. Kat replied it was possible for Rembrandt, or anyone, to feel lonely even if surrounded by wealthy people. And the fact that Jacob van Zweiten sent someone to visit the artist on legal business on July 26th of that same year—only six months after he had painted Marten Looten—could mean that Rembrandt was more settled in Amsterdam, and consequently less lonely. Dr. Kat didn't think it was too difficult to understand. And frankly, Mueller, neither do I."

He went on: "Although the biographical details are scanty, I've formed sort of a mental picture of Marten Looten. A man who aspired to, but could never quite reach his goal—that lofty pinnacle of success occupied by his brother—might react in one of two ways. He might be envious, even perhaps a trifle bitter. Or he'd feel inferior, inhibited—conscious of the fact he, personally, lacked that elusive something which balances the scales between a mediocre and an outstanding success. This feeling of insecurity might make him understanding of others striving to gain that elusive recognition. Which was precisely Rembrandt's position! And Rembrandt—like most great artists—was a student of psychology. He felt this compassion in Marten Looten, and responded to it. I'm rather inclined to agree with Dr. Kat's version."

Mueller did not pass judgment, but said:

"I agree that Dr. Sterck's opinions are too depreciatory. Listen to this one: 'I cannot condemn too strongly discoveries based on vague and unproven facts. We have already had enough of our Klaas Klan, of the Ora Linda Bok, and the First Supplement of the Charter turning our scientific knowledge into a laughing-stock abroad. We hardly require a 'Looten Letter' as well!' "

Mueller added his own conclusion. "He's a sarcastic gentleman, and doesn't seem to leave any room for reasonable inquiry. He's too uncompromising. And Dr. Bredius, who at first agreed with Dr. Kat and later retracted, saying he felt obliged to submit the letter to further investigation, did not help to clarify the situation."

"It says here how Dr. Bredius is famed for his great work in both the National and Municipal Archives. Apparently Professor Brugmans and Professor Bredius were in agreement with Kat at the beginning," interjected the American.

"Yes! Then Bredius wrote to Brugmans from Monaco, replying to a newspaper clipping which someone sent to him. It appears to have annoyed him. Dr. Bredius said these good people were all barking up the wrong tree; that his learned friend Brugmans maintained that all seventeenth-century letters began in similar fashion and greeting as did the Looten letter, therefore no special significance could be attached to it. In order to defend his earlier position, Dr. Bredius added that anyone believing they had extracted a definite meaning out of scribblings was obviously in a stronger position to argue his point, since he had a positive and not a negative view."

"Say, there's a letter here from Mensing! I had no idea that he was involved in this round-robin discussion. He sent a letter of denial all around. This is really something, Mueller. I wonder whether anyone outside of this country knows these details? It's getting exciting."

Mensing's letter read:

"*Admirers of Rembrandt,*
The words which Rembrandt painted on the portrait of Marten Looten have not been read by me as meaning that Rembrandt was lonely in Amsterdam. I have not succeeded in deciphering the whole of the printed text. In order to avoid further incorrect variations on this theme, I beg of everyone who feels himself constrained to write about this matter, to postpone it until I have had sufficient opportunity of learning the opinion of a number of experts. I beg that Dr. Kat's suggested version will not be circulated further.
(Signed) Anton W. W. Mensing."

43

The Dutchman's bland countenance was unusually alert and expressive. "It *is* exciting," he agreed, "even for a hard-headed dealer like myself. We seldom delve deeply into the background of any art object. That the work is genuine and has a brief authentic history of ownership is as far as we get."

"Practically all of the expert graphologists repudiate Dr. Kat's claim, even to calling it an elegant hypothesis," said the American. "Dr. Schmidt Degener says the word 'Marten' is actually Matcio, the Latin dative. He's convinced the letter isn't just idle scribblings, but does contain a message, possibly a business message relating to his client. Perhaps confirming a sitting? All in all, I believe Dr. Kat's interest in the 'Marten Looten' must have added to its value. Your government should have been on their toes to acquire a Rembrandt which was so highly publicized—apart from any other factors! Of course, this article ends like so many do: 'This portrait has been bought privately by an unnamed American, and will therefore leave this country.'"

It was obvious to Mueller that his companion was becoming increasingly sensitive about these references to himself. At first irritated, he later discounted them as being unimportant—even amusing. Reading article after article, in which the same note was struck, he grew thoughtful. The art dealer who had always respected his client's desire for anonymity, was puzzled.

Now, thumbing through Professor van Dillen's extensive study, he said: "We're most fortunate that Professor van Dillen preserved these old documents. He unearthed them while working in the Municipal Archives. Interesting references are made to your Rembrandt, and he quotes Jan Veth, who praised the Nicholaes Ruts painting so much, but says the Looten is far more sensitive and appealing."

"In my opinion, that's easily explained by Rembrandt having a warmer and more personal interest in Marten Looten than in Ruts."

"Van Dillen quotes Dr. Schmidt Degener, who says the

Looten is a faithful work, but a very beautiful painting. And also Emile Michel, who says the work is a jewel, studded in a glorious way, yet at the same time firm, supple and very gently handled. He says it's in the style of Thomas de Keyser, but without a trace of effort or restraint."

"It's gratifying to know that the critics' opinions are almost unanimous. I'm fortunate to have acquired this fine painting, and appreciative of the efficient way you handled this deal, Mueller." The American changed the subject. "Let's meet for luncheon tomorrow, and finish our story afterwards. I believe I'll quote from Professor van Dillen's article at length. I can use parts that do not repeat the material we've already decided on."

After Mueller left, the American checked the Looten story, adding incidentals, changing phrases, yet keeping the overall data intact. He wrote that in the year 1631 Marten Looten was taxed as being worth thirty thousand guilders—which was accounted on the low side. And that in 1644, after many years of successful trading, his dealings with the Exchange Bank were listed at approximately seventy-one thousand, three hundred and thirty-nine guilders. Still a mere bagatelle in comparison with the fortune of brother Charles! He re-read parts of van Dillen's article, which he had personally commissioned to be translated from Dutch into English. It told of the Looten portrait having been cleaned some few years before he had acquired it, and how—in the opinion of many—this was done too heavily; of the startling announcement made by Dr. Kat, and subsequent arguments that his interpretation of this letter was too romantic for such an ambitious young painter. And once again he re-read the original of an old newspaper clipping which Mueller had given to him some ten years previously:

"Must this old Amsterdam figure be doomed to continue its nomadic existence and perhaps even cross the ocean to America? It is to be hoped not, yet it looks as if our fears are

45

justified." And, further on: "It happened as I feared it would. The Looten has been bought on behalf of an unnamed American for the low sum of one hundred and two thousand guilders. It is still not known whether it has finished up in a private collection. Or is it still wandering around the international art trade?"

An hour later, in bed, he continued reading:

"In an interview with an Editor of the *Telegraaf*, Dr. Schmidt Degener announced that the Rembrandt Society, assisted by a number of private individuals, had made an attempt to secure the 'Marten Looten' for this country. The price, however, was higher than they could afford. It became known later that the unnamed American was prepared to bid up to one hundred and fifty thousand guilders—or even higher.

"Dr. Schmidt Degener continued: 'It is a great pity indeed that this Rembrandt has not remained in the Netherlands. We are falling behind, and the Government has made no money available for a number of years now. In England and other countries it is different.' Little needs to be added to this. It is a very great pity, as well as shameful, that at an auction held in Amsterdam, one of the very few portraits which Rembrandt painted of an Amsterdam merchant in the Golden Age should have been snatched by America for a comparatively low price. As has already been stated, Rembrandt's portrait of another Amsterdam merchant, Nicholaes Ruts, is already in the United States in the collection of Pierpont Morgan.

"Apparently the Netherlands cannot bid against America. This fact raises the question as to whether anything can be done to remedy the situation. The Government today is apparently not afraid to introduce restrictions on international exchange traffic when they consider that it is in the national interest. The question is, therefore, if it isn't possible, as has happened in other countries, that the Government be granted power to forbid the export of paintings or other works of art in special cases where their retention, from the point of view of their connection with the nation's history, as well as from the artistic point of view, is of primary importance.

"A great many objections may be raised to this proposal, but a 'sale' on a greater scale would be even worse."

As he switched off his bedside lamp the American resolved to meet Professor van Dillen before leaving Amsterdam.

The art dealer was amazed when his client announced his intention at luncheon the next day.

"Do you wish me to reveal your identity? How else can I arrange a meeting? Professor van Dillen is occupied in teaching at The Hague University. You can't expect him to come to Amsterdam for an appointment when he doesn't know whom he is to meet, or for what purpose."

The American's eyes glinted with cold determination. "It's a question of principle," he insisted. "I had the same right as anyone else to bid for the Rembrandt. It was a fair and responsible transaction. You know that I seldom use my name when bidding. And you also know that I never discuss my possessions, or my power to outbid others. It didn't occur to me that your fellow countrymen would adopt such an attitude. I know the Dutch people to be courteous and friendly. I'd like to straighten out the matter with a minimum of publicity. Honestly, Mueller, their attitude makes me feel uncomfortable. Professor van Dillen doesn't pull his punches either. He writes and says what he thinks."

The American observed how Mueller's eyes blinked more rapidly than usual—an unmistakable sign that the Dutchman was agitated, despite his bland calmness.

"I don't want to embarrass you," he hastened to add. "After all these years, knowing public opinion, you might be criticized; which would be unfair. You only bid for me—anonymously—at my request. And I won't hesitate to say so."

47

Mueller had no arguments to present. "I'll try to arrange the meeting, sir," he said, bowing to the inevitable.

. . . Van Hoboken, who had been of such valuable help at the Municipal Archives, acted as their intermediary. In due course, the art dealer and his client found themselves invited to tea with Professor van Dillen on the one afternoon a month he spent in Amsterdam.

Pledged to secrecy, van Hoboken—a former colleague of the Professor's—had not divulged anything beyond the fact that an American who admired his writings was anxious to meet him whilst sojourning in the city. . . .

The van Dillen apartment was on the top floor of an old, narrow house in Ruysdaelkade, a street alongside a canal. The American learned that in picturesque old Amsterdam, streets in residential quarters bore the illustrious names of Holland's great painters. Ruysdaelkade was of especial interest since a landscape by Ruysdael was in his collection.

It was quite a climb, for the stairs were steep. But a view of the slow-moving shining waters of the canal, flanked on either side by majestic lushly green and verdant trees, was ample compensation.

Professor van Dillen and his wife spoke fluent English, and before long all four sat around a tea-table chatting, comfortably at ease. Many topics were touched upon lightly before the Professor broached the subject of Looten's portrait by Rembrandt.

"I understand that you are especially interested in my articles on Marten Looten," he said to the American. And, still unaware of his visitor's identity, entered into a lively discussion.

The American claimed that, despite the passing of years, fundamental characteristics of humans had changed little—if at all. He illustrated his point by the Looten family, who were pilloried and persecuted for their religious beliefs.

48

Throughout the world at the present time—a supposedly enlightened and civilized world—human beings were still being pilloried and persecuted for their religious and political beliefs. "Conditions change, science advances. But fundamentally man himself seems neither to have advanced nor changed," he maintained. "In some phases, our twentieth century competes with the darkest chapters of the world's earlier history."

Mueller sat back and enjoyed this outburst of loquacity as his client continued: "Despite Charles Looten's great success, nothing remains. Everything he so arduously built up appears to have been swept out of existence. Yet their family name lives on—and will probably live on for ever through the talented brush of a then almost unknown painter."

"You sound like an incurable sentimentalist," commented Professor van Dillen. "As you know, I personally have never concurred with Dr. Kat's findings. I do believe, however, that Marten Looten and Rembrandt were acquainted with each other from their home town of Leiden. Perhaps the older man —who was already an established figure in Amsterdam—felt generously inclined to give Rembrandt a helping hand with his first commissions. It has never occurred to me, as you now so deftly suggest, that such a gesture resulted in anything other than Marten Looten getting an excellent portrait of himself. Nevertheless, your point is clear. The family of Looten, once so highly esteemed in the business and political life of Amsterdam in our 'Gouden Eeuw'—the Golden Age—has faded into relative obscurity. Yet Marten, the less prominent of the successful brothers, has possibly—through a kindly action— brought immortality to their name."

Professor van Dillen displayed a lively curiosity concerning life in general in the United States.

His host had a pleasant and surprisingly informal manner for a renowned scholar and Professor of Art at one of the world's leading universities, thought the American.

In turn, the former seemed agreeably surprised and even impressed by his visitor's conservative attire and unaffected personality.

They were about to leave when he said:

"I am sincerely flattered by your interest in my articles. May I enquire whether you have any specific reason for wanting all these details of the Marten Looten portrait?"

The American walked to the window and stood in contemplative silence. Then, facing the room, he said with quiet dignity: "Professor van Dillen, I am your 'unnamed American'."

The Professor, unprepared, was momentarily taken aback. He listened politely, as his guest resumed:

"I found your writings highly informative, Professor; I admired their honesty. It isn't pleasant for a nation to lose any part of its heritage. But great works of art are valuable ambassadors, spreading culture and giving pleasure to those less fortunate than yourselves. There was only *one* Rembrandt. And he belongs now, just as he belonged then, to the people of Holland."

He proceeded to enlighten van Dillen, telling him where the "Marten Looten" had been exhibited since he acquired it; of the countless thousands of people who had now been able to see this fine painting.

"Some day," he concluded, "I'd like to bring the Rembrandt back to Holland and loan it to the Rijksmuseum, or to any other Dutch exhibitions."

The professor and his wife had listened intently. Now Mrs. van Dillen said: "When you do, I feel sure that 'Marten Looten' and yourself will be most welcome."

Neither made reference to the unexpected disclosure, but a cordial invitation to visit them again, whenever the American might be in Amsterdam, was proof that he had gained the Professor's confidence and dispersed any feeling of resentment harboured against the "unnamed American".

Some days later, packing in preparation for his return to the United States, he told Mueller:

"You've been generosity itself. I just don't know how to thank you for giving me all your time, for your efforts, for placing your contacts at my disposal."

The art dealer beamed. "It's been as much my pleasure as yours, sir, as well as an enriching experience."

"I'm happy that you think so," the American's voice held an eager note, "because later—when I have the time—I'd like to visit other birthplaces of my works of art, and venture to reconstruct the lives of their subjects and artists."

Without hesitation the Dutchman said: "And when you do, sir, I'd like to help; regardless of whether the works of art in question were acquired through me or not."

"Fine! But, Mueller—forget that 'sir'. This is not a business deal. In this adventure we'll be colleagues. I'll surely depend on you when I'm ready. And in the meantime, if you should find yourself in the States, come out West and visit me at the ranch. I've built a special wing on to the place to house my collection—sort of a private museum."

"I would be delighted." They parted with a warm handshake, the American for Rotterdam, where he intended to board ship, the art dealer for his home in the suburbs of Amsterdam. En route Mueller mused over events of the past weeks, and of the character of his client.

"In some ways he's strangely reticent. I've been doing business with him for years, now—yet I still know little about the man himself, beyond the fact that he's an 'Important Collector'."

Thumbnail Biographical Sketch of Rembrandt

Born in Leyden (spelt Leiden in Holland) in the year 1606, Rembrandt's father was a prosperous miller, his mother a baker's daughter.

They wanted their son to study law; instead, he studied painting with Jakob van Swanenburch, whose greatest value to his pupil lay in the fact that he was an accomplished etcher. Later, Rembrandt studied with Pieter Lastman, a devotee of the then fashionable "dark manner" of painting, which stemmed from the Italian, Caravaggio, and which relied more on the use of light and shade than colour to create effects of solidity and space.

After successfully painting the portraits of two prominent Amsterdam merchants, Nicolaes Ruts and Marten Looten, Rembrandt in 1634 married Saskia van Uijlenburgh, a wealthy heiress in Amsterdam.

He spent much of her fortune on a fashionable house filled with a collection of paintings and valuable objects of art. The young Rembrandts lived beyond their means, and after painting the controversial "Night Watch", the artist's fortunes began to decline.

In 1656 he went bankrupt. Later in that same year he lost his beloved wife, who had so often acted as his model.

Rembrandt van Rijn died, heartbroken and in poverty, in Amsterdam in 1669.

[NOTE. *The "Marten Looten" portrait has recently been presented to the Los Angeles Museum by J. Paul Getty.*

· II ·

The Ranch

IN his own country, the "unknown American" could not remain incognito. There his name, J. Paul Getty, was widely known. Three months after his return to the United States, twelve days before Christmas, he received a letter from Mueller. Getty noted with surprise the Java postmark, and opened the envelope with keen interest.

Since his return, business and personal matters had claimed his time and attention, detaining him in Southern California and delaying his plan to revisit Europe before the end of the year.

Never a good correspondent, Getty had, with the best of intentions, meant to keep in touch with the Dutch art dealer. But after a brief interchange of letters he lapsed into his usual habit of cabling or telephoning, methods of communication he preferred for their speed and direct contact.

Mueller wrote that business connected with family properties had taken him to the Dutch East Indies; that he could offer some important works of art to museums in the United States, and would therefore be flying to San Francisco within a few days. His address in that city would be the Mark Hopkins Hotel.

The postmark date indicated that Mueller might have already arrived in Northern California. Getty at once placed a long-distance telephone call, and within a matter of minutes was connected with the Mark Hopkins Hotel in San Francisco.

"Yes," he was told, "a Mr. Mueller is expected any time now."

During the course of that evening the art dealer returned his

53

client's call, and without hesitation accepted the invitation which Getty made to him in Holland. Three days later the two met at the main railway terminal in Los Angeles.

"I hope you intend spending some weeks with me at the ranch," invited Getty as they shook hands. "Maybe later we can travel over to Europe together."

"I'd be delighted," beamed Mueller, "to co-ordinate our plans."

As they drove through busy Los Angeles, the Dutchman expressed his surprise at the changes that had taken place since the time of his last visit to the city in 1937.

"Most places I've revisited, postwar, have suffered some physical damage. And those showing no surface damage usually reflect, in some form or other, the emotional stress their citizens have undergone. This is such a direct contrast! All that Los Angeles appears to have done is grow, grow, grow. From infancy to childhood, and childhood to adolescence, and . . ."

Getty distracted his attention from current traffic problems for sufficient length of time in which to retort:

"I'll finish it for you, Mueller. We're still adolescent—and we're still growing. Look!"

The Dutchman looked at the industrial plants, schools, streets, apartment houses. In all directions, new, modern, streamlined developments. The down-town traffic congestion was, in itself, a revelation. Scarcely a pedestrian could be seen. There were few street-cars and fewer buses. Some taxis, mostly the gay "Yellow Cabs", mingled with the rest of the traffic. Never had Mueller seen so many private automobiles converging from every street-crossing into a caterpillar of moving mechanism.

"Does everyone living in Los Angeles own a motor car?" he asked in amazement.

"No; they don't. But most everyone drives some sort of automobile. Distances out here are a real problem. The city limits extended too rapidly for our public transportation system. But this is a mere nothing! I'm glad you didn't time your arrival for the early evening. Around five-thirty, when our stores and office buildings close for the day, automobiles travel bumper-to-bumper. *Then* you really see traffic congestion! From downtown Los Angeles clear out to the beach at Santa Monica, where we're going now, the roads are jammed solid."

Whilst they were driving along Sunset Boulevard traffic congestion eased somewhat. The afternoon sun shone brilliantly, and giant palm trees spread their fan-shaped branches heavenwards as if in supplication to a radiant blue sky. The purple range of the Hollywood Hills rising on their right, and the ever-growing, sprawling city of Los Angeles sloping downwards on their left, made an inspiring panorama.

As they approached Beverly Hills, its wide streets each named after the species of tree lining it—Maple Drive, Palm Drive, Sycamore, Oak, its beautifully tended residences of brick or stucco, in white or pastel tones, blending into landscaped gardens ablaze with the vivid colours of poinsettias—now in their season—and of orange trees, the art dealer voiced his appreciation.

"Sometimes, Mueller, I believe our Chamber of Commerce's boasts are justified. Especially on a day like this. Midwinter, and a mild seventy all day. And—no, oranges are not confined to the groves. Out here they grow everywhere."

Observing his companion as he deftly handled the steering wheel of his heavy Cadillac, Mueller noted the light sun-tan now accentuating the depth and blueness of eyes, the familiar tense set of jawline now relaxed, the almost mask-like coldness of face warmed to friendliness as Getty pointed out various landmarks.

They passed by the fashionable Beverly Hills Hotel and, continuing along Sunset Boulevard, came to Bel Air and Brentwood—neighbourhoods of luxurious homes; the famous Uplifters' Club, the Polo Grounds, and the Will Rogers

Memorial Park. At the foot of the boulevard they turned on to Pacific Palisades Highway, from where the ocean could be seen. Even the Pacific Ocean was justifying the Los Angeles Chamber of Commerce boasts that day, for the water was clear, calm and exceptionally blue. Turning right, they reached the beach-front. Driving along for another mile or so, the Dutchman saw a stone wall about ten feet high and, later, an iron gate.

Getty turned his car as though intending to drive straight through this gateway when, at a thirty-foot distance, it suddenly swung open. Mueller now observed the electric eye which was fitted on to the Cadillac. This device automatically operated the heavy iron gate. Intrigued with this method of entrance, he inquired whether anyone could gain access to the ranch grounds without this unique car attachment.

"There's a telephone concealed in the wall—just outside the gate. Most people visiting the ranch know about this. If not, they are informed of it. All they have to do is call the house from there, and identify themselves. Then the gate is opened by an electric eye operating from inside the house."

Upon entering the grounds the massive iron gate closed automatically, as it had opened. Ahead of them the winding road was bordered by beautiful old trees alongside a stretch of lawn and a natural stream. After approximately half a mile, passing a fruit orchard, an olive grove, stables and some guest cottages, they reached the main house.

They drew up inside a large square courtyard whose entrance was guarded, on either side, by the challenging stance of a life-sized lion sculptured out of white marble. A man-servant was waiting to take the guest's luggage.

The Dutchman's anticipation of a California ranch had evidently been very different from the reality. Getty smiled as he helped his surprised companion out of the car.

. . . The courtyard, paved with irregularly shaped flagstones, was walled in. An assortment of multi-coloured flowering

THE COURTYARD AT THE RANCH, SHOWING
MARBLE LIONS AND MONKEY FOUNTAIN

(*Chapter "The Ranch"*)

STATUE OF THE YOUNG
"HERAKLES"

*(Chapters "England: a Gainsborough—and a Roman
Statue" and "A Journey from Corinth")*

LEFT VIEW OF THE YOUNG
"HERAKLES"

THE THEATRE ROOM IN THE RANCH MUSEUM. TINTORETTO'S PAINTING "LA TOILETTE DE VÉNUS", HANGS ON THE RIGHT

(Chapter "The Ranch")

shrubs lined its walls. In the centre stood a tall marble fountain of the Italian Renaissance period; three life-sized monkeys cast in bronze sat around its base. . . .

From the doorway of the house a breathtaking view revealed itself. There was half a mile or more of gently sloping lawn—rich dark green and smooth with age; giant trees, of varied species, in abundance; a natural crystal stream which Mueller saw was fed by a spring trickling down from the canyon wall. And beyond this panorama—glistening in the distance—was the blue Pacific Ocean.

Getty—with justifiable pride—showed his guest a view from the back of the house. Its vista was equally enchanting. Wooded hills in varying shades of green clambered terrace-wise into the tall, dark canyon above, which in itself seemed to blend with and then disappear into the horizon.

A Giant Schnautzer and a clean-cut Pointer bounding over to hail their master interrupted their reverie.

"Hello. Hello there. Down, no—down, Hilda. There's a good girl." He gently called them to order, and in dog fashion the animals turned their attention to their master's companion, sniffing guarded approval. Getty hid a smile as the big dog, accepting a new friend, boisterously jumped up to greet the fat little Dutchman. Standing up on her hind legs, Hilda, the Schnautzer, was actually taller than Mueller!

Recovering his balance, the Dutchman was startled by the roar of a lion—apparently only a few feet away.

His host hastened to assure him that wild animals rarely roamed down from the canyon. At night one could hear coyotes. But only twice within four years had a mountain lion visited the ranch. Wildcats were frequent—but generally harm-less—guests. That roar came from Teresa, his lioness, welcoming him home. Teresa was tame, a ranch pet, and safely enclosed within her wire fence. Getty promised to show his guest Teresa and the remainder of his animal kingdom next day.

"Now it's more than time for some refreshment after your long ride," he insisted.

The interior of the ranch house proved as surprising as its grounds. Although within the Los Angeles city limits, the grounds adjoined the Santa Monica Mountains, making an estate of unique location. There was nothing rustic or ranch-like such as Mueller had envisaged; his knowledge of ranches and ranch life having been acquired through the medium of America's "Western" movies. This house, he discovered, was furnished essentially as a home—an elegant home—might be furnished anywhere, whether in city or country. Its furnishings were for the most part antique—rare and genuine pieces, yet all easy to live with. Its carpets and draperies were handsome. Harmony prevailed and everything unobtrusively blended into an artistic setting.

"It isn't a very large house," Getty explained, "yet it's spacious. All the rooms are of fair size and have french windows leading on to terraces, similar to this one. It's well-planned, and, most important these days, easy to run."

The art dealer looked around with an eye sharpened by long experience. "Your attention to detail is commendable! What a beautiful marble fireplace!"

"Yes. Isn't it? My father bought it in Italy many years ago. It used to be in the living-room of my parents' home, here in the city. After they passed on, some of their furnishings came to this house."

"I'm eagerly looking forward to seeing your collection."

"Tomorrow," Getty promised. "Tomorrow we'll spend as much time as you like in the new wing—which I call my museum. I'll also take you on a tour of the ranch, and tell you some of its history. It has quite an interesting history."

. . . "This is my miniature zoo." Getty showed his guest around. "As you'll notice the animals are in their natural habitat—similar to Hagenbeck's Zoo in Hamburg. Of course, the facilities here are very limited. It isn't much of a zoo, I'm afraid. Just my lioness, Teresa, two brown bears and their two tiny cubs, a pair of bison, and one white wolf. There was a pair of white wolves, but one of them ran off into the canyon and hasn't returned. She will, though, one day when she's hungry enough.

"The animals are better cared-for and fed here than in their wild state. And you'd be surprised how well they know it! Why, even if Teresa were permitted to roam around, she'd soon come back. Where else could she get her ten pounds of meat a day? And regularly?"

He hastened to dispel the look of consternation on his guest's face. "Don't worry. I'm not going to let Teresa loose—although she's as docile as can be. She'd growl at you to be sure. But that's merely Teresa's way of making conversation."

The lioness's "conversation" drowned Mueller's response, and the two men continued their sightseeing tour.

The Dutchman was fascinated by some Barbary sheep, a breed of animal unfamiliar to him. "What pretty things they are! And those gazelle! What food do your wild animals in captivity need?"

The American hesitated a moment before replying.

"I'm not too sure," he said slowly. "Although I guess it's fairly accurate to state that a lion eats ten pounds of meat a day for six days a week, and fasts on the seventh day. It's supposed to be good for them; for their digestion, their coat, their condition generally. Bears eat everything—bread, vegetables, milk, fruit. Fish, sometimes! I never give them meat. They don't need it, and meat tends to make them fierce. It costs more to feed one lion than it does to feed three full-grown bears. The bison eat hay, like most cattle."

"Have you any cattle?"

"Only two cows and a steer. And there are two saddle

horses; though in the old days this used to be quite a famous cattle ranch."

"Its history?" the art dealer inquired with mounting curiosity.

"This place was originally a Spanish grant," Getty began. "Way back in the days when Gaspar de Portala was exploring California, he and his men—including one named Marquez—followed the sea-coast north. One night they camped by a spring near the present house—the spring which comes down from the canyon. A range of mountains running into the sea immediately north of the spring seemed to shut off access, so they turned inland, looking for a pass through the mountains.

"The explorers were much impressed by the natural beauties of this country. Some years later, Marquez succeeded in getting the land as a grant from the King of Spain. And he started what became known as the famous Santa Monica Ranch.

"One of his descendants—Pete Marquez—now about eighty and the only surviving representative of his generation of this fine old Spanish family—occasionally visits here. Pete, his father and his grandfather were all born on the Santa Monica Ranch!

"Pete told me that when his grandfather inherited this property—the land you see now and its surrounding terrain—there were one hundred and forty-four thousand acres. But by the time his father inherited, only forty thousand acres were left. The rest had been absorbed in the growth of the city.

"By the time Pete's father died, the property had dwindled to a mere thirty-eight acres and forty thousand dollars in cash. According to Pete, the lawyers wound up with the forty thousand cash and the five heirs, of whom he was one, with seven and a half acres each; all they could salvage out of a one hundred and forty-four thousand acres estate! Approximately half a million people now live on the acreage which was originally their family heritage. It's all been annexed by Los Angeles' greater city limits. Had this land remained in the Marquez family, at present-day values they would surely be

60

listed among the world's richest," the American concluded.

Fascinated by the story, Mueller was eager to hear more detail. "The interior of your house reflects many periods and styles, yet its exterior is obviously Spanish and Italian. Has this any significance?"

"None. Except that the interior was re-designed to suit my personal tastes. The exterior—which I believe could be improved upon—was not my choice. However, it has one important virtue—it's unobtrusive and it blends into the landscape. Actually, I've made very few architectural changes. Even the museum addition is scarcely noticeable, although the house is now in two distinct sections."

"This landscaping is a masterpiece. It defies any suggestion of artificiality."

Getty warmed to his guest's appreciation. "Nature, in a beneficent mood, created this beauty and tranquillity. Usually one can't improve on nature. Yet I believe man's handiwork, in this particular instance, has proved an asset. Claude Parker, from whom I bought this property, is entitled to much of the credit."

He went on to relate how Claude Parker, who had long wanted to acquire the Santa Monica Ranch, eventually secured it in summary fashion.

Shortly after World War One, the ranch-house was a small building situated near the olive grove, and the property itself comprised some forty acres. Driving up the canyon one day, Parker found a Charro party in progress.

"Charros are Mexican riders with broad-brimmed hats and fancy saddles," the American explained to his guest.

Large numbers of Charros were enjoying an open air barbecue as guests of Perfecto Marquez, who then owned the ranch.

"Claude was introduced to Señor Marquez," continued Getty, "and, drawing him aside, enquired whether his property was for sale. Somewhat to Claude's surprise, Marquez replied: 'Yes, it is—at one thousand dollars an acre.'

" 'Isn't that pretty high?' questioned Parker.

" 'Sure it's pretty high,' agreed Marquez. 'But that's my price and I wouldn't consider a cent less.'

" 'Okay,' said Parker. 'You've just sold your ranch, Señor.' "

The Dutchman's eyes blinked rapidly. These impulsive Americans with their quick-on-the-trigger decisions were a source of wonder to his slower, more deliberate reasoning processes. He learned, also, that upon securing this property Claude Parker had built the present house. Getty had enlarged it after taking possession of the estate, but left the gardens and their landscaping more or less unchanged.

After luncheon they went to the ranch museum. It adjoined the theatre room, which was equipped for various uses—as a ballroom, for theatrical entertainment or concerts, or as a movie theatre.

The museum section began with a long gallery in which were hung a collection of paintings. These belonged mainly to the seventeenth-century Dutch School, the art dealer observed. Kalf's "Still Life", conceded by many expert judges to be one of the finest examples of still life paintings known, and Pickenoy's "Portrait of an Unknown Lady", which Mueller had purchased for Getty, were displayed to good advantage. Rembrandt's "Marten Looten" was, as always, a joy to behold. Seeing it again evoked pleasant recollections in both men.

A full-length portrait of King Louis XIV of France, wearing his magnificent Coronation robes, the crown resting on a cushion at his side, was of regal splendour. Known as "Showing a Leg", this painting by Hyacinthe Rigaud attracted the Dutchman's eye.

This portrait of the King hung in the Tuileries Palace until the French Revolution, he was informed now. Don Jaime, a direct descendant of Louis XIV, inherited some of his ancestor's private collection of works of art, and when he died in Frohsdorf, Austria, his daughter, upon inheriting these treasures, had put them up for sale. Several paintings from this celebrated collection were bought by Getty, including "Showing a Leg".

. . . The picture was notable for both its fine quality and historical interest. In superbly painted detail it depicted the personality of one of the greatest kings in history, a man who symbolized autocratic rule by grace of birth.

Often referred to as the "Sun King", Louis was lavish in clothing beyond the conception of the modern age. History records that he was inordinately proud of his legs and feet; hence in this portrait he turned a leg to the world, and to posterity.

His pose was both haughty and jaunty, and the dashing red heels of his shoes completed a vivid canvas. History likewise records that His Majesty invariably wore shoes with built-in lifts or higher than average heels, since his height was not to his royal satisfaction. . . .

An exceptionally fine portrait by Gainsborough invited comment.

"That's a work I'd like to explore when I visit England again," Getty volunteered.

"James Christie, by Thomas Gainsborough," the art dealer read. "Was he in any way connected with Christie's?"

"He *was* Christie's. The actual founder of the present-day Christie, Manson and Woods. It's almost two paintings in one! Notice how he leans on a framed canvas. It's a miniature landscape—an original—also painted by Gainsborough."

"I'm surprised that Christie's allowed an important painting like this to leave their family—or to leave England, for that matter."

"It has always surprised me, Mueller. I've often wondered why an ancestral portrait like this should have been sold. That's another phase of the Gainsborough I'd like to investigate. Here is what I call my 'Louis XV Room'—here, down this staircase."

A shallow flight of marble steps led them into a room

perfectly proportioned to display its treasures. Mueller was an appreciative and a discriminating audience. "These I list among the most beautiful things I have ever seen!" he exclaimed.

This magnificent array of eighteenth-century French tapestries never failed to elicit enthusiasm.

He examined one of the tapestry panels. Adapted from the legend of Psyche, according to the *Fables of La Fontaine*, this panel was one of a celebrated set of five woven on the Royal Beauvais looms, some forty miles outside Paris, when they were under the jurisdiction of Nicholas Besnier and Jean Baptiste Oudry. "Psyche" was acknowledged to be the most successful series of tapestries designed by the renowned artist, François Boucher, during the years 1741 to 1753.

Mueller knew that companion-pieces to these tapestries were in the Swedish Royal Collection, the Royal Italian Collection, and in the Petit Palais in Paris.

"This is the smallest panel of the five," Getty told him. "But it's as perfect as a flawless gem."

The art dealer continued his examination through his pocket-sized magnifying glass. After a while he said: "What detail! What mastery of weaving! This panel must surely be considered one of the greatest documents of the Golden Age of tapestry weaving in France."

"I believe it's generally accepted as such," replied his host with some pride. "I own four out of the set of five. This one— 'Psyche in the Boudoir', or as it's often called, 'La Toilette de Psyche'. Then there's 'Psyche at the Fisherman's', 'The Arrival of Psyche at Cupid's Palace' and 'The Abandonment of Psyche'."

"Their titles tell their story. Have you ever located a fifth panel?"

"Oh, yes! But unfortunately it's not for sale at any price. The late Mrs. Hamilton Rice owned a complete set of this series. She paid seven hundred and fifty thousand dollars for them—*pre-war* dollars! She bequeathed her collection to the

Philadelphia Museum. Her tapestries are in the 'Rice Room' there."

"Too bad," Mueller shook his head. "A complete set would be a magnificent possession."

Getty smiled ruefully. "I guess I'll have to content myself with an incomplete set. I've been looking for a fifth panel for the past fifteen years."

"Here's another beauty." The art dealer stopped before a larger tapestry in the corner of which was woven the initial "C" and then "Beauvais", indicating that this panel was woven by André Charlemagne-Charron, who directed the looms at the Beauvais factory from 1753 to 1780.

"It's one of the famed 'Loves of the Gods' series—'The Abduction of Europa'. I've others, also, from this same set. Here's the 'Bacchus and Ariadne'."

. . . By their elegance and refinement this series of tapestries is prized as representing French eighteenth-century art in its finest and most characteristic phase. . . .

"They're beautiful beyond my limited descriptive powers," said the Dutchman reverentially. "I've never seen such a collection of wonderful tapestries under one roof."

"Here is my finest." Getty stepped some paces backward to view the largest tapestry panel in his collection. "This is one of only two examples known in the world. Two subjects of the 'Amours des Dieux' series are woven into the one panel, as you can see. It's in its original state of preservation, and frame."

"What exquisite colouring!" exclaimed Mueller. "Where is the other panel?"

"When last heard of, it was in the Royal Palace in Budapest. Mine originally came from the Royal Family of Portugal."

"It must be the largest tapestry Boucher ever designed."

"I'm told that it is," said Getty, who was thoroughly enjoying this opportunity of sharing his treasures with an erudite and sensitive art adept.

E

65

. . . This tapestry was representative of François Boucher at the height of his career. In it he combined the classic and the romantic with equal skill. The architecture and sculpture were reminiscent of his private residence in Rome, the foliage and sky reflecting the influence of the Chinese paintings and porcelains that the artist loved so much. The female figures were a tribute to his exquisite wife, who nearly always modelled for him.

The large panel proved that François Boucher was a greater tapestry designer than he was a painter. Composition and colouring, both of immense importance, were supremely decorative and through the strong line contrast of tapestry-texture achieved full expression more powerful even than paint illusions.

Acknowledged as the master of his period François Boucher was, in style, the Louis XV period incarnate. This tapestry picture was a synthesis of the "back to Nature" movement as inspired by the Chinese. Art was under the domination of Nature. In the period of Louis XIV, people, architecture and foliage were all strongly sketched and contrasted. Boucher countermanded this. No longer were the figures statuesque, the foliage cultivated and formal, the architecture hard and symmetrical, the draperies stiff and regular. Life made itself felt everywhere. Architecture and sculpture were shattered by the hand of time, overgrown with vegetation. The cupids' bodies while still retaining an appearance of marble, had a pinkish flush. The figures were nymphs and gods who belonged to field and flower. It was an operatic setting for the ancient myths of Greece and Rome. . . .

"Isn't *she* the Antiope of that famous Greek sculpture group in the Naples Museum?" enquired Mueller after a detailed examination.

Pleased by his guest's knowledge of Greek mythology and ancient marbles, the American plied him with eager questions.

"I've read most of the mythological works. They've always fascinated me. Other than paintings, sculptures of the ancient world have long been close to my heart," the art dealer admitted.

"We can parallel some mythology with present-day situations," Getty declared. "A change of scenery and costume is all it takes."

"Plus your especial faculty for transporting yourself to other epochs," said Mueller with a broad smile.

"As I stand and look at this tapestry, its figures seem alive. To me, they're not merely characters woven in Haute Lisse. I imagine them alive and breathing—part of today's tapestry of life."

"Are you familiar with the history of the large panel?"

"Presumably it was given to the King of Portugal by the King of France. After the Portuguese Revolution it was sold to Jules Porgeis, a rich Parisian banker. Later, the tapestry found its way into the hands of French and Company, the New York art dealers. You know them, I'm sure.

"They sold it for two hundred and fifty thousand dollars. Their client ran into financial difficulties and asked whether another buyer could be found. It was during the depression of the early 'thirties, and few people were interested or had the space to hang such a large panel. I offered French and Company sixty-five thousand dollars. I hardly expected my offer would be accepted."

"But obviously it was! You seem to have a flair for lucky buying," Mueller declared. "Its present value must easily equal its original price."

"I believe it does. And there's little doubt that this panel is one of the greatest tapestries ever created. Only the greatest examples of fifteenth-century Gothic tapestries equal it. Outside of those, it stands alone."

"Except for its companion-piece in the Royal Palace in Budapest," the art dealer reminded him.

"Yes. Have you ever been to the Gobelins, or to Beauvais, and seen tapestries being woven?"

"I haven't. Yet I've always wanted to visit those factories. Perhaps next time I'm in Paris . . ." Mueller promised himself vaguely.

"We'll go together," his host said.

"I've never been particularly interested in acquiring nineteenth-century French furniture," Getty told him some time later. "As you can see, I've kept my collection largely to the eighteenth century. These ten chairs and this settee—Beauvais of the Empire period—are an exception. Originally, they belonged to the Empress Josephine."

"Imagine," said the Dutchman retrospectively, "Napoleon himself probably sat on one of these very chairs—just as we're doing now."

"I warned you it was infectious," smiled Getty. "We begin by reading a brief catalogue description of our treasure. Then we elaborate on it. And the next thing we know we're reconstructing its life—creating a history, plus."

Admiring the Queen Anne panelling, the eighteenth-century dining table and set of Queen Anne chairs in the gracious, formal dining room of the ranch-house, Mueller learned that the chairs were a test for any expert. Two were authentic of the period; the rest were skilful copies executed by an English firm of fine art and antique dealers, Frank Partridge & Sons, in London. They had been made as recently as 1937.

"It's always interesting—even amusing—to see whether my visitors can tell the new from the old. You'd be surprised how many experts have been fooled by these chairs," Getty told him.

Exquisite wall-brackets and a chandelier of Irish Waterford crystal dated 1760 enhanced the beauty of this room.

"It's a fine example," the American agreed. "The chandelier came from the British Embassy in Lisbon." Mueller's attention became riveted upon an enormous pair of silver candelabras; each stood on a small side-table set against the far wall.

"They're about the largest pieces of English silver I have, and are of the William IV period. My silver is mostly Georgian, and some of it by Paul de Lamerie. I'm especially fond of Lamerie, so was delighted to find a cake-basket and set of four salt-cellars by this great silversmith."

"That's a fine portrait—that one hanging above the sideboard. She's a pretty woman, beautifully dressed. I like the way you've got it lighted," observed the art dealer.

"It's quite a lovely thing, isn't it? Although who she is, or who painted her, is something of a mystery. Our distinguished art critic, Dr. Valentiner, thinks it's a seventeenth-century portrait by Vanderlyn. But there are conflicting opinions. One is that it might be the work of Peter Lely."

"I'm intrigued by your 'Madonna of Loreto'," Mueller confessed. "With your flair for 'buying right', that painting could even turn out to be the famous missing Raphael."

"I couldn't be that lucky! By the way, it came from the Don Jaime collection with my Rigaud and the two Van Huysum flower pieces. It holds a story to whet one's imagination."

. . . The "Madonna" hung in the Loreto Church in Rome until 1799, and when French troops occupied the city the Pope hastily sent his nephew to remove the precious portrait to safety and substituted a copy in its place. From then onward the original painting disappeared. . . .

"Whenever any 'Madonna of Loreto' shows up it always creates excitement," Getty concluded. "Mine is undoubtedly only a copy. There's not one chance in a million that it's the priceless Raphael."

"Nevertheless, so far as old paintings are concerned the unexpected has been known to happen," said the art dealer, with authority. "I'd suggest getting further expertize on it, regardless."

"I'll think about it," his host promised. "Tell me, how do you like my chandeliers?"

"I can only fall back upon my first impressions and compliment you on your good taste. Obviously you're a perfectionist! And I again repeat myself: you've been lucky. Even with the financial means to buy top quality art, it's increasingly difficult to find rare pieces. You've also been fortunate in acquiring fine works of art at reasonable prices. Your chandeliers are as perfect as your tapestries. I've rarely seen finer examples of rock-crystal, or lovelier cutting."

"Thanks." Always responsive to praise of his choice of *objets d'art* Getty went on:

"The deep depression of the 'thirties saw great works of art, as well as stocks and bonds, at prices which now seem ridiculously low. So deep was this depression in business that works of art and blocks of stock which seemed to be in the strongest hands and lost to the market forever, suddenly became available for purchase. And at prices often only a tenth of their former cost.

"Due to my father's prudence and business foresight, I was fortunate enough to have cash during the depression years. Some of it I've devoted to works of art—and I've never regretted it."

Mueller was surprised that apart from his host's secretary, no one visited the ranch during his stay there. In Europe, he had heard many and various rumours concerning the American collector's great wealth. The bulk of this immense fortune was reputedly inherited from his father, who had also been a shy, retiring figure—a powerful tycoon who shunned the limelight and chose to remain behind the scenes.

The art dealer saw in Getty a reflection of the father: an astute business brain, an agile though conservative mind, an insatiable thirst for knowledge—which he appeared to absorb with the minimum of effort—and a reticence which made "knowing him" difficult. He wondered whether anyone really "knew" this complex individual, whose personality embodied so many and such varied facets. Even living under the same roof, eating meals together, sharing a knowledge and love of art, revealed nothing beyond his client's magnificent collection and wealth. Propinquity brought him not an inch closer to the man himself.

Yet he admired Getty's restraint. His unpretentious dignity carried with it a touch of humility.

Of his personal life, the American volunteered the information that his family were out of town. He spoke of them affectionately to Mueller, made glowing reference to his five sons—of whom he seemed inordinately proud, and then, having touched briefly upon family life, abruptly steered the conversation into more impersonal channels.

The library with its Henry VII English oak panelling, its French windows opening on to a terrace and the panorama of cascading hills and canyon, was another room in which the Dutchman found much that was unique.

"I'm not strong on books," Getty said with a tinge of regret. "I guess my tastes are unorthodox in that direction. My few first editions are of no particular monetary value."

The library, however, contained a remarkable collection of eighteenth- and nineteenth-century guide and travel books on North America.

"They fascinate me," announced the Dutchman. "Most Europeans would probably react as I do. Some day your collection of travel books will rate as a major asset."

"My library's only claim to fame; plus these early-day photographs."

"Your collection of eighteenth- and nineteenth-century guide books represents a country in the making. Those must be the first guide books ever to be printed on and about this continent."

"They are! They're most interesting. I prize them because they're something different in the way of first editions."

"I would enjoy spending days in here, just browsing through them," said Mueller.

"You will have to come back to the ranch for a longer visit. Have you seen these?"

"These" were a collection of rare nineteenth- and early twentieth-century photographs. They were catalogued in modern albums, each page covered with a protecting cellophane sleeve.

"They are street scenes, mostly. Strangely enough, I came across a photographer in New York who was retiring from business because of age—he was eighty. I bought his entire stock. Shortly afterwards—here in Los Angeles—I discovered another old photographer who was going out of business. He was also an octogenarian, and had collected photographs of early American street scenes. These prints have now become America's history. Here's New York without any skyscrapers. And look at that horse-traffic."

"They have scarcely faded," his guest observed. "Between these photographs and your travel and guide books you have a unique story of America's progress; adventure and history combined."

"These pictures only cover New York, Los Angeles and San Francisco—our east and extreme west. It would be interesting to add to them—Boston, Washington, D.C., Chicago, etcetera."

"You're confirming my conviction," warned the art dealer. "Once a collector . . ."

". . . always a collector! No. I haven't got the virus that badly—as yet. It just occurred to me that my photographs only show three giant cities in their making. And those, while symbolizing America, are *not* America. America is made up of hundreds of small towns and cities in her forty-eight states, from coast to coast. To get a comprehensive photographic history of this great country in the making, I would need early pictures of the frontier towns—one-horse towns, hick towns, tank towns, we call them—which once were mere trading posts and even Indian territory."

"It would make an exciting collection. Exciting to own and exciting to collect."

"Mueller, you're a bad influence. You ferret out my weakness and encourage it." Getty's tone of voice belied his facial expression. Pioneering another phase in collecting was an appealing challenge.

The art dealer smiled—a smile of long experience.

His host went on to say how most visitors to the Santa Monica Ranch enjoyed the old photographs and found them entertaining. He concluded: "This room is where I enjoy seclusion. It has an atmosphere that inspires study and meditation. I spend some part of each day in here, working on my maps and business reports."

Life at the ranch slipped by quietly and pleasantly, one day drifting into another. Mueller, through long-distance telephone calls and mail, adhered to his object of negotiating the sale of works of art to various museums in the United States. The museum authorities of both San Francisco and Cleveland were interested to acquire certain paintings, subject to price adjustment.

To the Dutchman's surprise Getty extended him an invitation to travel as his guest, for three months or longer, and revisit England, France, Germany and Italy.

"Frankly, Mueller, I believe in the old adage that two heads are better than one. And your knowledge of ancient marbles will be helpful. I want to look around for some worthwhile sculpture in between my business activities. These, of course, always dominate the scene and take priority over personal pleasures."

"I'd be delighted to accept if I can also combine business and

73

pleasure," responded the Dutchman. "As you doubtless know, I'm the travelling member of our firm. My partners normally do the selling, while I treasure-hunt for paintings and bronzes to replenish our dwindling stock. It should be possible to synchronize my schedule with yours."

"We could start out right after the first of the year, if that's okay with you." The American, once he had made a plan, was always eager to carry it out.

With quickening interest the art dealer studied the remainder of his host's varied collection. He spent much of his time in the museum section of the house and made copious notes for reference. These, he thought, might be useful when investigating those art objects whose backgrounds they proposed to explore when in Europe.

The "Louis XVI Room", he discovered, was as impressive as its companion, the "Louis XV Room". A "bureau à cylindre" signed B. Molitor attracted his experienced eye.

This desk, fifty-three inches high, sixty-eight inches wide and thirty-three inches deep, had a cylindrical top and stood on four fluted legs mounted in ormulu. Around the upper part of the table and the top of the cylinder were a succession of frieze-like panels in chased ormolu, composed of vine foliage with delicate tendrils, and amorini blowing trumpets.

"The mounts are by Gouthière. They're really exquisite examples of gilt-bronze *ciselure*. This desk once belonged to King Louis XVI. It is said to have come from the Château de St. Cloud," Getty explained.

"The famed Molitor desk!"

"Yes. It's one of the best eight or ten examples which have come down to us."

"I suppose you look back with varying emotions on your many purchases now that they've stood the test of time," mused the art dealer.

"I do," his host said firmly. "Whatever I bought that

was of top quality *has* stood the test of time. It is always a pleasure. But anything of second-rate quality became boresome and an eyesore.

"Whenever I think of my collection, I recall my best art objects—not my worst. Unhappily for a collector, the public—when viewing a collection—often remember its worst examples and forget its best. Maybe there's a touch of malice in public reaction?

"When one invites someone to see his collection there is obviously a background of pride and esteem; otherwise there'd be no collection. And pride often goeth before a fall! The visitor says to himself consciously or unconsciously: 'All right, let *me* see what is considered so fine, so precious. Let *me* see this "Collector's Choice" and I'll form my own opinion as to whether it's choice.' Safely off the premises, he's likely to express surprise at finding so many third-rate art objects in what was reputedly an important art collection."

Mueller urged his companion on: "In French furniture, which pieces are your special favourites? How did you acquire them?"

Getty half-smiled. "It's a long story, so I'll try to condense it. The Schiff sale in June of 1938 was a fortunate event for my collection. Mortimer Schiff, son of the great banker, Jacob Schiff, owned an important collection of eighteenth-century French furniture and some fine carpets and porcelains.

"I visited the sale rooms with an acquaintance, Leon Lacroix, who's a good judge of quality, and selected the objects I wanted to acquire. Departing from my usual habit, I also went there on the day of the auction. The Paris and London dealers appeared in full force, for it was one of the most important sales of the decade.

"The room was packed. But times were not good, and it became evident that the public was there to see rather than to bid. Again departing from my usual habit, I did my own bidding. The dealers, sensing my determination to secure certain objects, had little interest in bidding prices up in vain, so resigned themselves to the inevitable.

"I acquired some wonderful pieces for the proverbial song, including my two Carlin Sèvres plaques Gueridons . . . a Carlin Sèvres plaque side-table . . . the famous Molitor desk . . . the Tilliard damask sofa and chairs. And my unique Louis XIII Savonnerie carpet. The dealers left almost empty-handed.

"When these treasures were added to the tapestry panels and furniture I had already procured through Mitchell Samuels of French and Company, I found myself with a first-class collection.

"Also from the Schiff sale are this pair of eighteenth-century Chinese porcelain vases with French ormolu mounts. Before the depression these sold for twenty-five to fifty thousand dollars a pair. Thus, the history of my French furniture collection can be divided, like Gaul, into three parts: pre-Schiff, Schiff and post-Schiff."

A superb Louis XVI Secretaire signed "M. Carlin" next demanded attention. Martin Carlin, a cabinet-maker to King Louis XVI, was appointed Master Cabinet-maker to the royal household in 1766.

"This came from one of the Rothschild collections. There's a companion-piece in the Wallace Collection in London," Getty volunteered.

"I've seen it there," said Mueller. "Which branch of the Rothschilds owned this lovely desk?" He read its catalogue description:

"Top of white marble enclosed by a pierced ormolu gallery; the frieze fitted with a drawer. The fall-front enclosing an interior with numerous drawers is inset with a large circular Sèvres porcelain panel painted with a basket of flowers suspended from ribbon ties, framed by a border of brilliant turquoise blue, decorated with little medallions of roses. Each side has three shelves. The lower part is fitted with a drawer, inset with Sèvres panels painted with sprays of flowers, supported by circular fluted legs, decorated with ormolu mounts and female masks. Period 1775. French."

"The Vienna Rothschilds," replied Getty. "Baron Alfons and Baron Nathaniel, from whose collection I also acquired this second cabinet."

It was another superb Louis XVI secretaire, signed "Adam Weisweiler", with bronzes by Gouthière. The art dealer read its catalogue description:

"Top of white marble enclosed by an ormolu gallery. The frieze of bronze doré decorated with two fauns and children with trumpets. The front inset with three very fine Sèvres porcelain panels painted with bouquets of flowers, the fall-centre enclosing an interior with numerous small drawers flanked by columnar pilasters with women's heads; the side panels inset with circular Sèvres porcelain panels decorated with flowers. The lower part is fitted with a drawer decorated in bronze doré with two amorini riding on lions. The four feet with interlaced stretchers. French. Period 1780."

"All the plaques are *pâte tendre* Sèvres of the finest quality and colours. Adam Weisweiler was made Master in 1778," Mueller observed.

"Yes. Later on I'll tell you something about these lucky buys," his host promised, "and this. . . ."

"This" was a small but extremely fine and rare Louis XV work or coffee table of green lacquer. Decorated with a blue and gold design, it was exquisitely mounted in bronze doré and fitted with a small drawer and shelf. The top was formed by a Sèvres porcelain plaque which had a rose Pompadour ground decorated with blue and gold ornaments and a reserve panel depicting a shepherd's love scene. The Sèvres plaque bore the markings "K" for Dodin, and the letter "I" for the year 1761. This table was signed "B.U.R.B.M.E." on the bottom of the drawer.

"The Guerault table! I was under the impression that it had never been out of the Louvre."

"There's a companion-piece," the American told his surprised guest. "It's similar; not identical. This small Riesener table is another favourite of mine. It came from the English branch of the Rothschild family."

"Your French furniture parallels the rest of your treasure trove!" exclaimed the art dealer. "You have some exceptional works of art. Why don't you give the public an opportunity of seeing them? It's criminal to hide all this beauty."

"One day I will," Getty promised. "I've always had an idea at the back of my mind that this little museum might some day belong to the nation." Not wishing to commit himself further, he changed the subject. "We must visit the Los Angeles County Museum. I've loaned them some paintings and carpets I'd like you to see."

The settee and two armchairs upholstered in early Régence eighteenth-century Gobelin tapestry were at one time owned by the Marquis Boni de Castellane.

Mueller was intrigued by the Gobelin tapestry design which covered the Régence settee. Under a canopy of land-scape, monkeys played musical instruments. The seat of the settee showed a leopard flanked by dogs.

"I wonder why monkeys were used so extensively in eighteenth-century *décor*? Your Cressent commode from the Gould collection is decorated by gilt-bronze children playing with a monkey."

The Dutchman learned that, like most of his purchases, Getty had bought the Régence Gobelin set, which was made around 1725, advantageously. The cost of these three pieces in Paris in 1904 was three hundred thousand gold francs—then about sixty thousand dollars. The suite was acquired for a mere sixteen thousand dollars! Its previous owner had been George Blumenthal, once President of the Metropolitan Museum of Art in New York.

"Why did you specialize in collecting eighteenth-century

French tapestries and furniture, seventeenth-century Savonneries and sixteenth-century Persian carpets rather than paintings, which are the choice of most collectors?" he questioned.

"Partly for that very reason," Getty told him frankly. "I never like to follow the crowd." He began to expound his theories of collecting. "A good painting is fine to look at—or to own. But pictures have become too fashionable. People will pay a hundred thousand dollars for a second-rate picture by a second-rate master, and believe they're getting value."

The art dealer found that his client objected to the division of artistic endeavour into major and minor art. As he said: "Why should a painting be major art and the Ardabil carpet minor?" And although Mueller's ideas did not coincide with those of the famous painter Whistler, who once publicly expressed his opinion that the Ardabil carpet—as a work of art—was worth all the pictures ever painted, he readily understood Getty's point of view.

"Pictures—whether in oil or watercolours—by their nature, the application of paint to wood or canvas, tend to be cold and stiff. Their decorative value is limited. I get annoyed by the importance given to paintings by the majority of people. In their ignorance, they interpret art as being of one sphere only—paintings.

"For instance, the guides at the Wallace Collection in London take visitors into rooms there and expatiate on the pictures. They don't even mention the wonderful furniture! Yet, at an auction, the furniture in some of those rooms would undoubtedly yield far more than the pictures. The furniture is first-class, while some of the paintings are nothing to rave about.

"Why should past generations be considered less intelligent and less educated, art-wise, than the people of today?" he went on. "It's a known fact that up to a hundred years ago the best paintings by the best masters were often valued below furniture, carpets and tapestries.

"In classic times, Roman collectors paid up to fifty thousand dollars for a small wooden table. Very few masterpieces of painting or sculpture would have fetched a tenth as much! Maybe our ancestors over-valued their furniture and under-valued their paintings. But our generation has gone to the other extreme.

"As a collector, I don't believe that artistic merit follows a value as set by the market place; I don't care to pay unrealistic prices for anything in life. A collector doesn't have to be impractical. He can appreciate art and revel in its beauty, yet still want to invest his money wisely."

Mueller, agreeing in some respects, disagreed in others. "My views are, of necessity, realistic, since I am a dealer. If I were a collector, my judgment would be determined by the beauty of the work of art and its appeal to me, rather than by any value placed upon it commercially."

He agreed however when Getty said: "If I limited myself to 'Old Masters' in paintings I'd have to content myself with a second- or third-class collection since practically everything first-class is in public museums. Even so, the best public museums have relatively few first-class pictures. The proof of this could be found by our going into any large picture gallery together. Presuming we each owned an undivided half-interest in its collection, and wanted to divide it equally, I'll make a bet you wouldn't agree to my choosing twelve pictures as my half and offering you the rest. Even on the assumption that there were five hundred pictures left."

The Dutch art dealer smiled broadly as his companion said: "I could select twelve paintings at the Louvre, far more valuable than all the hundreds I'd leave behind. I could undoubtedly do the same at the Rijksmuseum, the Prado, the Vatican or the National Gallery."

"You would seriously devalue any collection by taking your choice of twelve pictures. The importance of a collection is not its possession of numerous excellent works of art, but of a few great masterpieces."

"Ah . . ." said Getty, "in classical statuary, French furniture, tapestries and carpets I consider I have such masterpieces. Yet if paintings were my preference, I could never hope to compete with the Louvre, the Uffizi, the Prado or fifty other fine collections where paintings predominate. So—I have little desire to collect them. Oh, sure, I'd like to include a few good works in my little museum. Paintings, however, are not the be-all and end-all of artistic creation to me—as they are to so many collectors."

The Rothschild family, unquestionably the foremost collectors of French eighteenth-century furniture during the past hundred years, were seldom known to sell any of their treasures. Once works of art came into their collections they usually remained there. But when political trouble developed in Austria, rumour reached the international art market that some of the rare possessions of the Vienna house of Rothschild were about to change hands.

Visiting Vienna in 1938, Getty went to the Rothschild palace, but found it already occupied by Nazi police.

Many of Baron de Rothschild's incomparable works of art were on loan to the Vienna Museum, and these were also seized. All automatically became the property of the Third Reich.

The three brothers Alfons, Louis and Eugene were the last generation of the Vienna Rothschilds. Louis was arrested by the Nazis and thrown into prison. Alfons and Eugene escaped to the United States.

In 1939, the Rothschild brothers signed a deed and bill of sale to the Nazi Government. It covered their entire vast possessions in Austria. Their reward was to be the release of Louis, who was still held as a political hostage. It was a high price, but they did not hesitate. Freedom from tyranny was worth any sacrifice of material possessions. . . .

Among the works of art ultimately salvaged from this

F

priceless collection were the Sèvres plaque secretaires by Carlin and by Weisweiler. These two superb examples of French eighteenth-century decorative furniture were valued at a minimum of two hundred thousand dollars each during the first thirty years of this century. Difficult times of the 'thirties, however, wars, revolutions and the high taxes of later years led to the disappearance of collectors with relatively unlimited resources.

Getty, when offered these secretaires at one hundred and twenty-five thousand dollars for the pair, made a counter-offer of seventy-two thousand dollars. At first rejected, his offer was accepted some months later by the recently widowed Baroness Alfons de Rothschild.

. . . "Your Louis XV Gueridon tables by Carlin are most handsome. I expect you date them as being about 1775," said the art dealer. "The large Régence bureau plat is also—without doubt—important. It has such graceful, clean-cut lines, and its ormolu mounts of satyrs and females are unusually fine."

. . . "I take the liberty of quoting from your book *Europe in the Eighteenth Century*," he continued some time later. " 'Not many of us are privileged to own genuine Savonneries because there are probably not more than a hundred of them extant, and half of these are in public collections.' Yours, Mr. Getty, are superb!"

"Thanks, Mueller. I'm especially fond of my carpets. In fact, I enjoy everything that goes to make up my collection."

" 'Everything of equal standard' is an excellent axiom. You are obviously trying to live up to it."

"I am," said the American seriously. "I've followed the path of most collectors in so far as gradually weeding out less important pieces in order to make a balanced collection. I believe I have learned to evade the pitfalls, and thus now own mostly choice items. My little museum is about as complete as I expect to make it. Unless, of course, I get a most unusual buy."

The art dealer seemed amused. "Mr. Getty," he said, "in all my travels I have yet to meet a collector whose collection is complete—who isn't on the look-out for that unusual buy."

"I mean what I say," his client protested. "The only additions I intend making are some ancient marbles, if, as and when I'm lucky enough to find them."

Mueller who had not been active in the international art world for thirty years without understanding the psychology of collectors, smiled knowingly. "We shall see," he said. "We shall see."

"One could, I suppose, find fault with some of my things," said Getty in a critical mood. "The walls of my French rooms, for instance. But I intend replacing them with suitable *boiseries*. In fact, I propose having the work done while I'm away in Europe."

"An excellent idea," concurred the Dutchman. "Stucco walls are 'wrong'. But I didn't like to hurt your feelings. Believe me, though, no one could be constructively critical of your classical room."

. . . The classical room contained only a few choice and rare antique marbles. Its floor was an arresting mosaic, a Roman first-to-second-century specimen. It was a fine as well as an important example, its colouring unimpaired by time. Made up of twenty-two parts, the large central medallion contained figures of animals and a portrait-head enclosed within a honeycomb of hexagons. The remainder of the floor was an allover geometrical design of interlaced circles containing cruciform devices, and displaying square tiled panels of bird figures of brilliant plumage. . . .

"I would say it depicts the story of Bacchus, God of Wine. The figures around him seem representative of goddesses, birds and animals relating to mythology," offered Mueller, thoughtfully examining the mosaic design.

"And possibly you'd be right. I have no knowledge of mosaics other than the known fact that mosaic floors were used extensively during five centuries of Roman architecture."

"We'll doubtless find many fine specimens in Italy," said the Dutchman. "With your usual flair, Mr. Getty, you might discover that your floor came from Nero's villa at Antium or Hadrian's villa at Tivoli. Or perhaps from one of those numerous villas Tiberius once built for himself on the Island of Capri."

"All right," said Getty good-humouredly. "I can take it. Here is Livia, wife of the Emperor Augustus. This is one of the two or three portrait-busts of her now extant which show her as a young woman. It must have been made shortly after she became Empress. As you can see, she's indeed rare. The sculpture is undamaged, and dated as approximately 20 B.C." He went on to say that he had bought this work of art in Italy through his usual dealer, Barsanti of Rome. Prior to that time, it had been in a private collection in Florence. And, continuing, by way of introduction: "Here's Agrippina, whose mother, Julia, was the only child of Augustus. I always visualize Agrippina standing upright and dignified in one of those large niches in the Pantheon in Rome. Her father, the good and wise Marcus Agrippa, surely had her there—in the place of honour —on completion of his wonderful building."

"It's an idea! Only her head stands on this lovely column of rose marble. What's happened to the rest of her?"

"That is an interesting story. Maybe when we're in Rome— *quien sabé*—we will find the answer." Getty shrugged his shoulders. "*Quien sabé.*"

"This is a splendid torso of Venus," observed the Dutchman, critically examining the seven-eighths life-sized marble figure.

"Doubtless 'Venus with the Looking-glass', and as usual, mutilated. I wonder why the misguided zeal of fanatics always led them to mutilate statues of gods and goddesses?"

"Evidently they had no interest in art," replied his host. "It was considered a meritorious act to strike off their heads and limbs, like my poor little Venus. Her torso is so exquisite! She must have been a joy to behold with head and limbs. She, too, came from Barsanti. Incidentally I'm told on good authority that she was discovered in the ocean, right in front of Nero's villa at Antium."

Antium, as Mueller knew, was the present-day Anzio. Many fine examples of early sculptures and marbles had—even of fairly recent date—been found in the ancient seas around Rome and Greece.

A week after his arrival at the ranch the art dealer received a cable from Amsterdam. It appeared to cause him distress. "I am afraid it's imperative that I leave here within two days. I have to return to Holland on urgent family matters," he confided to Getty. "But you may depend on me. I shall arrange my business so that we meet again in London, and can then travel together wherever you wish."

His host, although disappointed, was philosophical about changed plans. As he told the Dutchman, "Actually I seldom plan ahead. I much prefer to do things as and when the spirit moves me: even to travelling. Will you go by sea or air?"

"By air. I enjoy flying, and air transport is a boon for long-distance journeys."

"For myself," said Getty, "I prefer to stay closer to the ground. I was a passenger once in a 'Jenny' back in 1917. And in '42 I flew from Chicago to Tulsa, Oklahoma. Since then I've remained faithful to automobiles, trains and ships. I'm a good sailor and always enjoy life on an ocean liner. But my favourite means of transportation is a Cadillac—with myself at the wheel. Driving is my greatest relaxation. I guess I've driven pretty much all over these United States and Europe—several times."

There was still sufficient time left for a visit to Los Angeles and its County Museum, where, among other exhibits, the American's treasured "Coronation Carpet" was on display.

It was a magnificent example of Persian art, and had at one time belonged to a Scottish family. They had loaned it to Westminster Abbey for King Edward VII's Coronation. Hence its title.

This historic carpet was later purchased by an American art collector, Clarence Mackay, for the sum of one hundred and twenty-five thousand dollars.

The "Coronation Carpet" remained in his country home on Long Island until after his death. Then it found its way back to England, where Getty acquired it. Thus once again this treasure crossed the Atlantic, this time to Santa Monica, California.

Mueller enjoyed seeing the exhibits and meeting some of the Museum officials. But he told his host there was not a carpet to compare with the large Ardabil which, only partly unrolled, was in the ranch museum. A fabulous example of Islamic art, it stimulated Mueller's interest in Persian arts and crafts.

From the sacred shrine of Safi in Ardabil, Persia, this carpet had elicited the challenging declaration: "This is too good for Christian eyes to gaze upon." Only one companion-piece exists, and it is on display in the Victoria and Albert Museum in London.

. . . Back at the ranch, Getty's two huge dogs boisterously greeted their master and sniffed his companion with familiarity: a week of seeing Mueller around had made him part of their animal pattern-of-living. The lioness, Teresa, roared out her welcome. By this time, however, the Dutchman was somewhat accustomed to the menagerie and their "language", although amazement at his host's deft handling and subtle knowledge of these wild animals remained.

86

In response to his compliment, the American explained: "They recognize their kinship to man; wild animals have an almost uncanny sixth sense in relation to humans. Fear, mostly, creates the barrier between us. When my grown bears were younger—me too—I had great fun boxing with them. They were always playful, and always gentle."

Enjoying a pre-dinner *apéritif* in the Lanaii, Mueller recognized the Delft ashtrays—souvenirs acquired by his host when visiting the Island of Marken. "I must confess that I didn't understand what you meant when you said, 'These will be fine for the Lanaii'," he admitted. "In fact, I've often wondered what a Lanaii was." He looked around him with curiosity, observing the gay chintz covers, the ultra-modern furniture, the wall of glass, with alongside it boxes of growing plants and flowers. Lightness, brightness, and informality were the key-notes of this room.

"Hawaii originated the Lanaii," said the American, "and our southern California climate favours these terrace-cum-den combinations. This is where I lounge around and relax; listen to the radio or gramophone records; or, once in a while, watch television."

"Lanaii life" and his host's interest in classical culture seemed worlds apart. However, it was not the first time the Dutchman had been surprised since he had been at the ranch.

"The Lanaii is a fashion I would like to introduce to my own country," he announced, draining his glass.

Anticipating a visit of longer duration, Getty had expected to show Mueller something of Los Angeles and its environs: to drive along the beautiful coast to Santa Barbara and, further north see some of the old Spanish Missions that still remained in southern California. "I guess the local sights will have to suffice," he concluded somewhat regretfully.

. . . Mueller was positive he would always remember the sight of those gaily ornamented floats and automobiles along

Hollywood Boulevard on that summer-like winter's evening. It was a sight which inspired mixed emotions.

As far as the eye could see, the wide thoroughfare was festooned with multi-coloured illuminations. Windows of all stores lining the boulevard were massed with Christmas merchandise, glittering and decorative.

Pavements were jammed solid with people watching this seasonal procession. The floats competed with each other. Blazing electric lights were massed together to create tableaux and portraits which were works of art in themselves, some of religious or Biblical subjects. And over all presided Santa Claus in traditional red costume and flowing white beard.

Later, at the near-by Beachcomber's Restaurant, famed for its Hawaiian delicacies, Getty introduced him to their "special" —an excellent after-dinner drink, coffee grog.

In Hollywood's legendary Brown Derby, Mueller expressed his disappointment at not seeing even one movie star.

At the Cocoanut Grove, internationally famous room in the Los Angeles Biltmore Hotel, where palm trees miraculously grew out of the dance floor, there were still no recognizable movie stars.

"We'll see if we can't find you at least one," his host promised, as their car drew up outside Mocambo, an exclusive intimate club on The Strip—a short strip of road which serves as a connecting link between two sections of the city of Los Angeles.

Mocambo was filled to overflowing, and the art dealer noted that here, as elsewhere, his companion was well known.

"You forget that I was practically raised in this town," Getty retorted to his chiding. "I seldom get around to the night spots, though. This is quite an event for me, too."

To Mueller's satisfaction, Mocambo provided several movie stars. Like most people, however, he was disillusioned to find

MECHANICAL TABLE BY OEBEN. A SOMEWHAT SIMI-
LAR PIECE IS IN THE LOUVRE

(Chapter "Rome")

ONE OF A PAIR OF FLOWER PIECES BY VAN HUYSUM

(*Chapter "A Tapestry of Paris"*)

BLUE SÈVRES VASE WITH MOUNTS BY GOUTHIÈRE

(*Chapter "Rome"*)

"REST ON THE FLIGHT INTO EGYPT" BY ORAZIO GENTILESCHI. FROM THE COLLECTION OF SIR HAROLD FARQUHAR

(Chapter "All Roads Lead to Rome")

that without their screen make-up movie stars looked hardly more glamorous than the average run of people anywhere.

Next morning the American sentimentally pointed out a frame and stucco mansion on Wilshire Boulevard, at the corner of Kingsley Drive. Much of his youth had been happily spent there; this residence had belonged to his parents.

"Like everything else, it's changed, evolutionwise," he observed regretfully. "This neighbourhood used to be one of the choicest in Los Angeles. When my parents first settled out here in 1907, all this property—clear out to my place at Santa Monica and beyond—was nothing but wild ranchland."

. . . Before Mueller left for Holland, he and Getty discussed those works and objects of art they had decided to "explore".

"I don't agree with you about your fountain," the art dealer said firmly.

"Do you still believe it to be of any importance?"

"I do. True, it's not unusual as to the pedestal. But its subject-matter—three bronze monkeys sitting around the base—leads me to believe it is representative of an important Renaissance sculpture. Perhaps a first copy, if not an original."

"All right, we'll include it. Though I've never felt that my monkey fountain might be a copy of a Giambologna or a Tacca. The only information I can contribute is to tell you that I bought it many years ago from Crowther's in London. They, as you know, specialize in garden sculptures. They said it was formerly the Earl of Effingham's property, used as an ornament on his estate in England, and indicated its origin was Italian."

"It's possible that those bronze monkeys signify monkey gods and illustrate a fable. I should like to trace its background," Mueller insisted.

The great bronze door which served as an entrance to a new wing of the ranch-house had likewise whetted his curiosity.

It was in pure Renaissance design and of superb patina. Its lower panel represented a battle scene and its upper panel a triumphal scene. The surrounding ornamentation was symbolic of war, with figures bearing shields and trophies. Men and horses standing out in bold relief gave an impression that, by placing one's hand around any of the bronze figures, one could lift them intact out of their panels.

The great bronze door both enhanced and completed the courtyard as a pictorial scene, the art dealer maintained. In origin and period it paralleled the monkey fountain which was the central ornament there. "It might easily have been the entrance to an old *palazzo* in Rome or in Florence," he said.

Getty related one of the many legends of his ranch—of the huge California Oaks—and of the allegedly largest oak tree in the whole wide world, said to be over a thousand years old, which was swept away like a leaf out of the ranch grounds by a fierce storm.

"One hears a lot of tall stories about these old Spanish grant properties," he told the Dutchman.

Arranging to meet in London early in the following year, Mueller took his departure, declaring that his unfortunately curtailed visit had none the less been a memorable and enriching experience.

. . . Aboard the aeroplane, *en route* east to New York on the first lap of his return flight to Amsterdam, the Dutch art dealer, before relaxing into a comfortable doze, reflected upon the events of the past weeks, and of his host.

"Strange," he mused. "I suppose I can now call the American a friend rather than essentially a client. Yet by and large I still know little of J. Paul Getty—the man himself—beyond the fact that he's an 'Important Collector'."

· III ·

England: a Gainsborough—and a Roman Statue

SUDBURY, in the county of Suffolk, England. It was a quiet little village in the year 1746, and a wedding being solemnized in its old church was an event calculated to bring Sudbury's residents, young and old, out of their homes. On this bright Saturday morning one and all turned out, dressed in their best for the marriage of Sudbury's native son, Thomas Gainsborough, to her native daughter, Margaret Burr.

Gainsborough, a young man of nineteen, had recently returned from London, where he was studying painting with the famous artist, Baymann. Formerly he had studied with Gravelot, a well-known engraver. Sudbury's small church was crowded with family friends and well-wishers, and soon, the wedding ceremony concluded, the happy pair walked up the aisle arm-in-arm to the organ strains of suitable wedding music as chosen by the bride.

An unknown but aspiring young painter, Thomas Gainsborough was destined to gain early recognition. Pioneering naturalism in landscapes, his subtle handling of tone and delicate feeling of colour speedily brought his work to the attention of the world of art. In 1760, with considerable artistic achievement to his credit, Gainsborough, an astute businessman as well as a man of genius, moved from Ipswich, where he had made his home since his marriage, to Bath.

. . . According to fable, Prince Bladud, a leper, found a cure in Bath's mineral springs and waters nine centuries before

Christ. In the seventeenth century a visit by King Charles II and the Duchess of Cleveland made Bath fashionable. The famous diarist, Samuel Pepys, gave it honourable mention, and then in the eighteenth century—under Beau Nash's direction—Bath became known as the most exclusive watering and curative spa in England. . . .

It was obviously an excellent choice of *locale* for an ambitious young portrait painter. For Gainsborough had decided to emulate his contemporaries, George Romney and Sir Joshua Reynolds, and concentrate mainly on portraiture.

Bath, with its wealthy and fashionable clientele, proved ideal. Within a few years, Thomas Gainsborough became the rage of Society. To be painted by him was synonymous with social success. The lion's share of portrait painting, however, still went to Romney and Reynolds in London. In 1774, Gainsborough, realizing that Bath had its limitations, changed residence again—this time for London.

In the Metropolis, he became one of the original members of the Royal Academy, which was honoured by the direct patronage of King George III. (Gainsborough contributed regularly until 1783, when a dispute over the hanging of one of his pictures caused him to refuse to exhibit at the Royal Academy again.)

During this period there was a man in London already famous in artistic circles, a man whom both artist and art dealer called friend, a man who created one of the most unique business enterprises of his time—James A. Christie, founder of Christie, Manson and Woods, auctioneers, universally known as Christie's.

. . . Getty put down the article he was reading and looked at his wrist-watch.

"The sale begins in half an hour," Mueller observed pointedly.

"We'll be on time. It's only five minutes' walk from here."

Christie, Manson and Woods were holding one of their weekly sales at their auction rooms in London. The huge rooms were almost full by the time Mueller and the American arrived there. They managed, however, to secure two seats at the back and, catalogue in hand, prepared to sit through the two hours' auction.

Most of the important dealers in antiques and fine art from the English provinces, London and continental Europe were present that day. It was an exceptional sale featuring the furnishings and effects of one of the stately homes of England.

"It's really tough," said Getty, "that after such a hard-won war, Britishers have to liquidate their family treasures to pay death duties on family estates. It seems a gross miscarriage of justice!"

"It is indeed," the Dutchman replied, and then listened attentively as the bidding opened.

Several more or less unimportant pieces were offered and sold for fair prices, until a more imposing item was offered— the normal routine adopted by auctioneers.

"One thousand two hundred guineas! Am I bid one thousand two hundred guineas? One thousand three hundred guineas! Am I bid one thousand three hundred guineas? One thousand five hundred guineas! Am I bid . . . ?"—and so the auctioneer, standing upon his rostrum, continued until: "Going—going—gone!" And "Lot No. 15" went to the highest bidder for two thousand guineas.

"It was a good buy," Getty whispered. "Why didn't you outbid him?"

"It might have jumped the price to two thousand five hundred. Too high. Besides, there are more attractive items in the catalogue."

The atmosphere became tenser as the sale proceeded. The Dutch art dealer made several bids, apparently with restraint. Whenever competition became over-keen he retired. There were some beautiful pieces, yet little of major importance. Strong in one period of old English furniture and in Georgian silver, the sale was weak in paintings and bronzes—the works of art he especially desired. Prices were good. It was evident that there was still a healthy demand for fine art objects.

Not interested in buying, Getty compared postwar values. He was gratified to find that prices for works of art had not only maintained their high level, but in some phases increased. A variety of comments from buyers and would-be buyers around him confirmed his suspicion that many of these treasures would find their way across the Atlantic, due to changed circumstances and Britain's austerity programme. People who normally indulged their tastes for antique furnishings, silver and those appurtenances associated with the great town houses and country estates of England's nobility and landed gentry could no longer afford to do so.

"Evolution," he decided. "Social evolution. Nothing remains static."

As the sale proceeded excitement mounted, and with it—so it seemed to Mueller—the temperature of the room became stiflingly hot. Distracting his client's attention from the auctioneer for a moment, he said:

"There's an unhealthy lack of ventilation in here."

Subconsciously, his companion reacted by putting a hand to his throat and loosening his shirt collar.

"*Yours*, sir!" shouted the auctioneer, pointing to him. "*Yours*—for one hundred guineas!"

"Great Heavens!" exclaimed Getty. "What has been wished on me?"

There was subdued laughter from those around him. If, while the bidding was in progress, a person absent-mindedly smoothed his hair, stroked his chin or lifted his hand, it was often mistaken for a bid and the item on auction was consequently knocked down to him. This time—and for the first time in his art-buying career—Getty was the victim.

"It's No. 18A," said the Dutch art dealer, thumbing through his catalogue. "A watercolour of Old London, a street scene of about 1845."

"I'll be darned!" ejaculated his client who none the less accepted the accident with good humour. "I'll be darned! I have no use for a painting like this. I'll have to put it back for sale."

. . . And thus, by a strange quirk of Fate, was laid the foundation of a small collection of paintings which the American always alluded to as "My Moderns" . . . .

After the sale ended both men went into Christie's private offices, Mueller to complete his purchase of a pair of bronze figurines by Rodin, his sole acquisition from that day's auction, his companion to renew acquaintance with the partners and staff of Christie, Manson and Woods.

"We hoped we might see you in England about this time, Mr. Getty," Christie's manager said in greeting. "You usually arrive in London during the month of June. Did you find anything that you liked today—other than your surprise purchase?" He seemed amused by this incident. Getty smiled ruefully. "Once in the life of every man," he quoted. And then: "There were some very fine things, but not in my line. I'm only interested in ancient marbles this trip. Do you know of any?"

"I wish I did, sir. Since the war, and the embargo on exporting works from Italy and Greece, there's nothing worthwhile available. The few ancient marbles in private collections remain there. And should anything of importance get on to the market it's immediately snatched up by museums, here and in the United States. There's an absolute famine in Greek and early Roman works. I shall be surprised if you find any important sculptures."

Mueller, occupied in concluding his transaction with the

cashier's desk, now joined in the conversation. It veered to his last visit to the United States, and his impressions of the current and increasing demand there for fine works of art.

"May I offer you gentlemen some tea?" Christie's manager asked. "It's four o'clock—tea-time in England."

While he was speaking, a young girl appeared with a tea-tray set with three cups and saucers. It was evidently a foregone conclusion that whoever was in the manager's office at tea-time had tea, regardless.

Over tea and sweet biscuits, the Dutch art dealer broached the subject of Gainsborough's "Christie".

"Mr. Mueller has kindly agreed to co-ordinate his European travels with mine," Getty explained. "He's looking for bargains, and I'm entertaining myself in whatever time I can spare from business by delving into the backgrounds of certain of my art treasures."

He went on to tell Christie's manager about his trip to Holland: about the facts unearthed relating to Rembrandt's "Marten Looten", saying, in conclusion, "I'm equally anxious to learn something about Gainsborough's 'James Christie'. Other than its catalogue description, I know precious little about it."

The Englishman showed surprise at anyone taking the time and trouble to investigate a work of art they had already acquired. Diplomatically—in his punctilious and polite manner —he indicated that this must be an American foible.

"We Americans always like to find out what makes the wheels go round. Making my collection has preoccupied me. I know little of the individual histories of my works of art. Exploring their whys and wherefores is exciting—as exciting as collecting itself."

"You will find it interesting, no doubt," the manager politely agreed. He pressed a button on his desk and the girl who had brought in the tea-tray reappeared.

"Ivy," he said, "please bring me the catalogue of our sale

of May 20th, 1927, and anything else you can find connected with that sale."

Ivy departed as silently as she entered.

"You have an extraordinary memory, sir!" the Dutch art dealer exclaimed.

"Thank you," replied the Englishman. "Unfortunately, I don't always remember the specific date of a sale, although I was working with our firm in 1927. But I always recall the sale of *this* particular Gainsborough."

"I wonder why Christie's permitted this portrait to leave their family," Getty asked eagerly. The manager's attitude reflected that he, likewise, wondered why: and regretted its disposal. Before any further comment could be made, Ivy re-entered with an armful of files.

"Mr. Wilson told me to bring them all. He said you would sort out what you want."

Sorting out several files, they came to one containing a photograph of the Gainsborough portrait. Another provided some relatively unimportant data.

"Here it is, sir." The American was handed a catalogue, which read:

SALE, FRIDAY, MAY 20th, 1927   LOT 29
The following is the
property of JAMES A. CHRISTIE, ESQ., M.P.
Picture
THOMAS GAINSBOROUGH, R.A.
Portrait of James Christie, Esq.
Founder of the firm of Christie, Manson and Woods.
Born at Perth, Scotland, 1730, of English and Scottish parentage. He served for some time as a midshipman in the Royal Navy, and later settled in London as an assistant to an auctioneer in Covent Garden named Annesley.

About 1766 he started business on his own account at the rooms in Pall Mall formerly occupied by the print-seller, Richard Dalton, and in 1770 removed to 125 Pall Mall, next door to Schonberg House. He died at his residence in Pall Mall on November 3rd, 1803.

In brown coat with rolled collar, brown vest, and breeches, white frills at the neck and wrists; a watch-fob with two seals hangs from his pockets; powdered hair; leaning on a framed landscape by Gainsborough and holding a paper in his right hand; red curtain background.

Painted, 1778.

$49\frac{1}{2}$ in. by $39\frac{1}{2}$ in.

Exhibited at the Royal Academy, 1778.

Exhibited at the National Portrait Exhibition, 1867.

Exhibited at Burlington House, 1891.

See Sir W. Armstrong's *Gainsborough*, p. 193.

See James Greig's *Gainsborough*, p. 123.

Bought by Agnew for seven thousand, five hundred and sixty pounds.

"I bought it in 1938," Getty volunteered.

"From Colnaghi's, not Agnew's. And you paid seven thousand five hundred pounds for the painting," Christie's manager informed his listeners.

"You certainly know the history of Gainsborough's 'Christie'," said Getty. "I envy you your prodigious memory."

The manager seemed embarrassed; like most Britishers, he was unaccustomed to praise. His position with the firm demanded tact, a basic knowledge of the art-world in general, and, of course, a good memory was always an asset in business.

The phlegmatic English people, whilst appreciating services rendered, were seldom effusive with their praise. On the contrary, Americans invariably said what they thought at any unexpected moment. This spontaneous compliment inspired a response. The manager relaxed. He began to express his personal feeling of disappointment that his firm had not reacquired this portrait of their founder when, upon the death of James Christie's great-grandson in 1927, the painting was ordered to be put up for auction.

Mueller and Getty learned that this canvas had hung in the gallery at Christie's auction rooms for a hundred years before its removal to the home of the great-grandson who inherited it. In the 1920's, when works by Romney, Reynolds, Lawrence and Gainsborough were in great demand and fetching enormous prices, the firm of Christie, Manson and Woods reluctantly decided they could not afford the capital investment necessary to purchase this portrait from the then deceased great-grandson's estate.

"I believed that I was actually overpaying for the Gainsborough," said Getty. "As you know, English works fetched high prices in the 'twenties. But in the 'thirties, Romney, Reynolds and other famous artists sold for a fraction of what they'd brought ten years previously. Yet I paid the same figure this canvas yielded in its heyday."

"You still bought 'right', sir. I haven't seen the Christie portrait for many years now, but it's universally considered to be one of Gainsborough's masterpieces."

"At the time," Getty went on, "I was sitting for a portrait by Gerald Brockhurst. I wanted to acquire one outstanding painting of the English School and saw the Gainsborough—quite by accident—at Colnaghi's Gallery. I asked Brockhurst if he would expertize it for me. And he did. He too considered it to be one of Gainsborough's best and advised its purchase even though the price was high. He also told me that the painting would have been of greater value commercially—although not artistically—if its subject were a lovely woman, or even a child."

Christie's manager smiled. "Of course, sir, we've always held the opinion that this particular portrait could not be improved upon. Mr. James Christie, you will no doubt agree, was a handsome figure of a man. He made a fine portrait."

The three of them entered into a lively discussion apropos of the psychological reasons which made paintings of children, girls or pretty women of greater commercial value. Facts were cited to prove or disprove this or that theory. Mueller vehemently disagreed. Subject-matter, he insisted, would never take precedence over composition and technical execution with any art expert.

"I wonder how and where James Christie and Thomas Gainsborough first met?" Getty ruminated aloud.

"Supposedly on an Opening Day at the Royal Academy some short time after Gainsborough came to live in London," said the manager.

"I'd sure like to know something about that meeting. Do you have any of the details?"

"No, none, Mr. Getty. It's just hearsay—and more or less a fable nowadays. It's a long time ago—in the 1770's!"

"Maybe we can all lunch together tomorrow, and you'll tell me whatever you know. Any scraps of information will be welcome."

Christie's manager again pressed a button on his desk and in a moment Ivy reappeared.

"Have I got a luncheon engagement for tomorrow, Ivy?" he asked. The girl, of wraith-like personality, disappeared without a word and in a few moments was back, appointment-book in hand.

"No, sir. You have an engagement at Hove in the afternoon. It is a two hours' drive, sir."

"Thank you, Ivy." He turned to the Dutch art dealer and the American as, noiselessly, the girl departed again. "I can manage an early luncheon—if that will suit you?"

"Fine! Come over to my apartment at the Ritz at 12.30," cordially invited Getty.

"I shall look forward to seeing you, then." The Englishman shook hands with each man in turn and bowed them out.

. . . Many heads turned to look, with curiosity, as the two

men, an oddly-assorted pair, walked briskly along Piccadilly back to the Ritz Hotel. The contrast between them could not have been more pronounced. Mueller's sojourn in his native Holland had increased his corpulence and made his short legs look even shorter. In appearance, he might have sat to a cartoonist as the typical Dutchman of popular conception depicted in old-fashioned lithographs. The American, on the other hand, having lost a few pounds in weight, looked taller and even more loose-limbed. His face still bore traces of a California suntan.

It was an effort for Mueller to keep pace with his companion's long-legged stride, and the latter, realizing this, apologetically slowed down.

London, striving to regain an atmosphere of pre-war gaiety, was inaugurating the Festival of Britain. The great city was crowded with its own natives and a motley of peoples from different parts of the world. Among them were many visitors from the United States.

"You can spot an American a block away," exclaimed Getty. "It never occurred to me before, but we Americans have a tell-tale walk—almost a strut. I guess it's sort of a defence mechanism. A challenge from citizens of the New World to subjects of the Old World saying: 'Sure, here we are, independent, enterprising, and all set to enjoy *your* culture with *our* dough'."

"If we could but see ourselves as others see us there might be more laughter in the world and less tragedy," the Dutchman said, noting that in London, as elsewhere, his client's trenchant interest in all phases of daily living was evident.

"In a nutshell, Mueller, I'm a rabid Cook's tourist. I have a blinding, restless urge to see and participate in everything that's happening regardless of where I am. I'm afraid it's a strain on my friends, and on their stamina," Getty said, his half-smile broadening.

"I hope mine will stand the strain!"

"It should. You, Mueller, are quite a few years younger than I."

"Only two or three, I imagine. And without your boundless energy and physical endurance. However, I'll try to keep pace with you, and hope for the best."

"Swell! Tonight, let us go over to the South Bank. I'm anxious to see the Festival of Britain. Aren't you?"

. . . The Festival Pleasure Gardens, situated on the South Bank of the River Thames, covered a large acreage. The Festival of Britain itself was in the nature of an exhibition resembling the World's Fair in America, Getty told Mueller. Excepting that here, British and Dominion wares, arts and crafts were solely represented, whereas its American counterpart had International pavilions displaying the works, culture and crafts of many nations.

Highlights here were the Dome of Discovery, in which was housed the Hall of Science; an immense Concert Hall; panoramic Pleasure Gardens. For miles along the Thames Embankment gay illuminations pierced the evening darkness, and throngs of automobiles and chartered buses brought sightseers from far and wide to the banks of the river affectionately referred to the world over as "Old Father Thames".

"It's well worth seeing!" exclaimed Getty. The Dutchman agreed, but after two and a half hours of constant walking declared that whilst he had gained in knowledge he had seen quite enough for the time being.

"You're a quitter," announced his companion. "There are days of worthwhile sightseeing here." The art dealer was relieved when he suggested "Let's take in the variety show they advertise."

They were fortunate in securing two vacant seats for the last performance. The length and breadth of England had been scoured for quality performers and only top talent was enlisted for the much publicized Festival of Britain. The especially erected Royal Festival Concert Hall, whose architecture provoked both controversy and admiration, was filled to capacity with a warmly responsive audience. To Mueller's astonishment, his companion relaxed under this spell and somewhat shyly joined in the community singing in which both artists and audience participated.

. . . The Ritz Hotel, quintessence of luxury and refinement, is a fashionable rendezvous at all times.

Its main restaurant, overlooking the Green Park, was crowded for luncheon that day. Several people paused to greet Getty on his annual return to London. The three men had reached their dessert course by the time they were able uninterruptedly to concentrate on the subject of James A. Christie.

"As you might possibly know," said Christie's manager, "Christie's was established in 1766. Some of the most famous sales in history have been made by us. In 1882, the Hamilton Palace Collection realized over three hundred and ninety-seven thousand pounds—a fabulous fortune in those days! Before that—in 1875—the Manley Hall Collection yielded one hundred and fifty thousand pounds. We had the Bernal Collection, the Fontaine Collection, the Dudley's, the Magniac's— and many others of equal importance. We sold Sir Julian Goldsmith's pictures, Sir John Pender's pictures, and the jewels and paintings belonging to the Duke of Cambridge. I think it's safe to say that a large percentage of important sales are still effected through our firm. More recently—in 1951—we raised approximately thirty-seven thousand pounds for the Red Cross by selling miscellaneous articles sent into our auction rooms by anonymous donors. The contribution was listed briefly as 'From a Sale at Christie's'."

"I've attended Christie's sales for at least twenty-five years myself," said the Dutch art dealer.

"What was your last purchase at Christie's, sir," the manager asked the American, "other than your accident-bid of yesterday?"

Getty thought for a moment before committing himself to a reply. "If I recall correctly, it was a very fine Savonnerie carpet. And talking of my 'Modern'—which is, I believe, a Victorian work—I rather like street scenes, so I've decided to keep it after all."

The manager produced a few sheets of paper on which were written whatever story he had found relative to James Christie and Thomas Gainsborough.

"Thanks. I certainly do appreciate your going to all this trouble."

"You are very welcome," the Englishman assured him. "I only wish that it were possible for us to provide something more tangible for you, sir."

"Find me some ancient marbles," said the American with a smile.

The manager deliberated a moment. "I prefer not to be quoted, but there might possibly be something in the Marquess of Lansdowne's Collection, if you can induce the family to sell. Unfortunately, they haven't sent anything in to us. But you might try negotiating with them through Spink's. You know them, of course? Among other things, they specialize in ancient marbles. They have a splendid classical section."

. . . Spink & Son, of St. James's; Frank Partridge & Sons, of Bond Street; T. Crowther & Son, of Fulham; Cameron's of Grosvenor Square; Botibol's; Colnaghi's—all "fine art and antique dealers" of renown and reputation—contacted Getty during his first week's sojourn in London.

"One would have to be a billionaire," he quipped to Mueller as they crossed Piccadilly into Bond Street, on their way to keep an appointment at Frank Partridge & Sons. "But I must admit I enjoy all this courtesy and consideration. Should anything exceptional come on the market, I've requested that they cable my lawyer in New York. He always knows where to reach me. But I've not been steered on to anything spectacular since the Rembrandt. Your firm has always been right on the beam. Too bad you don't handle marbles. Why not?"

They waited for the traffic lights to change before crossing the narrow street, which was, as always, congested, and were on the opposite pavement before the art dealer spoke.

"Having built our reputation on fine paintings of the Dutch School, we concentrate mainly in that direction, with bronzes as our second feature. Perhaps we ought to expand our interests—I don't know. Antique marbles are so difficult to find. And handling them creates many problems for a dealer."

. . . Bond Street, with its innumerable speciality shops catering to the highest clientele, was a scene of discreetly well-dressed women, with only a sprinkling of men. Cartier's, their windows adorned with a handful of priceless jewels, attracted the Dutchman's eye.

"I love beautiful gems," he confided.

"Jewellery never attracts me," said the American as they passed by Asprey's, with its array of gold and silver trinkets of the superb craftsmanship for which they were famous. He paused, however, to admire a desk-set of English hogskin displayed in their side window.

"How different from 1949! When I first came back here—four years after the war in Europe was over—it was pathetic; most everyone still looked careworn and sort of shabby. Quite some percentage of the stores had been bombed, and very limited merchandise was available—let alone displayed. I'll never forget my first sight of the City and the East End—they'd been blitzed almost to obliteration! What a nightmare for anyone to have lived through!"

"My first postwar visit was in the winter of '47," said Mueller. "I was under the firm impression that my people had suffered—until I saw London. Why, Dutch food rations were a feast as compared to England! And our clothes rations were an extravagance by contrast."

"And there's still some rationing here—the only country in Europe where it still exists. I'm forever amazed by the British people's endurance. They accept these things so philosophically. One just has to admire their spirit."

By this time they had reached their destination.

Inside the sumptuous antique galleries they were greeted by Claude Partridge, who invited them to look around whilst waiting for his father to arrive. An appointment had been made to see a pair of ancient marble columns and some sculptured figures.

"I'm not over-optimistic," confided Getty, "and I said as much to Partridge when he called me this morning."

"Still, there's nothing to be lost by seeing them," was Mueller's advice.

With the arrival of Frank Partridge, they all got into a taxicab and drove to a warehouse in Marylebone Road where the marbles were stored.

On first sight the American was impressed. The Dutch art dealer, however, was dubious.

"They are only fair," was his verdict. "Of course I'm no great authority, but in my opinion these columns are much superior to the figures. I would say the columns are good Roman examples, but far from being first-rate. The figures are Roman also, but of poor quality. They are about second century A.D."

Frank Partridge agreed that these works of art were not of museum quality, and showed an evident surprise at Mueller's undoubted knowledge of ancient marbles.

"Paintings are my business; sculptures are only my hobby," said the affable Dutchman.

"You've evidently taken your hobby seriously," commented Partridge.

Getty declared that he was only interested to acquire works of art which could be rated as being of top quality, so the three of them returned to the Bond Street galleries. Some handsome English furniture of the Queen Anne period and some finely-cut crystal chandeliers attracted the visitors.

"They're not as good as the pieces I sold you some years ago; but they are quite beautiful. Too bad you're not a Hepplewhite collector—this set of chairs is magnificent. And this Chippendale dining table and sideboard are as fine as anything we've ever had in our showrooms."

"You can't tempt me." Getty determinedly shook his head.

Nevertheless, Frank Partridge's trained and discerning eye did not miss the implication of a detailed scrutiny of a Louis XV period French commode. Almost reverently the American's hands were lightly passed over its inlaid woods, which gleamed dark and rich with a polish mellowed by age.

"It's got an exquisite patina. The Ormolu is not unlike the Gouthière drawer-fronts on my Molitor desk. Incidentally, what do you consider is the best way to clean ormolu?"

In reply, Partridge invited them to accompany him down to the basement. There, one of his staff of highly skilled restorers of antique furniture demonstrated his particular method of cleaning the gilt-bronze ciselure and ormolu mounts which adorn most cabinet work of French eighteenth-century origin. Afterwards, the man wrote out the details in full of this delicate process. He presented his information to the American, who had attentively watched the procedure of removing ormolu trimmings from their base in preparation for cleaning.

"Some people prefer not to remove the ormolu mounts, sir. But I always insist. They can't be cleaned thoroughly otherwise," the restorer maintained.

Shaking hands at the door, Frank Partridge said:

"You may be certain I'll let you know of anything worth-while that comes on to the market."

"I'm not interested," the American protested quickly, "unless it's ancient marbles."

With recollections of the past hour and a half, the English art dealer and the Dutch art dealer exchanged an experienced smile.

. . . Dinner at a restaurant in Berkeley Square—on the site where the Marquess of Lansdowne's Town House stood—brought to mind the suggestion made by Christie's manager.

"We'll call Spink's first thing tomorrow morning," Getty said. "I'm told that when this place was the Lansdowne residence, part of their famous collection of marbles decorated it. Nowadays all their statuary is at Bowood, their country seat."

Mueller, once a week-end guest at Bowood, on the occasion of his sale of a renowned Old Master to the then Marquess of Lansdowne, was able to recall and describe some of the ancient marbles there.

"I've always been interested in their 'Herakles'," his companion confided.

"I remember it well," said the Dutchman. "It is larger than life-size, and there was some speculation as to whether it was Roman or Hellenistic. It's referred to as both the 'Hercules' and the 'Herakles'."

"The marble is Greek—Pentelic—but the statue is Roman or Hellenistic. It would be a priceless possession if it were Greek of the good period—fourth century B.C. or earlier."

A lively discussion apropos of the artistic and technical merits of Roman *versus* Greek sculpture, and of the reason for the enormous disparity in their relative value, continued as they leisurely strolled back to the Ritz.

Whenever some phase of life or art intrigued Getty's versatile mind his family rarely intruded until the phase had exhausted itself.

An extremist, the urge to acquaint himself more thoroughly with the intricate worlds of art became the motive transcending all else—apart from business—during this period of his life.

When travelling, he spent many hours of each day—whether late at night or in the early morning—attending to his voluminous daily batch of mail and cables, which arrived with clockwork precision wherever he was. And, in nearly every city he visited, business people and business discussions awaited him, by arrangement.

Once Mueller found him on his knees poring over several large maps spread out over the carpet. Absorbed in their intricacies, Getty had forgotten all previous appointments.

"They're geological maps," he explained apologetically.

"Do you understand them?" the art dealer asked with genuine surprise.

"Oh, sure! I studied geology for a while, just to make myself familiar with things. It helps a little. At least I can try to offer an intelligent answer when a problem is presented to me. Which, by the way, happens too frequently for my liking. Sometimes I've cursed the invention of the telephone; it makes one so accessible. Yet, on the other hand, immediate problems are often solved by a long-distance call." The telephone bell rang, interrupting him. He picked up the receiver. "Excuse me, Mueller. I'm expecting a call from San Francisco."

... Rudolph Forrer, general manager of Spink and Sons and expert of their antique department, knew Getty slightly. With British diplomacy he evinced no surprise on sight of Mueller, although the art-dealer-and-millionaire-client association was causing lifted eyebrows as, together, the two men were constantly seen around the sale rooms, exhibitions and museums.

"Yes," Forrer, acknowledged as an authority on ancient marbles, informed the American, "there might be a possibility of securing the Lansdowne 'Herakles'."

... Generally considered to be the best statue in the celebrated Lansdowne Collection of ancient marbles, and known to museums and students of art the world over, the "Hercules" or "Herakles" was awarded a place of honour—the catalogue frontispiece—when this collection was offered at auction in 1930. This statue had been favourably mentioned in the learned books of Michaelis, Furtwangler and Richter.

To the surprise of those in charge of the Lansdowne sale, the "Herakles" did not attract heavy bidding. It was bought back by the Marquess himself for the low figure of five thousand, eight hundred pounds. Bidders knew the Marquess had placed a high reserve price on the statue, and there was obviously no point in bidding unless prepared to exceed the reserve.

The sensational piece in this sale proved to be the "Wounded Amazon", a statue usually considered second to the "Herakles" in the Lansdowne Collection. Brisk bidding for this sculpture carried it up to twenty-eight thousand pounds, with John D. Rockefeller, Jr., as its purchaser.

During the depression years, the late Marquess of Lansdowne had firmly refused all offers of under ten thousand pounds for the "Herakles". So this early Hellenistic or Roman statue still remained in the Lansdowne family. ...

Negotiating for his firm, Rudolph Forrer had lost opportunities to sell the "Herakles", for the Marquess refused to compromise on price. Now he said: "Of course, since his Lordship's death, things might have changed. Anyway, I can find out. The present Marquess spends much of his time travelling. Bowood is practically closed, except for a few rooms. They might even be dismantling their sculpture gallery. I'll start enquiries without delay."

According to Forrer, the "Herakles" was in an excellent state of preservation. The statue was in one piece and the head belonged to its body and was not, as was often the case, a body with a head which was not originally its own, joined on. The amount of restoration work on the sculpture as a whole was very slight indeed, he told them.

"Fine!" exclaimed Getty. "You follow through on the details, and I shall be ready to drive out to Bowood any time you say."

Promising to contact him the moment he had any specific news to impart, Forrer took his departure.

"A highly knowledgeable gentleman," observed Mueller, with respect.

. . . Visiting some of the "Stately Homes of England" now open to the public was part of an itinerary decided upon by the Dutch art dealer and his client.

"Let us start with Blenheim Palace, the Duke of Marlborough's home—that's Churchill's family," Getty suggested.

"And afterwards, Longleat, the Marquess of Bath's seat. It isn't many miles from Bath itself, Gainsborough's former home. We could spend the night there."

"Fine! Let's get started." As always, once he had made a decision, Getty was impatient.

Mueller needed no urging. In addition to a normal interest, a desire to see the interiors of England's historic homes, he also possessed that inherent impulse and curiosity of the art dealer.

It was the sort of day over which writers wax lyrical in prose and which poets weave into verse—a rare, typically English summer's day. Warm yet not too hot, it was sunny without the sun's blinding brilliance; mellow, ageless and calm as only the cool greenness of the English countryside can be.

The drive from London to Oxford, through Woodstock, the discreetly well-bred Georgian houses with shining brass knockers on their doors, the perfumed climbing roses, the mild elm-studded Oxfordshire landscape—everything they encountered was sheer enchantment.

And when the two men finally passed through the arched

entrance to Blenheim Palace, that often-quoted "finest view in England" burst upon them. Its lake, its bridge, the miles of magnificent park with its old and stately oaks was a breathtaking sight.

To their left, in the near distance, was the immense palace itself. To their right, the Column of Victory, topped by the Duke of Marlborough's statue, rose nobly above the trees. And beyond, was the great lake and its poplared island with Vanburgh's Grand Bridge and Capability Brown's hanging beechwoods.

They admired this scene—a model of effortless and natural beauty. Mueller, well-versed in the history of Queen Anne's gift of Woodstock Park to the first Duke of Marlborough, observed:

"Yet it was all thoughtfully and laboriously planned to the smallest detail."

"Even Turner's famous painting doesn't do it justice," said Getty, enthralled by the scene.

"The Great Lake at Blenheim provides an endless source of argument for landscape gardeners all over Europe, and especially in Holland."

On arrival at the north front, a main entrance to the palace itself, they joined a line of sightseers already congregated on the palace steps. Visiting the Stately Homes of England had become a major tourist attraction.

After the guide completed his present tour of the palace they would be allowed to enter, the doorman politely informed everyone.

Meanwhile, the American, with his usual interest for detail, took stock of the surrounding architecture, and picked up interesting scraps of information. Of all the stately homes now open to the public Blenheim Palace was the prime favourite, due to its association with that great man of modern history, Winston Churchill. A member of the illustrious Churchill family, he was born at Blenheim.

PORTRAIT OF JAMES CHRISTIE BY GAINSBOROUGH

(Chapter "England: a Gainsborough—and a Roman Statue")

THE LIBRARY AT THE RANCH HOUSE

(Chapter "The Ranch")

Quoting figures—the number of visitors who passed by him during the course of each day at two shillings and sixpence per head—the doorman said the revenue yield was several thousands of pounds for the season.

Getty deplored the changed conditions which made it necessary to open England's historic homes to public viewing, but he wondered how else the man in the street would have had an opportunity of studying such a magnificent social and cultural monument as Blenheim Palace.

After a twenty-minute wait, one file of sightseers came out of the palace while another, including Mueller and himself, entered.

The Great Hall, the Grand Cabinet, the Saloon. The Long Library, the Chapel with its famous Rysbrak Monument, the family paintings—among which were portraits by Reynolds and Sargent—all proved of immense interest. But to the majority of visitors the most interesting sight was the bedroom in which Winston Churchill was born. All the appurtenances used when he was an infant were still there, even to the bed upon which the great statesman had first seen the light of life.

In the Saloon, Getty discovered a French eighteenth-century desk of quality similar to his Molitor treasure. To his surprise a framed photograph of mutual friends stood upon it.

Blenheim Palace, splendid relic of the age of Anne, preserved its original atmosphere. Their visit inspired thoughts of a Golden Age that had passed, leaving behind this national monument as an intrinsic part of Britain's history.

In characteristic fashion, the English climate, as capricious as a pretty woman, changed overnight. On the morning following, the skies were overcast, and before long threatening clouds turned into rain. It was not that sharp shower which clears the air and leaves the earth and all growing things pungent and fresh. It became a steady drizzle, which, with a dropped temperature, made the American shiver as he stood before his sitting room windows overlooking the Green Park.

"Only Britishers can take this sort of climate for long," he remarked.

"Scotland is even worse," declared the Dutchman. "And my country is almost as bad."

Of necessity they postponed their proposed visit to Long-leat, going instead to the British Museum. They lingered with pleasure in the section which contains superb ancient Greek sculptures and parts of the Parthenon frieze from Athens, "The Elgin Marbles".

With still a couple of hours left before the exhibition closed, the two men went to the celebrated Wallace Collection.

Comparing the Gainsborough, Reynolds and Romney portraits of Perdita Robinson, Getty said:

"Each interpretation is so different that I've often doubted whether the subject was one and the same woman."

Both agreed that the paintings of these great English cöevals possessed a quality in common: a calmness, a sureness, a poised grace, courtly manners. They were part of the aristocratic life before democracy, anarchism, socialism, fascism, nazism and communism bedevilled man's existence.

"How bourgeois and colourless it makes our daily dress," deplored the Dutch art dealer as he contrasted the colourful costumes of that romantic era, the leisurely eighteenth century.

An admirer of the French artist, Watteau, he told his client the Louvre and Wallace Collections each possessed nine of Watteau's paintings and that the last German Kaiser had owned the world's largest collection of Watteaus. Of the French School, Getty declared a preference for Fragonard, whose most important painting, "The Swing", was in the Wallace Collection.

They lingered over the wonderful French furniture, and especially over a Louis XVI secretaire by Carlin, whose companion-piece was in the ranch museum.

"It might be pure imagination," said Mueller, "but to me the Carlin secretaire in your collection looks finer than its companion here."

"There's less competition in my little museum," said Getty. And he went on to compare the manner in which his own art treasures were displayed.

"In 1938, Lord Duveen told me that if Gainsborough's 'Perdita' was ever sold at auction he would open the bidding with an offer of two hundred thousand pounds. Duveen was a patriotic Englishman. It was largely due to his love for and interest in the eighteenth-century English School of portrait painters that works by Romney, Reynolds, and Gainsborough reached such fantastically high prices during the 1920's. Today many of them couldn't be sold for more than fifteen per cent. of their peak prices."

And, with his eyes still on Gainsborough's portrait of Perdita Robinson, the American concluded:

"Now perhaps you appreciate what I mean by the value of a pretty woman as subject-matter."

Whether the Dutchman appreciated it or not, he stubbornly refused to concede that subject-matter was of any major relative importance. Technical execution, composition and artistic quality were the prerequisites for a good painting, he maintained.

The next day the sun, as though trying to make amends, shone clear and bright again.

The first view of historic Longleat House, the Marquess of Bath's country seat, from its park entrance known as Heaven's Gate, impressed Getty as a gentle sepia engraving. This immense house was lapped in a broad valley of wooded park, which blended gently into the landscape and the surrounding countryside.

There were almost as many sightseers as there had been at Blenheim, although the types of people differed somewhat. Blenheim Palace attracted a mixed crowd of Britishers and overseas visitors, with a large percentage of British provincials.

At Longleat, judging by their varied accents, overseas visitors predominated.

The inevitable photographer on business bent among the tourists, induced the Dutchman to have his photograph taken, with the American at his side.

The routine at Longleat was similar to that of Blenheim Palace. An experienced guide, familiar with the history of the house, its owners past and present, and some of the art treasures, conducted them around.

From its beautiful wide staircase—one of James Wyatt's renowned examples—and its magnificent formal dining room and huge drawing room a warmth exuded, giving the great house a feeling of being lived in. Immense as this mansion was, it was also a home—unlike Blenheim Palace.

Both men admired the many richly encrusted and painted ceilings, which were of exquisite colouring and craftsmanship. And in the smaller library Talleyrand's desk, upon which the historic Treaty of Vienna was signed, gave them food for thought.

Getty was fascinated by the Thynne family's State Coach, which stood at the foot of the staircase. The State Coach was highly ornate, painted bright mustard-yellow, and resplendent with embossed silver trimmings. Also displayed was its matching coachman's uniform—an outfit of great elegance—complete with knee breeches, powdered wig and a black cocked hat, similar to the style worn by British admirals of that day.

"What gracious and cosseted lives people lived in the eighteenth century," he observed. "I believe I'd like to have lived in that era myself."

Mueller looked at him, speculatively. Although of the New World, his companion appeared equally if not more at home in the Old World. Casually, even carelessly dressed, he yet had a certain easy grace of manner epitomized by life in the eighteenth century,

"It would be a simple matter to transplant you," declared the art dealer, "except for your restless, driving energy."

"I was born and raised in a country whose immigrants derived their pioneer driving energy from a romantic past. Maybe that explains many things!" The American appeared to be talking to himself rather than to Mueller, as though he had only just realized the truth he uttered.

After inspecting a series of sculptured figures adorning the parapet of Longleat House, they continued their journey to Bath.

"With all due deference, I don't believe either Longleat or Blenheim houses finer works of art than those of my little museum in Santa Monica," Getty confided as they drove along.

. . . Entering Bath from the main Bath road, they stopped at the foot of a steep incline. Above them, set step-wise on varying levels, stood row upon row of immaculate tall and narrow three-storied houses on crescent-shaped terraces. It was early evening and the sun had not yet set, for England was still adopting extra daylight-saving time. From this vantage-point the sun's rays, momentarily imprisoned and reflected in that crescent of glass window-panes, resembled a veritable rainbow of gold.

"It's like an eighteenth-century print!" the American exclaimed aloud in admiration. "Look at it, Mueller! Have you ever seen such symmetry in architecture? It must be perfect of its kind. It's enchanting—just like an eighteenth-century print!"

They tasted the curative waters at the old Roman Baths and later attended a concert in the famed Pump Room. As in Georgian days, it was still a centre of social activity.

The Pump Room, with its glittering array of old crystal chandeliers, had retained much of the pomp and formality of the Beau Nash era; but full evening dress was no longer *de rigeur*.

"I imagine that Bath has scarcely changed since Gainsborough's time." The art dealer's *sotto voce* remark reached a dignified dowager seated on his left.

Annoyed by this distraction from the Philharmonic Orchestra, she interjected: "Bath *never* changes, my dear sir. That is why *I* come here."

. . . The notes provided by Christie's manager confirmed both rumour and fact that Thomas Gainsborough had been as astute a businessman as he was a gifted artist.

Romney and Reynolds were still in great demand as portrait painters of the dandies and famous beauties of London in that era. And, after almost four years of residence in Britain's Metropolis, Gainsborough still encountered a competition unknown in Bath.

He decided that he needed publicity. A commission to paint Royalty would have been an ideal solution—he was to achieve this honour later. Now, the artist cast his imaginative mind around. The annual exhibition at the Royal Academy was scheduled to open during the forthcoming week. Gainsborough, in the company of his contemporaries, Romney, Reynolds and others, was to have his work exhibited there. Opening Day at the Royal Academy was an important social event on the calendar of the London Season. Sometimes it was attended by members of the Royal Family.

Thomas Gainsborough's principal objective on that summer's day in 1777, however, was to capture the attention of one man—and one man only—James A. Christie.

. . . A "Society to cultivate the Arts" was initially formed in 1754. The "Academy of Art" was founded on December 10th, 1768. King George III, anxious to foster interest in art and artists, granted it a Royal Charter in 1769. Sales were held at Lamb's Auction Rooms and, later, space for hanging was allotted in Somerset Palace. Then the National Gallery was built in Trafalgar Square, and several spacious rooms were reserved for the use of the then-titled "Royal Academy of Art". . . .

The fashionable world, the aristocracy, the élite of county and London social life arrived at the National Gallery on the Opening Day of the Academy's Annual Exhibition of Art.

In company with his fellow artists, Thomas Gainsborough welcomed the great ladies and their gallant escorts, walked around with them, discreetly admired the works of his con-temporaries and listened to flattering comments on his own talent. Abruptly he excused himself to the lady of noble birth whose portrait, recently executed by him, was hung among the exhibits.

"How rude!" the lady of noble birth exclaimed to her husband.

"How wise!" retorted her husband as he observed Gains-borough greet that somewhat unique figure in the art world, James A. Christie.

. . . Tall, handsome, vigorous and forty-eight years of age, Christie was a Scotsman with the suavity of a public school Englishman: his parents were English on the one side and Scottish on the other.

Acting as brokers, the firm of James A. Christie, auctioneers, became something in the nature of an insurance to an artist. If, for example, someone had acquired a painting and then tired of it, the work could be sent to Christie's for sale on a commission basis. In many cases its original cost was redeemed and even, on some occasions, netted a profit. Should a death occur and a family and a home consequently break up, Christie's proved that paintings or portraits were never a lost investment. The firm developed into a clearing house for art objects and furnishings of all kinds. . . .

Christie could claim friendship with many of the artists of the period. He admired the works of Thomas Gainsborough, although his personal preference was for the latter's landscapes rather than his portraits. Gainsborough must have found it difficult to convince the auctioneer to sit for a portrait.

Perhaps with visions of the large vacant space on his dining room wall just above the sideboard, Christie listened to the artist's proposition.

Gainsborough offered to paint his portrait without any fee; it would be an excellent advertisement for them both, he declared. Christie would pose holding the canvas of an original landscape (by Gainsborough) in his hands, which he, the subject, was presumably offering at an auction. An important proviso made by the artist was for the auctioneer to display the finished painting in a prominent position in his galleries, where all could see it.

The auctioneer's preconceived notion of a decoration for the blank space on his dining room wall vanished. Being a keen-minded businessman, however, he recognized that a portrait of himself holding a Gainsborough landscape bore all the earmarks of good advertising.

Thomas Gainsborough's enterprising scheme developed to its conclusion. He painted Christie's portrait, although in a slightly different pose than was at first discussed.

Aware of the potentials of this unusual commission, Gainsborough undoubtedly put all he knew into the portrait—this picture within a picture—and it created immediate interest, and provided much discussion. The numerous art dealers and experts, regular visitors to Christie's auction rooms, were unanimous in their praise, declaring that some day this canvas would be acclaimed as a Gainsborough masterpiece.

Highly satisfied with his bargain, James Christie fulfilled his promise. He displayed the finished painting in a prominent position in his galleries, where all could see it.

Shortly afterwards the auctioneer took the advice of experts and loaned his portrait to the Royal Academy, where it hung for some time. A fitting tribute to Gainsborough—his artistry and his ingenuity—who, according to rumour, from that time on had little need to concern himself with any competition from his contemporaries.

. . . It was Opening Day at the Royal Academy, 1951. Since 1869 this former "Society of Fine Arts" had been housed in their own distinguished headquarters at Burlington House, Piccadilly.

"I guess Opening Day hasn't changed too much," said Getty, casting an admiring eye at the pretty girls and women who, in their summery dresses and flattering picture hats, were complemented by formally attired male escorts.

Automobiles drawing up at the entrance, however, spoke of a different era from the days when hansom cabs, coaches and footmen were part of London's everyday scene.

Inside Burlington House they met the urbane obliging manager of Christie, Manson and Woods, and all three walked around viewing the exhibits together.

"Thanks for the data on my Gainsborough," the American said. "I suppose it's about as complete a story as one can hope for."

"I'm afraid it's very sketchy," apologized the manager. "There may be some degree of authenticity, of course. On the other hand, it may just be imagination added to fragments of hearsay."

"Mueller and I both thought it feasible."

"Certainly it explains why one painting portrays two distinct subjects," added the Dutchman.

"I can visualize it hanging here—right where this painting is," Getty said. "It's about the same size. James Christie,

elegantly dressed, suave and convincing, auctioning a Gainsborough landscape to the highest bidder! You've got to hand
it to your venerable founder. It was certainly an ingenious way
of advertising Christie's for all time."

"You will no doubt agree that Gainsborough was no novice
at drawing attention to himself, either," the manager observed
drily. "Have you had any luck in negotiating for ancient
marbles?" he added.

"Not yet! But I'm hoping! I called up Spink's, who are now
enquiring about the "Herakles" in the Lansdowne Collection
—thanks to your constructive thinking."

"I wish you every success."

. . . In the weeks following, the Dutch art dealer grew to
understand something of what his client meant when he once
casually mentioned how difficult business problems presented
themselves too frequently for his peace of mind. Several
persons connected in some manner or other with Getty's
"Empire"—from the Middle East and Europe to the middle-
west of the United States and as far as Mexico—arrived in
London, at intervals. They claimed his attention exclusively,
sometimes for days at a time.

Emerging from these uninterrupted sessions of conferences,
Getty rejoined the Dutchman and made no reference to the
intervening days, nor in fact volunteered any information
whatsoever. The challenge of complicated problems and vital
decisions seemed to exhilarate him, to act as a stimulant. And
with his usual mental agility, he swung from the cold-blooded
jungle of international "Big Business" back into the humanistic
realms of art.

At the Victoria and Albert Museum in South Kensington
they saw the companion to the famed Ardabil, most magnificent of Persian carpets, in its full size and glory, complete
with beautiful borders. Its companion carpet at the ranch

museum was minus its original borders and slightly reduced in size on one end. In compensation, however, Getty's Ardabil was better preserved as to colour.

"It's badly displayed," said the American critically. "First of all, it shouldn't hang on a wall. And, secondly, it shouldn't be covered with glass."

"The glass distorts it somewhat," agreed the art dealer. "But keeping it covered has probably helped to protect it. As for hanging on the wall . . ."

"There's a good reason, sir," a museum official who was standing close by volunteered. "There isn't a large enough floor space here to lay it down so that it would be seen to its best advantage."

"It's a trifle larger than my carpet, one year younger, and, of course, the border is different. That glass certainly distorts its sheen! You've seen my Ardabil without any covering, Mueller. It looks like a sheet of silk with a high-sheen finish, and its dark though vivid colours glow like jewels." Occasionally the American waxed poetic with enthusiasm and love for his art treasures.

On a plaque fastened to the wall beneath the Ardabil carpet was a printed description:

ISLAMIC ART

Wool sehna knots with three shoots of silk weft on plied silk-warps. Three hundred and sixty knots per square inch. Persian, dated 946 A.H./A.D. 1540.

INSCRIPTION: "I have no refuge in the world other than thy threshold, my head has no protection other than this porchway.

"The work of the slave of this Holy Place. Maksud of Kashan, in the year 946."

From the Mosque of Sheikh Safi at Ardabil, 272/1893.

"The slave's inscription is translated from its Arabic counterpart. You can see it here—woven into this end of the carpet,"

Getty pointed it out to Mueller. Together, they deciphered the woven message and became lost in admiration of the Ardabil's beauty and design.

Another example of Persian art invited comparison. As in the sixteenth-century Persian Hunting Carpet in the Poldi Pezzoli Collection in Milan—the only carpet which Getty acknowledged as being comparable to his Ardabil—animals were its principal *motif*.

"It's quite beautiful," concurred the Dutch art dealer. "But its subject-matter is so restless—beasts of the jungle fighting each other, and stalking their prey. For my own taste I prefer a more peaceful design."

Once again they surveyed the treasured example of Islamic Art from the Mosque of Safi.

In both colouring and design the Ardabil carpet was calm and dignified—symbolic of a Holy Place and of Prayer. At either end a large lamp was meticulously woven into its pattern. This, they decided, was particularly representative, possibly being a replica of the actual lamps which once lighted the interior of the Shrine of Safi-ud-din.

. . . Ardabil—a Persian town—is in the province of Azerbaijan near the Karasu, a tributary of the Aray some forty miles from the Caspian Sea.

Because Ardabil was the main transit road for Russia and Persia through the Caspian port of Astara, it was important geographically. In addition to its renowned mineral springs, Ardabil became a favourite residence of the Persian Court in approximately A.D. 1540.

The illustrious Sheikh Safi-ud-din, famed as the learned individual who built the largest and most comprehensive library in Persia, was buried at Ardabil. So also was Shah Ismail, founder of the Safavi Dynasty. The holiest of its shrines most venerated and worshipped by the Persians, however, was the shrine of Safi-ud-din.

There were two large carpets and two small prayer rugs in this shrine—the Mosque of Safi. But in the early part of the nineteenth century all were removed. According to one story, they were pillaged by Russian soldiers; according to another, by custodians of the shrine, who bartered them for a great sum of money.

They remained in Oriental hands until 1890, when all four were acquired by a London art dealer named Robinson.

Robinson offered one of the two large carpets to the British authorities for an extremely high figure.

Anxious to acquire this historic treasure and under the impression that it was the only carpet of its kind in existence, they organized a collection. Contributions were obtained from all parts of Britain—from the rich, the middle class and even the poor, who, desiring to enrich their country artistically, made their humble donations. The famous painter, Whistler, was active in this campaign, and his statement that the Ardabil carpet was worth all the pictures ever painted has often been quoted.

The amount of money required for its purchase was raised. And so this exquisite example of Islamic art was duly presented to the Victoria and Albert Museum, where it has been on display ever since.

"It must have been an unpleasant surprise—in fact, a shock— to the British authorities when they discovered that a companion carpet existed," Getty told Mueller. "For Robinson, anxious to obtain dollars, sold it and the two prayer rugs to Yerkes in New York. He was one of the outstanding carpet collectors of all time.

"After Yerkes died his famous collection was sold. The large Ardabil was acquired by the fabulous Captain de la Marr. He placed this treasure in his town house in New York City, where it remained during his lifetime."

Lord Duveen—as colourful a character as Captain de la Marr himself—was on board a liner in mid-Atlantic when news that the Captain's effects and household furnishings were to be auctioned was announced and relayed to him. When Duveen found the Ardabil carpet was included in this sale, he ordered his New York office to buy it at any price up to two hundred and fifty thousand dollars.

Bidding at the de la Marr auction proved surprising. To Duveen's amazement, he became the Ardabil's new owner for the comparatively small sum of fifty-seven thousand dollars.

News that he intended to bid high had presumably leaked out through the "grapevine", and possibly other art dealers decided it would be a waste of time to bid against him.

Duveen did not buy the carpet for resale, but for his own use and pleasure. . . .

"I first saw the Ardabil at an Exhibition of Persian Art in Paris in 1938," Getty told Mueller. "I was so impressed by its majestic beauty that I wanted to see it again. I called up a friend—Leon Lacroix—who was deeply interested in Persian art, and he came along when I visited the exhibition a second time. Lacroix took one look at the Ardabil and said, 'Now I understand the Persian statement: 'This carpet is too good for Christian eyes to gaze upon.'

"As with Rembrandt's Looten portrait, I couldn't get the Ardabil out of my mind. Again I went to the exhibition. This time another friend of mine—an American-Armenian who's been in the carpet business for many years, an acknowledged expert on Persians—came along. His reaction convinced me that the Ardabil was the finest carpet he'd ever seen in his life."

"How did you eventually acquire it?" Mueller asked with eager curiosity.

The American related how, after his visit to Paris, he had

contacted Lord Duveen with a view to purchasing the historic Persian carpet. And how Duveen informed him that it was not for sale at any price.

During the war scare of 1938, Duveen changed his mind: he was now prepared to consider an offer for the Ardabil. Negotiations proved so lengthy that in the interim the world's stock markets weakened alarmingly. The war news was sadly discouraging: civilization seemed to be nearing disintegration. People were looking for shelter, not for art objects. Because of these circumstances, the negotiations were eventually concluded at a bargain price of sixty-eight thousand dollars.

"From the point of view of purchase, my timing was right," said Getty. "But the bottom appeared to be falling out of things otherwise. I acquired one of the two prayer rugs which also came from the shrine of Safi."

He went on to say that his former penthouse-apartment in New York contained a living room with sufficient floorspace to accommodate the large Ardabil. For some time the Persian carpet was used there. Later, it went on loan to the Metropolitan Museum.

"Some months afterwards, visiting Duveen's establishment on Fifth Avenue, I was shown the famous Anhalt carpet. The price quoted was one hundred and twenty-five thousand dollars. My curiosity aroused, I decided then and there to compare the Anhalt and Ardabil carpets—to lay them out side by side."

"Wasn't that difficult?" queried the Dutch art dealer. "Your carpet was on display at the Metropolitan."

"It had been released about a week previously and was being stored at Duveen's. Believe me, Mueller, side by side with the Anhalt—which is a fabulous carpet—my Ardabil proved it has no competitor for first place. Everyone agreed that it reigned supreme."

"And of course," Mueller thought, "if Duveen's price for

the Anhalt was a hundred and twenty-five thousand dollars, the Ardabil must naturally parallel, if not exceed, it in value."

As though divining his companion's thoughts, the American related the sequel.

"Shortly afterwards, the King of Egypt's sister was about to marry the Shah of Iran. A dealer reported that, assuming it could be purchased, the King wished to present my Ardabil carpet to his sister. It was a well-considered wedding gift. The return of the Ardabil—with all its historic significance—to its birthplace in Asia after its long absence in the western world would doubtless have delighted his future brother-in-law."

"Excellent diplomacy on the part of the King of Egypt," was Mueller's observation.

"Excellent," Getty emphasized. "But nothing and no one could induce me to sell a work of art I'd become increasingly fond of. The price suggested? It was in the region of two hundred and fifty thousand dollars, I believe."

. . . A communication from Spink and Son announced an appointment to visit Bowood had been arranged. The American was invited to go there at any time to suit his own convenience.

"After which I suggest we leave for the Continent, Mueller. If that suits your plans?"

"I shall arrange my affairs accordingly," said the genial and obliging art dealer, who had previously resolved to make trips to both Scotland and Ireland. He left Ireland unvisited, but went to Scotland while Getty visited a friend, an English baronet well known as a collector of eighteenth-century French furniture.

"His taste is impeccable and his choice of art objects superb. His estate in Cornwall is delightful. And his library made me uncomfortably aware of the insignificance of mine," Getty told Mueller when next they met. "Talking of books, let's

THE LANAII ROOM, SHOWING PAINTINGS BY THE
SPANISH ARTIST, SOROLLA

(Chapter "The Ranch")

THE MOLITOR DESK IN THE LOUIS XVI ROOM

(*Chapter "The Ranch"*)

browse around the old bookshops in Charing Cross Road before we leave London."

Charing Cross Road bookshops did not yield any travel or guide books of America's pioneer days to add to the ranch library. However, Getty unearthed one treasure—Pausanias' *Descriptive Guide of Greece* with ancient Greek and English texts. It was written in the time of the Emperor Marcus Aurelius, about A.D. 170. The American was as elated as a schoolboy over his "find".

"Can you read it in the original?" Mueller asked with astonishment. It seemed to him that his companion reacted somewhat in the manner of a schoolboy—embarrassed when discovered reading a book pronounced by adults as "beyond his years and over his head".

"Yes," said Getty. "I understand something of ancient Greek. At least well enough to read Pausanias, especially with an available translation to help me over the hard places. My Greek is, naturally, not as good now as it was when I was at Oxford. It used to be one of my best subjects."

"Do you speak modern Greek, too?"

"A little. Enough to get by on, anyway."

. . . Rudolph Forrer accompanied them to Bowood. They saw nothing of the great house itself, visiting only the sculpture gallery, which was, as Spink's expert had foreseen, in the process of being dismantled.

"Here it is, sir—the 'Herakles'." As they examined the large statue Forrer read its description aloud:

According to Michaelis: The marble statue of Herakles is one of the finest pieces in the Lansdowne Collection. It shows the hero as of youthful age. He rests on the right leg, holding the club over his left shoulder, in lowered right hand he holds the lion's skin, which hangs down to the ground. Sculptured in the manner of Lysippos, the head is of characteristic

ɪ

129

smallness. The workmanship is first-rate. Of Pentelic marble, the head has never been broken off. Restoration: the tip of nose, parts of left forearm and the right thumb, a piece inserted on the right forearm and the left shin between knee and ankle. Six feet five inches in height, this statue was found in the year 1790 at Hadrian's Villa at Tivoli, just outside Rome, in the grounds belonging to the Conte Fede. Later it was in the possession of the Marefoschi family. Jenkins, an English dealer who was travelling throughout Italy in search of works of art, apparently obtained this sculpture from the Marefoschi family. Jenkins in turn offered it to Lord Lansdowne. The purchase was completed in May, 1792. Lord Lansdowne paid six hundred pounds for this statue. It is judged to be either first century B.C. or first century A.D.

"It's an inspiring work!" exclaimed the Dutchman. "In my opinion it's Greek, Mr. Forrer. What do you think?"

"Well, since it was influenced by Lysippos and is sculptured out of Pentelic, I'm rather inclined to think it's Greek, too. Hellenistic, possibly. That's why I always speak of it as 'Herakles' rather than 'Hercules'."

"The British Museum's expert, Bernard Ashmole, prefers to date it as a Hadrianic copy," Getty declared somewhat ruefully.

"It's really all a question of theory," Forrer told them. "And after my own careful study, I believe this sculpture is just too good to be a Roman copy."

"Assuming that you can obtain the 'Herakles' for me, how will it be listed?"

Forrer thought for a moment and then volunteered the diplomatic reply: "Well, sir, in deference to the opinion of the British Museum expert, I'd suggest that we leave it flexible: first century B.C. to first century A.D."

"I've only had the pleasure of meeting Mr. Ashmole on one occasion," said the American, "and I asked him then what actual difference existed in sculptures executed between the two periods, first century B.C. and first century A.D. He thought for a while, and then told me that he personally could see little difference, if any."

"Most statues are copies of original bronzes of the fourth and fifth centuries before Christ, so these differences of opinion only amount to splitting fine hairs," said Mueller brusquely.

Getty continued to examine the "Herakles" critically. He particularly studied the face. "It's late," he observed; "very late. It can't be earlier than late Hellenistic—say, 150 B.C. It might easily be a Hadrianic copy. Obviously it was made in Greece, for it's out of Pentelic marble. Freight was high, sculptors were numerous and needed employment and, as we've always read, Hadrian loved Greece and worked untiringly for her prosperity.

"One of her few industries was sculpturing the native marbles. Since a sculpture was only half as heavy as the marble block before chiselling it into shape, and freight based largely on weight, it was only practical to chisel the work in Greece before shipment elsewhere.

"In my opinion, therefore, this statue was made in Greece. Not before 150 B.C. though, and obviously not after about A.D.130—the date of Hadrian's villa at Tivoli. Too bad Greek sculptors didn't remain as they were in the fourth and fifth centuries B.C." Getty's voice conveyed more than a tinge of regret. "Herakles shows signs of being a work of the decadence. His body is reminiscent of the Golden Age, but his face is very late. Very weak in character. None the less, I'm impressed with this sculpture as a work of art, Mr. Forrer. If it's available at a reasonable figure, I'd be interested to buy it."

The conversation turned to what would be considered a reasonable figure. In view of the late Lord Lansdowne's insistence that a ten thousand pounds minimum be quoted, Rudolph Forrer did not think there would be too much difference in the asking price at the present time.

"I'll make an offer of six thousand pounds."

"I will gladly submit your offer," Spink's expert shook his head, "but I very much doubt whether it will be accepted, sir."

"This is an interesting piece," the Dutch art dealer observed, moving towards a group of statuary, "Leda and the Swan". Its description in Michaelis read:

> "*Michaelis: No. 78.* A marble group of Leda and the Swan. Leda, half-sitting, presses the swan to her embrace, while the cloak held up with her left hand is to protect him from the threatening eagle. The chiffon is delicately and finely worked, the body is fair. Restoration—left arm with cloak, right arm as far as wrist, sundry pieces of drapery and the head and neck of swan. Out of Pentelic marble, the head, though found with the statue and of the same marble, may not belong. It is, however, beautiful and it fits. Height four feet two inches. Roman."

Forrer related how this statue was found in 1775 by V. Abbati Rancouriel at the Villa Magnani on the Palatine Hill in Rome. "The piece is unquestionably Roman, even though it's sculptured out of Greek marble." And of how Gavin Hamilton, who subsequently acquired it, offered it to Lord Shelbourne for one hundred pounds. There was considerable negotiation until Lord Shelbourne finally purchased the sculpture for sixty-five pounds. "I don't know when the Marquess of Lansdowne procured the 'Leda'," he concluded.

"It's an attractive piece," said Getty. "Of course it doesn't begin to compare with the 'Herakles' as an important work of art. It's a nice garden ornamentation, though. How much do you consider it to be worth, Mr. Forrer?"

"Oh, somewhere in the region of five hundred pounds."

"Fine! You have my authority to offer six thousand pounds for the 'Herakles' and five hundred pounds for 'Leda and the

Swan'. How long do you suppose it will be before you know whether or not my offer is accepted?"

"Within the week, sir."

Before leaving Bowood, they examined other marbles of the famed Lansdowne Collection, and beyond all doubt its most important work of art was the "Herakles", whether first century B.C. or first century A.D.

The sculpture gallery also contained a life-sized white marble statue of a hermaphrodite. The American questioned why artists employed their talents on these indelicate and inartistic subjects. "Or maybe it's just that I don't especially care for Carrara marble," he shrugged his shoulders.

Replying to Forrer, he said that research on his art treasures had yielded mainly superficial data.

"I've acquired some sketchy details which are, I'm afraid, more supposition than fact. To do research on a work of art comprehensively means breaking down theories and methodically following clues. And I don't have that much leisure time! So I utilize whatever scraps of information I can dig out, a little invention—or author's licence—plus my imagination."

"How do you find it affects your relationship with the work of art involved, sir?" asked Forrer with professional interest.

After some deliberation, Getty said: "I feel closer to the work of art. For instance, I've gained more understanding— even affection—for Gainsborough's 'Christie' since I have some vague idea of the reason that prompted its creation. These scraps of what I call backstage information personalize my treasures, if you know what I mean."

"I know precisely what you mean. And if I owned a collection of works of art I would certainly follow your example. It seems an intelligent approach to artistic or intellectual pursuits."

"You flatter me. However, it's a safe bet to assume that both Mueller and myself are finding this experiment fun."

133

It was the first time the Dutch art dealer had ever seen anything approaching a twinkle in his client's eye or his smile so broad. Uncertain how to interpret this, he merely nodded in surprised agreement.

On the morning they were due to leave for Paris, Rudolph Forrer telephoned his American client and on behalf of Spinks said that—somewhat to the surprise of his firm—the Lansdowne family had accepted the offer for both the "Herakles" and "Leda and the Swan".

His news was received with elation. "I'll send instructions for shipping just as soon as you arrange for an export permit. And if you should hear of other Greek or even early Roman sculpture . . ."

"I very much doubt whether there will be any such likelihood, sir." Forrer's voice sounded regretful, yet decisive.

"Well, just in case of that one-in-a-million chance," insisted Getty stubbornly, "you can always reach me through the Ritz Hotel in Paris."

· IV ·

A Tapestry of Paris

IN Paris, a glimpse into the romantic history of tapestries revealed that the art of tapestry-weaving was known even in ancient Egypt and Greece. Byzantine tapestries were in existence from the fifth to the ninth centuries, but were created primarily as a decoration for monasteries and other ecclesiastical institutions.

By the close of the thirteenth century, tapestry-weaving as a means of artistic expression had become an important, widespread and accepted art, its principal centres being the northern sectors of Europe.

The town of Arras, in Burgundy, contributed fine examples of this craft in the fourteenth and fifteenth centuries. Brussels became prominent in the late fifteenth and in the sixteenth centuries. The later sixteenth century and early part of the seventeenth century produced Mortlake's contributions.

Cosimo established a factory in Florence, which survived until the eighteenth century. In Italy's dry and warm climate, however, paintings proved more durable and suitable for wall decoration just as, on the other hand, the climate of Paris proved more suitable for tapestry panels as wall coverings. Heating was a big problem in olden times; the majority of rooms were large and draughty, and tapestries covering vast wall spaces kept the rooms warmer. In consequence, they became popular, achieving a useful as well as a decorative purpose.

Now extinct in so many countries, the art of tapestry-weaving as begun in the fourteenth century in France is still practised at the Gobelins in old Faubourg Saint-Marcel, on the left bank of the River Seine.

On a Thursday, the day for public viewing, from two to four o'clock in the afternoon, the Dutch art dealer and his American client proceeded there.

Adopting a suggestion of the *concierge* at the Ritz Hotel, when they had enquired for the most direct route, they were travelling by Métro—the Paris subway.

... Rabelais mentions that in the year 1540 a tapestry-maker named Jean Gobelin established himself on the actual site of the present-day Gobelins factory. It is assumed that he must therefore have been one of the first, if not the first, tapestry-maker in Paris, since the earliest Royal Tapestry Workshop was established at Fontainebleau.

Rumour also has it that in the reign of Francis I, when the Paris of letters, of arts and sciences was born and became, according to Ronsard, "the town where the teaching and the glory of the Muses merge", a tapestry-maker named Jean Gobelin moved his residence from Rheims to Paris, where he set up a workshop on the banks of the little river Biévre.

Ostensibly his workshop was a dyeworks. From Venice, he introduced a vivid scarlet colour which became a Royal favourite—and thereafter—associated with the name Gobelin. This scarlet dye proved so expensive to manufacture, however, that only the Royal household could afford it. The Gobelins Workshop was not a financial success, and in later years it earned the unhappy title of "Folies Gobelins".

In 1604, when Brissac delivered Paris to Henry IV for a reputed sum of six hundred and ninety-four thousand livres, after the many years of siege and famine, the King, aided by his Provost of the Merchants, François Miron, applied himself to the interests of the French capital.

Among his numerous activities he created a Royal Manufacture of Tapestries and, anxious to build up a tapestry workshop in Paris, installed two Flemish tapestry workmen at the

Gobelins factory, Marc de Camans and François de la Planche.

Henry IV was assassinated on May 11th, 1610, in the Rue Ferronnerie in Paris, but many of his projects lived on. Tapestry-weaving became State-controlled, and thus incorporated the Gobelins Workshop.

In 1662, Colbert, who was then in charge, decided to concentrate all tapestry-makers scattered in and around Paris into one central factory.

Further to enhance this project, Colbert secured the services of the Royal painters, Le Brun and Vouet. These two inventive artists helped to create the tapestry designs, in addition to supervising every phase of work which, they insisted, be performed only by the ablest of workmen obtainable.

King Louis XIV ordered tapestry panels for his many Royal households, in addition to those intended as presentation gifts to other reigning monarchs, foreign ambassadors and numerous court favourites.

In 1667, by Royal edict, "La Manufacture Royale des Meubles de la Couronne" was formed. The Gobelins now included cabinet-making as part of its resourceful business endeavours.

The Revolution, and Napoleon Bonaparte, ultimately destroyed what had, by that time, developed into a remarkably successful enterprise. In 1826, however, the Bourbons restored The Gobelins to Royal favour and renewed popularity.

When the manufacture of carpets at La Savonnerie was discontinued, those *ateliers* were transferred to the Gobelins Workshop. Production of Savonnerie carpets was continued there, and they became the first factory in the world ingeniously to copy famous paintings on tapestry looms.

. . . "I've often heard it said that as an independent art tapestry-weaving lost its originality by attempting to imitate paintings, and by using portrait subjects," observed Getty. "Yet, how can one generalize? An artist is surely not expected

137

to create the subject-matter of his work. The 'Last Supper' was not Leonardo da Vinci's own creation. He simply depicted a scene which took place fifteen hundred years before he was born, and immortalized it in fresco." And then, as an after-thought: "If only it were transportable, painted on wood or canvas, so that all the world could share what is to me one of the most inspired of all works."

Mueller and the American had formerly discussed and deplored the fact that Leonardo's "Last Supper"—painted in 1495-7—was, by virtue of being a fresco, restricted to a wall of the Cenacola Vinciano in the Old Dominican Convent adjoining the Chiesa di S. Maria Delle Grazie in Milan.

In 1943 the Convent was mercilessly bombed. One wall was destroyed, its roof was badly damaged, yet the wall upon which da Vinci's immortal fresco is painted was spared, and it has suffered little except from time and the elements. Much restoration has, however, been necessary, that of recent date being the most successful.

Arriving at the Gobelins Station the two men ascended from the bowels of the earth into clear, crisp daylight.

Sewers almost completely cover the little River Bièvre which formerly washed the walls of the old Gobelins dye-works and tanneries, and the scene has lost some of the picturesque quality of past generations.

Rustic and vegetable gardens, once cultivated by workmen from the Manufacture des Gobelins, are replaced by a park. Its small chapel, now used as a museum, bears two marble tablets on either side of its projecting door, and on them are related a history of the Gobelins.

Part of the old building was burned down by the Commune in 1871, and it is generally conceded that the new factory built in 1914 is conventional and lacks character, even though surmounted by a square dome with an haut-relief by Landowski and decorated on the first floor by caryatids.

138

Behind it the old factory buildings, with their large chimney-stacks and fine style, still maintain a peaceful charm, reminiscent of the monastic air of the trade houses of old France. In the cobbled courtyard, which separates the buildings, a bust of Jean Gobelin, sculptured out of marble, gazes in silent retrospect.

Inside the factory, Mueller and the American learned from a well-informed guide that all Beauvais tapestry was now woven with a low warp or *basse lisse*, and worked on horizontal frames. Gobelins tapestry was worked on an upright frame with *haute lisse* or high warp. Both types, however, used a similar yarn of silk and wool-thread mixture.

The trend of present-day designs, the full-sized models or cartoons, especially created for Gobelins tapestry panels now in the process of weaving, dismayed Getty. Ultra-modern in conception, they were comprised mostly of circles, squares and hexagons interlaced into geometrical patterns.

"There's nothing subtle or romantic in these designs. They're significant of jets and rockets!" he exclaimed.

"It depends how one defines romantic," Mueller protested. "There's romance in our mechanical age, too. There's . . ."

"I'll grant you all that," his companion interjected. "Yet surely tapestries—an art one associates with the more leisurely past—needn't be impregnated with this lust for speed, for modernism. All this cubistic design and garish brightness of colour," he indicated with a gesture of his hand, "is harsh and disillusioning. More and more I'm convinced that modern art is decadent!"

The Dutchman did not share his client's view. "I am not a disciple of modern art, yet certain of its characteristics appeal to me. Its realism, for one thing. In essence, modern art is synonymous of our time."

Getty's voice conveyed regret as he said, "I guess the Golden Age and all its romantic illusion is receding further and further into the shadows. Future generations will doubtless refer to our time as an age of stark realism."

There were twelve high warp looms now being worked in the Gobelins factory, and three young people were employed at each one. The visitors learned that each loom yielded an output of one to six square metres per year per person, depending upon the intricacy of the cartoon they were following.

There were also three Savonnerie looms in work, and four low-warp looms. The latter, however, were used mainly for weaving small panels suitable for chair-seats and chair-backs. On these looms the output yielded by each person per year was similar to that of the high-warp. Although since the warp or cord of *basse lisse* tapestry was smaller than that of *haute lisse*, an operator could legitimately be expected to produce less in fair competition. Synthetic and vegetable dyes were used for all types of work.

More interested questioning elicited the fact that the tapestry factory at Beauvais had suffered some war damage in 1940; hence this transfer to The Gobelins and the ultimate incorporation of both factories into one unit.

The Gobelins museum, formerly the chapel, proved disappointing. For Getty, it contained only one outstanding example of a sixteenth-century Persian carpet, plus one long strip of carpet—a Louis XIV Savonnerie of exceptionally good colour, in addition to some few interesting seventeenth-century tapestry panels of fine quality.

"It's a poor display when one realizes that this is the very birthplace of French tapestries and Savonnerie carpets," he said.

. . . At the Petit Palais which shelters the Musée des Beaux Arts de la Ville de Paris and which, with its sister building, the Grand Palais, was constructed for an exhibition in 1900, they saw a magnificent Beauvais tapestry. Gifted to the French nation by an American, Mr. Tuck, it occupied a place of honour as one of the few important Boucher tapestries in France today.

Mueller referred to notes he had compiled at the ranch museum. "Louis XV Beauvais Tapestry: Nicholas Besnier and Jean Baptiste Oudry, *circa* 1750, 'La Toilette de Psyche'. Size eight feet ten inches wide by eleven feet high. The nude nymph, partly covered by a white robe, is seated cross-legged upon a cerise drapery on a gilded fauteuil. Two maidens, robed in pale yellow and rose, arrange her hair as she gazes at her reflection in the golden mirror placed upon a cherry-red drapery on a rococo table, supported by two other maidens, who glance admiringly at her beauty. At her right are two more nymphs, one seated and arranging a garland of forget-me-nots and roses, the other bearing a salver with a perfume bottle and powder jar. In the foreground are a large rococo ewer and basin, and at the left a pair of sandals before a marble fountain surmounted by statuary figures of cupids and dolphins. A prospect of summer woodland at night."

"According to its catalogue description, your panel is similar," Mueller told Getty. "Yours, however, has a plain blue selvage border and appears to be a trifle smaller. These Boucher masterpieces can be justly described as the greatest documents of France's Golden Age of tapestry-making. Their weaving is perfection itself."

"These companions to my own treasures impress two things upon me," said Getty thoughtfully. "Namely, my good fortune in possessing art objects of equal stature, and of their surpassing beauty. One is apt to lose sight of these facts when things are close at hand and can be seen at any given moment."

. . . François Boucher, they discovered, had led the life of a *grand seigneur*. He had lived at the rate of the then considerable sum of fifty thousand livres a year, subsidized ballet dancers and given artistic fêtes to which all the fashionable world of

Paris thronged. He himself was no indiscriminate art collector. He possessed an æsthetic and varied collection comprising works of gold, bronzes, Japanese wood engravings, Chinese porcelains, pictures and drawings by many of the great masters.

The period of his activity covered half a century, and until the last days of his life François Boucher worked ten hours a day.

Under the government of Madame Pompadour, especially, Boucher was the "man of the hour". Each day he appeared at the palace to give "La Pompadour" instruction in painting. He conducted all the court festivals and theatrical events which, in that era, were the vogue. He designed costumes for the great ladies who appeared at court. And, apparently inexhaustible in invention, he also furnished designs for sculptors, ivory-carvers, goldsmiths and carpenters; for wall-paper, furniture, sedan chairs, bookbindings, fans and jewellery.

He painted easel pictures, wall or ceiling pictures, screens, carriage doors. He became renowned as the greatest interior decorator of his day. Hundreds of apartments and mansions in Paris, Versailles and elsewhere owe their *décor* to this artist's impeccable taste. In every manner, light and shade, François Boucher, apotheosis of the aristocratic life of the rococo, typified it. . . .

"On the surface, Paris always seems unaffected by time and events," observed Mueller as they stood on the steps of the Louvre. Its wide expanse of Tuileries Gardens to Napoleon's small Triumphal Arch and beyond it, the pale pink granite Obelisk of Luxor in the Place de la Concorde which, flanked by the magnificent marble Horses of Marly, is a gateway into the Champs Elysées, where the imposing Arc de Triomphe de l'Etoile rises triumphantly at its head, was an inspiring view.

"Paris fulfils all expectation as one of the world's loveliest cities," said the American. "In some respects I prefer Rome. But for sheer physical beauty in architectural planning Paris, in my opinion, has no equal."

Inside the picture galleries occupying the first floor of the Museum's south wing they paused before an unfinished portrait of Madame Récamier, by Louis David. Getty scrutinized it through the pocket-sized magnifying glass he generally carried.

"This is the only Louis David painting I really care for," he said. "Like many things in the world of art, I suppose we can credit its artistry to Boucher."

. . . When Louis David went to study with François Boucher, the latter realized that this youth possessed a rare talent, but alas! not for the rococo. Consequently, he advised him to study with Vien, who at that time was the pioneer of classical painting in France.

Louis David followed this advice, and on Boucher's personal recommendation Vien accepted the youth as a pupil. Eventually the young artist went to Brussels and Rome, where the classical reaction was in full tide, and where his genius soon displayed itself.

The period of the rococo had begun to wane, and a fashion for imitating the ancients, even in dress, was emerging.

Years later, returning to his native France, Louis David was acclaimed, appointed the King's painter, and enjoyed an immense success. . . .

"David imitated the ancients to extravagant lengths," criticized the Dutch art dealer. "His style is, if anything, too severely academic. His colours lack richness. Even in its very perfection and draughtsmanship, his execution seems harsh and uninteresting."

"You've got to give Boucher his due," said Getty. "He always recognized talent, and gave it a helping hand."

Several paintings by Hyacinthe Rigaud were displayed in the Louvre.

"Do you consider this 'Showing a Leg' better than mine?" Mueller scrutinized the colourful portrait of Louis XIV in

his Royal regalia. It stood on an easel as a special exhibit at the
far end of the Long Gallery.

"It's an identical version. Artistically there's no difference
whatsoever," he replied.

. . . They had been in Paris for some ten or eleven days when
the American received unexpected news from Spink's. The
firm could now secure a large Roman statue from the Earl of
Pembroke's collection, and gave him the first offer of it.
Photographs were enclosed, and a description as translated and
copied from Michaelis, which read:

According to Michaelis: The statue of the elder
Faustina, Consort of the Emperor Antoninus Pius, Empress
A.D. 138, who died A.D. 141, at the age of thirty-seven.
This statue, similar to the "Matron from Herculaneum",
which is in the Dresden Museum in Germany, is of excellent
effort. The head, which has never been detached, is a definite
likeness of the Empress and is undamaged, except for its
nose and chin. The hair forms a crown of plaits on top of her
head. The lowered left hand is not hidden in the cloak; it
holds a stalk; she holds an object, perhaps a cluster of
wheat-ears. In excellent preservation. *Parian* marble. *Roman*.
Second century A.D. Height six feet eight inches.

Never had the Dutchman seen his client so exuberant.
"Seems like this is destined to be a lucky trip, Mueller! The
experts were all so dubious about my getting any ancient
marbles of importance. Yet I've already acquired the Lansdowne
'Herakles', and now I'm offered the Pembroke 'Faustina'."

In his enthusiasm he had overlooked the important detail
of price, Mueller gently cautioned.

Placing a telephone call to London, Getty confided: "I'd
just hate to miss this opportunity. Yet I don't feel inclined to
pay some fancy and exorbitant figure."

When he learned the price, however, and discussed its merit

with his companion, they decided it was reasonable. Thus this early Roman statue of the Empress Faustina became destined to cross the Atlantic.

"It will be shipped to Santa Monica just as soon as they get an export licence. My dream of a choice sculpture gallery might come true, Mueller. It's exciting, isn't it? This calls for a drink. What'll you have?"

... "Here it is," declared the American. " 'Guerault's Table'. I've been here—to the Louvre—at least twenty times with experts and connoisseurs of French furniture, and there's always been unanimous accord that this small table by Burb is one of the three most important pieces in the Louvre furniture collection."

"I knew of this piece, of course," said the Dutchman. "And of the similar coffee table—although it isn't by Burb—in the Wallace Collection. But I must confess my amazement at finding a companion-piece in your ranch museum. I had absolutely no idea that a companion-piece to 'Guerault's Table' ever existed."

"Nor did I, until . . ." And Getty proceeded to relate how this pride of the Louvre, this lacquer and Sèvres plaque work or coffee table had, many years previously, come into the possession of one Monsieur Guerault in Paris, a well-known dealer in antiques.

Practically every serious art collector interested in furnishings of French eighteenth-century origin had at one time or another bid for this outstanding example of the cabinet-maker's craft, but always unsuccessfully.

Comte Edmond de Rothschild, one of the most famous collectors of eighteenth-century French furniture in a family of famous collectors, had bid through Stiebel, his personal representative, twice making offers of ten thousand pounds. Monsieur Guerault, however, evinced little interest in the offer and always refused to sell, even when requested to name his own price.

"Had he been interested," Getty told Mueller, "Stiebel was of the opinion that Edmond de Rothschild would have even paid up to fifteen thousand pounds."

. . . Small but exquisite, this work or coffee table became known as "Guerault's Table". When its owner died in the early 1930's, it was inherited by the Louvre. . . .

In 1949, when visiting the galleries of Rosenberg and Stiebel, a firm of antique and fine art dealers in New York, Getty was shown some fine pieces of French furniture. They had become available from the collection of a branch of the Rothschild family, due to war conditions.

Choice though these pieces indisputably were, he was not disposed to purchase. Subconsciously he was looking . . . looking . . . for, in similar manner to the Ardabil carpet and Rembrandt's portrait of Marten Looten, the small Sèvres plaque and lacquer table had fired his imagination by its delicacy and superb craftsmanship. Its artistic quality struck a responsive chord.

He bade the art dealers good day and was about to leave their premises when, almost furtively, they called him back into their private offices. A door was carefully shut, an immense safe unlocked, and an object wrapped in a white cloth was brought out.

Unwrapped, Getty found it difficult to believe his own eyes. It appeared that two impossibles had happened. First, here was a companion-piece to "Guerault's Table", and, secondly, this creation by the cabinet-maker known as Burb was even finer than the original one in the Louvre. It had often been declared that it would be impossible to surpass this example. Yet here it was—surpassed!

"Timidly, I enquired whether this superb little table was for sale. Its price? They asked fifteen thousand dollars. I'd already decided that, if I were lucky enough to secure a first offer, I would readily pay up to three times that amount."

Having made it a cardinal rule only to purchase antique

furniture or any work of art, subject to reliable expert opinion, Getty immediately telephoned to Mitchell Samuels, a friend and an acknowledged authority on French furniture. In response, Samuels arrived at the galleries without delay.

Alone in the room together for a few minutes, Mitchell Samuels asked quickly: "Have you bought this table yet? If you haven't, I would like to buy it myself. This is probably the most important piece of French furniture in the United States today." Vague rumours were afloat to the effect that Rosenberg and Stiebel had a surprise in store, he went on. This, was evidently the surprise. "Had I seen this wonderful little table for only one minute before you did, I and not you would be its present owner," he declared in all seriousness.

. . . It was presumed that this work or coffee table had originally been the property of Madame Dubarry, and was given to her by King Louis XV. . . .

With his usual avid curiosity, Getty pressed for greater detail—the name of its immediate previous owner, etcetera, etcetera.

They were pledged to secrecy concerning the matter, declared the art dealers. And merely disclosed this treasure was formerly in England, intimating it had been in the possession of the highest nobility, possibly Royalty.

The table was a pure and delicate example of Burb's workmanship—Burb who for some hundred and fifty years or more has been an enigma to all the experts of antique furniture. Of consummate quality, skill and grace, any piece of furniture stamped with the initials B.U.R.B. is regarded as perfect of its kind. Yet the identity of this greatest cabinet-maker of all time, the enigmatic B.U.R.B., still remains a riddle.

. . . "Isn't there another Burb piece in your ranch museum?" asked the Dutch art dealer, thoughtfully.

His client smiled as he related an incident concerning the

Burb table, once part of the Countess of Londesborough's collection. A serpentine-shaped Louis XV writing table of tulipwood, mahogany and marquetry with gilt-bronze mounts of flowers, leafage and shells, it was likewise a relatively small piece of eighteenth-century French furniture, some twenty-nine inches high and thirty inches wide.

He had first seen the writing table together with a fine bureau plat at Botibol's, a firm of art dealers in London. Greatly admiring them, he was informed that neither piece was for sale. Nothing daunted, he said: "I'll make you an offer for both pieces. And I'll hold my offer open indefinitely. If you ever decide to sell them—and at my price—just cable me to Los Angeles."

That was during the summer of 1937. . . . It was May of 1940 when he received the cable accepting his offer. World War II had begun, and the dealer—afraid his treasures might suffer bomb damage—had decided to get them out of England.

Despite Hitler's submarine blockade of the high seas, the precious furniture duly arrived, unharmed, at the Santa Monica Ranch.

Six years later, a New York antique dealer visited the ranch. Getty, showed him around the newly-completed museum section. The dealer, seeing the Londesborough Burb writing table at a distance of ten yards said: "I'll give you twenty thousand dollars for that without examining it at closer range. We can make the deal right here, before we step one foot closer to the table itself."

"It's remarkable," commented Mueller, "that so many of France's great cabinet-makers of the eighteenth-century were, in actual fact, German." He cited Molitor, Oeben, Weisweiler, Riesener and possibly the mysterious Burb, who never revealed his identity by a completed signature.

. . . His business meeting concluded earlier than anticipated,

Getty sauntered along the Rue Faubourg St. Honoré late one afternoon. Some paintings in a window beckoned and attracted his perceptive eye.

Inside, he discovered this miniature salon was a haven for aspiring artists. They brought their work there, and left it to be sold on a commission basis. He looked at many canvasses of varying sizes and, impressed by their effectiveness and decorative value, earmarked four—a set of ballet scenes as portrayed by a *prima ballerina* solo, and by pretty young *coryphées* as a group.

"*Ah, ils sont très ravissants, monsieur.*" The *patron* clasped his hands together in an appreciative gesture. "*Mes compliments. Vous avez un goût exquis.*"

Before completing his purchases, however, Getty invited the Dutch art dealer's opinion.

"They're the work of a young Romantic, of course," the latter said as he studied the four paintings. "But even though immature, they are well constructed and balanced. This artist shows a decided ability in composition."

. . . "And so," Mueller later observed with some amusement, "you dislike modern art, yet you've just increased your collection of Moderns to a total of five."

Sheepishly, the American admitted: "I just couldn't seem to resist them. Their colours were so lovely; although of delicate pastels, they're positive. And the dancers looked so fragile and appealing."

"Where do you intend to hang your modern paintings?"

Getty thought for a moment, and then said: "I guess they'll look well at the beach-house. You didn't see my beach-house while you were on the West Coast. It's an unpretentious little place, but has a lot of charm. And it's right on the ocean front—within the sound of breakers. I love the sounds of the sea, especially at night when everything is dark and still. There's music in the sea, Mueller; a symphony as descriptive

149

and melodic as any composed by mere mortal. On occasions, when I've listened to the sea—myself in a contemplative mood—I've thought of man's persistence, of his efforts to emulate Nature's sounds and scenes and colours. And I always arrive at the conclusion that while an exact reproduction is beyond his powers, man all-in-all achieves some creditable results."

. . . The art dealer pointed to a stone mansion which faced them on the opposite side of the wide Avenue Montaigne. "Your out-sized tapestry panel, your Boucher of the two subjects—'Bacchus and Ariadne' and 'Jupiter and Antiope'—once hung in there." He explained: "After this tapestry left the Royal Family of Portugal, it went into the collection of Jules Porgeis, the banker."

"And Porgeis lived in that imposing edifice?"

"That was his residence in Paris," Mueller said, as they crossed the street to closer observe the great mansion, once the home of François Boucher's most magnificent of all tapestries, put on the looms at the Beauvais factory in 1749.

. . . This, the second lap of their travels, showed Mueller another aspect of the American. Although fluent in French, the latter practised diction daily, and read mainly French newspapers.

"I make it a habit," he explained, "to speak and read in the language of whichever country I'm in, wherever and whenever possible. It's the only way I can ever hope to improve my accent."

The Dutchman, whose French, while conversationally fluent, held a guttural overtone, said in self-defence: "I ought to follow your example, but I've too many things on my mind. Between your massive correspondence and other business interests, visits to museums and exhibitions—and studying—you must occupy yourself on an average of sixteen hours a day every day."

"That's about my minimum," Getty said in all seriousness. "Most times I find the days are all too short for everything I'd really like to accomplish."

"Just as a point of reference, how many works of art have you acquired from the various Rothschild collections?" asked the art dealer, changing the subject.

"Let me think. In tapestries I have 'The Abandonment of Psyche', 'The Arrival of Psyche at Cupid's Palace' and 'The Toilette of Psyche'. My fourth panel of that series came from Lord Iveagh, via the Walters collection. It has a companion-piece in the Stockholm Museum. In furniture, I have a couple of Gueridon tables and the two large secretaires by Carlin and by Weisweiler. From Hamilton Palace—and also from Edmond de Rothschild—there's the small writing table by Riesener and a Louis XVI upright secretaire by Leleu. That's about all. Oh! I almost forgot, I have a pair of black lacquer Louis XV encoignures by Dubois.

"I'd been in the market for such a pair for about fifteen years before I saw these at Partridges in London. Their beauty and elegance so impressed me that I bought them—regardless of their high price—without hesitation. Frank Partridge was under the impression that these also came from one of the Rothschild collections. But their previous ownership was never fully confirmed."

"You've been very wise to limit your buying activities to these and similar responsible sources."

"As you well know, one has to be a lucky buyer," Getty quoted his companion's often-used phrase with a significant gesture. "A work of art from any Rothschild collection is tantamount to a gilt-edged security! Art objects, even when authenticated and from responsible sources, can sometimes be doubtful. I've been duped, like most collectors, at one time or another. In my early collecting days I got stuck a few times. By the way, Stiebel once told me some interesting facts about the great art treasures of the Rothschild family. He said that Comte Edmond de Rothschild of the French house of Rothschild owned in the early twentieth-century what was generally accepted to be the finest collection of eighteenth-century French furniture in the world. Some parts of it were inherited, other parts were bought. Baron Nathaniel, head of the Austrian house, and his heirs, could apparently boast the second best. The third collection in importance belonged to Lord James de Rothschild at Waddesdon in England."

"If anyone is in a position to gauge the order of their merit it's Stiebel," declared the Dutchman. "His firm helped to make part of those collections."

"In the States," said the American, "our finest French furniture collections are in the hands of Forsyth Wicks, Mr. Dunlap, Mrs. Dilman Dodge, René de Becker, John D. Rockefeller, Jr., and . . ."

"And . . . yourself," added the art dealer.

Getty responded to what he knew was genuine appraisal. He felt relaxed with Mueller.

"Only a handful of public museums in America can boast of really fine French furniture," he said. "In New York there's the Metropolitan, of course, and the Frick. There's the Rice Room in the Philadelphia Museum, the Severance Collection in Cleveland, and the Huntingdon in Pasadena. The Spreckels in San Francisco about completes the list. Those are the only important ones that I actually know of."

"Your ranch museum can certainly boast its fair share of treasures. And additions like the 'Herakles', 'Faustina', and 'Leda and the Swan' add to its importance. Tell me, where do you propose placing these marbles?"

The American asked Mueller if he remembered a long gallery which served as an entrance to the museum section of the ranch house. It connected the theatre room with the museum. At the present time it was used mainly as a picture gallery. He went on: "There's plenty of space in there for the larger sculptures. The gallery is about forty feet long and

SÈVRES PLAQUE SECRETAIRE BY WEISWEILER

(*Chapter "The Ranch"*)

A BRONZE CAT, VERY RARE, ANCIENT EGYPTIAN
SAÏTE PERIOD, 600–400 B.C. SHE REPRESENTS THE GOD-
DESS BAST, FAMED AS A GODDESS OF BENEFICEN
ATTRIBUTES OF THE SUN, SUCH AS GERMINATION O
THE SEED (SIDE-VIEW)

HE FRONT VIEW SHOWS THE UTCHAT (SACRED EYE
MULET) WORN AROUND HER NECK. THIS LIFE-SIZE
AT WAS WORSHIPPED AS THE GODDESS BAST WHEN
UBASTIS BECAME EGYPT'S CAPITAL IN PLACE OF
THEBES

(Acquired 1955)

SÈVRES PLAQUE SECRETAIRE BY CARLIN

(Chapters "The Ranch" and "England: a Gainsborough—and a Roman Statue")

sixteen feet wide. And it's well lighted. It has windows at either end. Of course, I'll still keep the smaller marbles where they are now, in the classical room."

"I've often meant to ask you . . . how long did it take to lay the mosaic floor in the classical room?"

"Ah, now you've really got me on a favourite subject. It was a real headache, believe me. I think I told you how I bought the mosaic floor, in its many pieces, crated and sight unseen from one of the Randolph Hearst sales."

"Yes; you did."

"The difficulty of laying an ancient mosaic floor is formidable. It takes highly skilled mosaic workers, and there are few of them in the United States. I consulted a famous antique marble firm, and was told they knew of only two men in America capable of laying this floor. After some weeks they located one of the men and engaged him. For six weeks or more, he worked eight hours a day five days a week at five dollars an hour. It proved an expensive hobby! Installing a floor in a room only twelve feet by eighteen feet amounted to well over two thousand dollars. And, of course, this didn't include the cost of the mosaic itself."

"But what a floor! I doubt if there's a finer example of ancient mosaic anywhere in America. Its colours are so bright and clear that one can scarcely credit its antiquity."

"Oh, I'm well pleased with the result. Although I grumbled a bit about the cost. It seemed a mighty high price for such a little floor."

. . . This conversation reminded the American of an appointment to look at some boiseries while he was in Paris. If suitable panelling at the right price could be found, his instructions for shipment and its installation in both the tapestry and Louis XVI rooms of the ranch museum would follow.

"Nevertheless, I enjoyed watching my mosaic floor being laid. The workman was a skilled artist at his trade, and I tried to learn something about his art. I found that many of the ancient colours could no longer be matched as the quarries are lost in the mists of time. Trying my hand at setting the tiny coloured stones into their cement base, I soon realized the intricacies of this difficult craft," Getty concluded.

. . . At Jansen's in the Rue Royale the Dutch art dealer and his client met Monsieur Boudin, one of the most outstanding interior decorators, specializing in eighteenth-century *décor*, in Paris. They were shown some fine examples of boiseries. The prices quoted ranged from two to three million francs upwards. Admiring a small settee adorned with superb old gilding, they were told that this piece of furniture was formerly the Duke of Windsor's property. Jansen's were now asking two and a half million francs for it.

Mueller urged his companion to wait—to look at other examples of boiseries before making any definite commitment. "These are too fussy . . . too busy . . . for your rooms," he said.

Getty took the Dutchman's advice and was glad he had done so, for within a few days' time a telephone call from Jansen's told him they had obtained "some exceptionally fine panelling . . . exactly what Monsieur was looking for."

"I'm certainly anxious to see what else they have to offer," he told Mueller. "That other estimate of twenty-seven thousand, five hundred dollars for a modern Louis XVI boiserie seems rather high to me."

The Régence boiserie which Monsieur Boudin of Jansen's showed to them later that morning was both impressive and pleasing to the eye. Part of it was old, although well restored, and part was added.

Of carved oak, in a design of the first quarter of the eighteenth century, it was reproduced in the manner of the famous architect Gilles-Marie Oppenoord (1673-1742). Its original portions included two corner sections containing mirrors and showing in the *dessus de glaces* female masks, shells and swags of flowers, all carved in relief on a diaper- and fleurette-patterned ground.

Further illustrating what he desired to convey with the aid of a large photograph of the ranch museum's tapestry room, Monsieur Boudin indicated that the marble staircase along its left wall should have an iron and gilt-bronze banister—in the manner of François Germain—to replace its existing marble balustrade. This would blend in perfect harmony with the boiserie and so complete the tapestry room.

For the Louis XVI room he now offered a carved boiserie painted in grey and gold, dated *circa* 1780, with newer additions where architecturally necessary. Boudin envisaged that when completed, this Louis XVI room would, architecturally, resemble certain rooms at Bagatelle, the Paris house which François-Joseph Ballanger built for Comte d'Artois in 1777.

The price quoted for both sets of boiseries and their installation was in the region of eighty thousand dollars, which included two hundred thousand francs for piecing them out to fit each room. The banister was approximately seven thousand dollars, including whatever piecing and straightening work would be necessary.

Without a moment's hesitation, Getty agreed to place this contract. Skilled men capable of carrying out the work would be sent to Santa Monica from Jansen's New York office. The cost complete was in the region of one hundred thousand dollars.

For the first time Mueller saw how unimportant cost was to the American, despite his often repeated statement that he disliked paying inflated prices for anything in life. The keenness of his desire was the deciding factor. . . .

. . . Satisfied with his transaction at Jansen's and with the promise of an interesting afternoon to be spent at Versailles, Getty persuaded Mueller to rearrange his own schedule and join a business acquaintance, his wife, and himself for luncheon. "Although you might be bored," he warned, "I've been delegated by one of my associates in the States to show the town to a couple who've never been in Europe before. And they're not even remotely art-conscious, I'm sorry to say."

The Bar at the Ritz Hotel "on the Cambon side", fashionable pre-luncheon and pre-dinner rendezvous of cosmopolites and internationals, was, as usual, crowded. However, George, the barman, magically found a corner table for the party. He was evidently familiar with Getty's palate: a tumbler of ice, a beaker of dark rum and a bottle of Coca-Cola speedily appeared.

The guests, a typical young-middle-aged couple from Texas, insisted upon "Everything French for us! We get rum-and-coke all the time back home." Mueller seconded their choice of the Ritz "special"—champagne cocktails—and of their expressed "France is such wonderful wine country. Why drink hard liquor over here?" It was not warm enough to lunch outdoors in the hotel gardens, so they went into the Grill Room.

"I've been coming here, on and off, since before World War One," Getty told them. "In fact the first time I ever visited Paris was with my parents, in 1909. We stayed at the Hotel Continental. I remember it all vividly. The Continental hasn't changed—it's almost the same now as it was then."

"I'll bet nothing's been changed here either," declared the Texan, whose obvious preference was for everything bright, shining and new. His wife—a perfect example of the sleekly-groomed American wife—admonished: "That's the whole charm of Europe, Fred. Everything's so old. Remember how they told us back home how the Ritz is so much a part of Paris that it *is* Paris?"

Her husband nodded: "I guess you're right, honey. Europe should be kept European. That's its big attraction for us Americans."

. . . The Dutchman was far from being bored; he found these unsophisticated down-to-earth Westerners refreshing, even though his æsthetic senses were outraged once or twice during their afternoon visit to Versailles. . . .

Getty knew an official at the palace and he arranged for them to visit certain rooms not usually open to the public.

Mueller was delighted at this unexpected opportunity to explore Louis XV's private library, and Marie Antoinette's boudoir containing the famous mirror which had revealed to France's ill-fated Queen her fate. In the glass she saw herself headless, and ran screaming in terror from the room. The American and his party now gazed into that same mirror, fascinated.

Close examination revealed a flaw in its cutting and silvering. From a certain angle it reflected the body minus the head. Thus the mystery was explained.

Some tables of superb patina and with exquisite gilding delighted Getty. There was also a brocade love-seat whose beautiful proportion and symmetry were a joy to the eyes of a connoisseur. Apropos the several great carpets, he said, "Lacroix—the carpet expert—told me that none of these Savonneries equal mine. It's almost impossible to find another Louis XIII example. Mine is unique. I had it on display at the Gobelins Museum before the war, and their official pronounced it to be one of the rarest and most beautiful of all Savonnerie carpets. By the way, magnificent though these chandeliers are, not one of them is cut out of rock crystal."

The Galerie des Batailles was an outstanding example of Louis-Phillipe's atrocious taste, Mueller agreed with his client, whereas Madame de Maintenon's tapestry chairs, in their original frames, and now on display, epitomized good taste.

Like the majority of citizens of the New World, the Texan and his wife reacted as their art-loving host had anticipated. Dutifully awed by such grandiose surroundings and all the splendour of this epoch, they were amazed that a palace containing over a thousand rooms could not boast one single bathroom. This lack of even some primitive form of plumbing was incomprehensible to them.

"You wanted to see Paris," Getty warned them, "so Paris you are going to see. You've inveigled me into sitting through the Folies Bergeres tonight, so this afternoon you are going to visit still another old place. In its own way, it too is historically interesting."

. . . Jansen's Atelier in the Bastille district proved to be huge workrooms where over five hundred people were employed. The visitors saw *ébénistes* making furniture and *menuisiers* making panelling by hand. Sculptors carved wood, using one hundred different chisels. Gilders were applying water gilding on wood and an electric process on bronze. Mercury gilding, the visitors were told, was by far the best and most durable. However, this process and its use was now forbidden by law. It was dangerous to the health of the workers. Skilled artisans wrought heavy iron into intricate and unbelievably fragile design; upholsterers worked with precious silk damasks in a multitude of colours. All these tasks were expert, individual, and slowly and painstakingly performed by hand in the manner of earlier centuries.

"Back home, we'd produce all of these things in a fraction of the time and therefore at a fraction of the cost," said the Texan.

"But these are all antiques, honey!" His wife's voice reflected her irritation at her husband's "ignorance".

"How can they be antique when they're only just being manufactured?" he retorted practically.

"Most of the period designs are faithfully reproduced here," Mueller explained. "The cabinet-work, when completed—although it won't have the patina of age—will be as fine in craftsmanship as some of the work produced by *ébénistes* of the seventeenth- and eighteenth-centuries." . . .

While returning to the Place Vendôme—it seemed as if this tableau had been especially designed and presented to complete "An Afternoon in Old Paris"—they encountered a regiment of French cavalry dressed in the colourful uniforms of the 1790's. The winding, cobble-stoned streets with mounted riders clop-clopping towards them was a romantic and picturesque sight. Even the practical Texan exclaimed with pleasure.

Mueller was disappointed by the negative responses of certain antique dealers in Paris who, for some years past, had been commissioned by the American to locate a fifth tapestry panel with which to complete his set of Boucher's "Story of Psyche" series. (His ranch museum boasted four out of this set of five Beauvais tapestries.)

"There isn't much to report about your Rigaud, either," he said, disturbed. "The Director of the Louvre says that three portraits of Louis XIV, 'Showing a Leg', were commissioned at the same time. One, as we know, is on show in the Louvre. Another is at Versailles. The third was supposedly destined for the King of Spain. It conflicts with your information, Mr. Getty. Your Rigaud supposedly hung in the Tuileries Palace until 1830, when the monarchy changed and the ex-King went to Frohsdorf."

"But later on my particular Rigaud—as we know to be a fact—was inherited by Don Jaime and in due course by his daughter in Frohsdorf," insisted the American.

"Did you acquire the painting from her personally?"

"No; I got it in London. As I told you, my two flower pieces by Van Huysum and the disputed 'Madonna of Loreto' also came from the Don Jaime collection. I bought all four paintings at a sale at Sotheby's in 1938."

"I picked up one authentic scrap of information," said the art dealer with some slight show of satisfaction. "The Director of the Museums of France at the Louvre states that all three portraits were painted in 1704. Furthermore, he suggests that additional data might be available in the National Archives.

159

The Louvre Archives don't list anything which belonged to the Tuileries."

"Ummm-m! We found the Archives in Amsterdam invaluable. Maybe we ought to follow-through the same way here in Paris."

During the following week the American was fully occupied by business matters, so the Dutch art dealer decided to spend a few days in the château country.

Alas, they proved unproductive days, he told Getty when next they met, yielding nothing of interest, artistically.

The latter commented: "I'm afraid the Texan couple regard me as something of a curiosity, if not a crank. It's impossible for them to comprehend the depths and phases of art, or of how or why anyone should want to collect works of art. Mind you, they're all for enhancing America's cultural standards, for expediting her artistic development as a nation. But despite their own substantial fortune, they accept no personal responsibility for helping the development along; not even in time or effort.

"Sometimes, Mueller, I get good and mad at my fellow countrymen," he concluded sharply.

A visit to the National Archives of France left the American perplexed. Seeking to confirm and supplement his own information relative to Rigaud's painting, he told the Dutchman:

"I'm not concerned with the financial aspect of this portrait. No doubt it will always be worth what I paid for it. What does seem incredible to me is that Don Jaime owned anything other than authentic works of art. After all, he inherited the Rigaud; he didn't buy it. And the fact that this canvas was cut out of its frame, plus the further fact that Don Jaime's ancestors lived in the Tuileries and not the Louvre, tends to confirm my belief that my painting must be one of the original three versions, if not the original itself."

PRTRAIT OF THE DUCHESS OF CUMBERLAND BY
ROMNEY

(*Chapter "A Tapestry of Paris"*)

THE LOUIS XV ROOM, SHOWING BOUCHER
TAPESTRIES, THE JOSSE TABLE, AND THE NEW
BALUSTRADE AT FOOT OF WHICH IS A MARBLE
PORTRAIT-BUST OF MR. J. PAUL GETTY

(Chapter "A Tapestry of Paris")

The sparse records available at the National Archives of France referred to an *original* portrait of King Louis XIV, "Showing a Leg", as being in too tattered a condition to display. They dated it as being painted in 1701 and referred to three copies of this same subject being executed by Rigaud in 1704. All three copies—since each was painted by Rigaud himself—were equal in importance. Now, Getty was somewhat confused.

"By the same token," he said to the Dutch art dealer, "my 'Madonna of Loreto' is unquestionably only a copy of the famous Raphael, but nevertheless it's a good painting. Only good paintings were in the Don Jaime collection. After all, it was an art collection belonging to royalty. They had full and free choice of the best of all times."

Thinking out loud, a habit of his, Mueller mused: "Museum authorities prefer not to disclose the fact that art treasures once accredited to their museums have disappeared. Many of the recorded great works of art were probably salvaged from the Revolution, but are lost to France for ever."

. . . Concerning his "Madonna of Loreto", the American said that Gerald Brockhurst, an ardent student—almost a disciple—of Raphael, who acted in an advisory capacity to the late Lord Duveen, was also impressed by the picture.

In Brockhurst's presence, Duveen had said to Getty: "I won't tell you the Madonna is by Raphael, because if I did it would be worth seven hundred and fifty thousand dollars. But I won't tell you that it isn't." . . .

"There's a good Poelenburgh among your Dutch paintings—similar to the one in the museum at Dijon. The study of an unknown man, a sixteenth-century Flemish work, was another picture I liked. It impressed me, as did the studio piece painted by one of Rembrandt's students. Likewise, Berghem's 'Milking a Goat'. You disclaim being a collector of paintings, Mr. Getty, yet you possess an interesting variety. A painting can be a fine—sometimes a great—work of art,

L

even if it isn't attributed to a great Master," said the Dutch art dealer.

"A serious collector of paintings might argue that point. Unless a picture is attributed to an acknowledged 'Great Master', it's usually of little interest to him."

"You're proud of your Rembrandt because it's signed and dated. And of your 'two-pictures-in-one' Gainsborough. You overlook the fine Romney you have," grumbled the Dutchman.

"Anything that lives in the house proper and not in the museum section is apt to get overlooked. Romney's 'Duchess of Cumberland' hangs in the drawing-room. By the way, when I bought that portrait through Duveen, he told me he believed it to be as fine a Romney as existed. I'm fond of my paintings by Sorolla—the Spanish artist, and especially so of his 'Gardens of the Alhambra' with its wonderful portrayal of sunlight."

In the Rodin Museum they admired a small though life-sized terra-cotta head similar to one in the American's collection.

"It's a pretty little thing," observed Mueller, critically, "but it lacks character."

"I've never been too keen on French sculptures, yet I find this one charming. She has a winsomeness that's appealing. Her companion-piece is one of my favourite art objects—sort of a pet," said Getty.

. . . Coming originally from the Dowager Lady Sackville's collection, this terra-cotta head of a pretty girl by Rodin was the only example of modern sculpture in the ranch museum. . . .

In Paris, as elsewhere, there was gossip of the American's fabulous wealth, his control of "major business", the immense scope of his far-reaching financial operations. Mueller heard vaguely of oil, banking, Wall Street; of hotels, insurance and manufacturing. Their mutual interests, however, were restricted to the world of art, the only sphere in which the art dealer found his client voluble.

On occasion he imagined Getty to be on the verge of coming out of his shell, of opening up to the extent of discussing personalities, of exchanging confidences; a not unnatural supposition considering their constant association. Once, talking superficially on world affairs, Getty said: "I majored in political science and economics at Oxford some thirty-odd years ago, and the basic law of economics never changes, regardless of politics."

Mueller thought: "Many a world-famous figure suffers the tortures of inner loneliness, afraid, and a prisoner of his fame. Could a man also become the prisoner of his own great wealth?"

His companion's restless driving energy and lust for seeing more and yet more; his unquenchable thirst for knowledge; those endless hours of study and "escape into learning". Could it all add up to being a sedative for inner loneliness, for that spiritual isolation which great wealth with its accompanying responsibilities and fears so often engenders?

Through his acquaintances who were oblivious of the world of art, Getty realized an unexpected pleasure. In the hotel lobby the Texans met a friend who was the business adviser to the Duchesse de Talleyrand.

The latter, who started life as Anna Gould, daughter of one of America's first railroad tycoons, had also been the wife of the Marquis Boni de Castellane, celebrated and aristocratic boulevardier of the 'nineties. Now in her eighties, the Duchesse lives in the United States and seldom visits Europe.

Her business adviser intended checking the contents of her Paris home, the famous Palais Rose. "If you would care to see the house, you are all very welcome to come along," he invited.

. . . The Palais Rose stands on one corner of the Avenue

Malakoff, where it occupies a large area reaching to the Avenue Hoche. Built out of pink marble, its architecture was influenced by the Grand Trianon at Versailles.

Completed in 1898 at the reputed cost of thirty-eight million gold francs, the Palais Rose stands, still resplendent and set back in its formal grounds, coldly aloof from twentieth-century Paris. Most of the neighbouring mansions are now modern apartment-houses.

This relic of elegance, a glittering monument to the aristocratic life of Paris, looked lonesome, Getty decided, even desolate, with its shuttered windows.

The interior of the great mansion was of incredible beauty. Looking up at its wide marble staircase which graciously ascended from the centre of an immense entrance hall to a mezzanine and then branched off to the right and left, and continued upwards to the first-floor suites of rooms, the American exclaimed: "It resembles the Royal Palace at Naples! What banquets, what balls, what grandeur this house has seen! What exquisite taste!"

It was common knowledge that Boni de Castellane's flair for *décor* was responsible for the Palais Rose—its exterior and interior—which was acclaimed by the art connoisseurs of the world. The Marquis had exquisite taste and his wife the unlimited fortune which made it possible for him to indulge his taste.

Nowadays the house is stripped of its great art treasures; some have been sold and others shipped to the Duchesse in the United States.

Proofs of Boni de Castellane's impeccable taste in furniture were in the ranch museum. Mueller referred to his notebook and read about the Gobelins Suite from the Palais Rose, and the Commode from the collection of George J. Gould, former brother-in-law of Castellane: "*Gobelins Suite.* Tapestry, comprising one settee and two matching armchairs. French, *circa* 1720-5. Backs and seats are woven after designs of Claude

Audran the Younger or François Desportes. The gilt frames carved with shells, acanthus and paterae are of later date. (Personal notation: I was amused by its tapestry-design of monkeys playing musical instruments.)

Commode. French, *circa* 1735. Rosewood, mahogany and tulipwood. Body of slightly serpentine contour, contains two long drawers. Gilt-bronze mounts comprise sprays of endive foliage rising from claw feet and flanking a vignette of two children playing with a large monkey. *Jaspe Fleuri.* Height thirty-five and a half inches, length fifty-three and a half inches. In the manner of Charles Cressent."

Pierre, butler in the Gould family for forty-five years and now sixty-eight years of age, still lived at the Palais Rose, as did Jules the chef, whose service in the great mansion totalled some forty-three years. Pierre proudly informed the visitors that Jules' art was still incomparable.

Refreshments were offered and, wandering through the almost empty rooms, glass in hand, was a strange experience. All the furniture in evidence was shrouded in dust-sheets, while ghosts of more recent times haunted the enormous library.

. . . In 1948, the four major powers—"The Big Four"—held prolonged sessions at the Palais Rose. These sessions lasted approximately two months, during which time an agreement was sought with Russia regarding a permanent peace treaty with Germany and Austria. The conference terminated in a complete fiasco, since Russia would not agree to any of the proposals made by the United States, Great Britain and France. All were vetoed. . . .

The elaborate winter garden adjoining the library must have been a magnificent sight in its heyday, Getty thought during the tour of inspection. Deserted now, emptied of all growing, living beauty, adorned only by relics of the past—some statuary which was attributed to Houdon, and other scattered pieces—it was forlorn, almost pathetic.

165

"I wonder why the Duchesse doesn't dispose of this place," he ventured.

"I doubt if she ever will," he was told. "The Palais Rose is a romantic chapter in her long and colourful life. She's very sentimental about it."

. . . The Dutch art dealer was unable to satisfy his curiosity with regard to the monkey motifs used so extensively in eighteenth-century *décor*. From old French books on *ébénistes* and tapestries, he learned that in the earliest of tapestry designs, dating as far back as the medieval, floral garlands predominated. Later, these evolved into intertwining ropes or cords decorated with tassels. To relieve the monotony of such stereotyped patterns, and to fill in the many blank spaces created, it became necessary to invent further decoration. Obviously, only birds could perch upon garlands and monkeys clamber up ropes. Berain, it appeared, was the first tapestry designer to utilize such effects. Though hardly a satisfactory or edifying conclusion, it was the only conclusion Mueller reached.

The American was amused: "I didn't think there was any special significance; merely perhaps that monkeys—like Pekinese dogs—were used as pets, especially by the elegant ladies of that elegant era."

. . . "The last time I visited here, Stiebel was with me," Getty told Mueller.

"Here" was a mansion built and formerly occupied by the eminent Camondo family. Victims of Nazism and Hitler's insensate persecution, the last members of this respected and philanthropic family all perished in the concentration camp of Auschwitz. Their beautiful home with its great works of art is now a private museum. An engraved plaque fastened upon the outside wall of the house bears tribute to the Camondo family, whose cultured tastes remain—indestructible—for humanity to enjoy.

166

"There are quite a few private art collections in these old mansions around the Parc Monceau", Getty explained to his friends. "None, however, equals this one. The 'Jacquemart André' is possibly the next most interesting. Stiebel said the truly great examples in French furniture here are that pair of encoignures by Dubois, which are similar to mine; this Baroque corner commode by Cressent (which he claims is the most wonderful Baroque example in existence); and this small green Sèvres plaque bonheur de jour. He dated this piece as being about 1760, and maintained that it's unique. It reminds me somewhat of my little Burb table."

The Dutch art dealer enthused over a large bureau plat, likewise credited to the renowned *ébéniste*, Dubois. "I recollect seeing a similar bureau plat at the ranch museum. But it was unsigned. Have you any ideas as to whom it can be attributed?"

"We-ell ... there are theories. . . ." The American proceeded to relate how, when in London, he was anxious to secure seventeenth-century and eighteenth-century rock crystal chandeliers. They were extremely difficult to find, but at Cameron's, fine art and antique dealers of Grosvenor Square, he eventually saw the loveliest rock crystal chandelier of his life. It held twenty candles and equalled the best examples of the Wallace Collection. It was dated as 1690 to 1700.

"I'd been looking for just such a chandelier for fifteen years, so grasped this opportunity. I figured its cost would be at least four thousand pounds. When the price asked was only fifteen hundred pounds, I naturally didn't hesitate for a moment."

Getty also saw a small French eighteenth-century mechanical table by Oeben, and a magnificent bureau plat of earlier period. Both sorely tempted his instincts as a collector. However, the large bureau plat was a most expensive piece of furniture, and he hesitated.

The Oeben mechanical table had a companion-piece in the

Louvre, he was informed by Mr. Levy of Cameron's. "In the Louvre example, however, the table-top raises. This one, as you can see, slides," he said, demonstrating its mechanism.

On impulse Getty added the Oeben mechanical table to his collection.

"Like the Rembrandt, Ardabil and other art objects I've acquired, that bureau plat haunted me. I'd seen it before, but where? I knew the table was unsigned, but had a feeling that such a handsome piece of French furniture must be important. Finally, I decided to make an offer for it."

Discussing the matter with Frank Partridge, the latter suggested that he, as an art dealer, would evaluate and endeavour to secure this piece for him subject to an adjustment of price. It was, however, late on Friday afternoon, and Cameron's had now closed their galleries. There was no alternative but to exercise patience until they reopened for business on the following Monday. Partridge was leaving London for the week-end, so they decided that he would approach Cameron's (acting as Getty's buying agent) upon his return to town.

On Tuesday morning a telephone call from Partridge told of his seeing the bureau plat, and he advised: "Secure it without delay before opposition arrives." For Fabre, the Paris dealer, had, as soon as news of this table reached him in Paris, flown to London.

"I authorized Partridge to close the deal immediately. An hour later he called back to say it was a *fait accompli*. At noon I went to Cameron's to take a look at my newly-acquired treasure."

Monsieur Fabre acknowledged Getty, with whom he was acquainted, introduced his client—a wealthy French collector, Monsieur Vergé—and resumed his examination of the ormolu mounts on the bureau plat. He spoke to his client in rapid French, and explained that this was doubtless the famous Josse table which the Germans had seized during the war. It was allegedly purchased by the Reichsbank. How the table had eventually reached England was a mystery.

In May, 1894, the large bureau plat was the frontispiece of a catalogue of the celebrated sale of works of art belonging to Monsieur Josse in Paris. *Ebénistes* seldom signed their works before approximately 1750. Both Levy and Fabre now dated this piece of furniture as between 1690 and 1710, further corroborating that it was indeed the Josse table.

"All of a sudden I realized that Fabre was right. I remembered seeing this bureau plat at his place in Paris before the war. I wanted to buy it then, but his price was too high. Monsieur Vergé was quite obviously disappointed when he heard this lovely piece of furniture was already mine. Fabre asked whether I would relinquish my purchase to him—at a profit."

. . . "You have other bureau plats in your collection." The Dutchman referred to his trusty notebook:

"*Writing Table*. Tulipwood and kingwood marquetry. Gilt bronze foliated mounts—a seated figure of Justice ornaments the frieze at either end. Oblong with three drawers at one side; top covered with dark leather. Manner of Charles Cressent. Height thirty inches. Length seventy-eight and a half inches. From the collection of William Randolph Hearst."

"Presumably that table was used in the Royal Law Courts of France—it bears an appropriate title 'Jury and Justice'. It could probably tell us many interesting tales, Mueller. However, it's no longer in my collection. I recently presented it to the Los Angeles County Museum."

A wave of business associates, geologists and engineers from the Middle East again descended upon the American, keeping him in conference for some days, after which both Mueller and he were scheduled to leave Paris.

The art dealer was bound for Geneva and the tiny independent Duchy of Liechtenstein, which is sandwiched between Austria and Switzerland. An important collection of paintings was to be sold there. The American's business activities were now taking him into Germany. The looseness of their association pleased Getty, whose idiosyncrasy in regard to plans and timing was now well known to his companion.

"Let us keep the date of our next meeting flexible," Mueller suggested. "It's less difficult for me to accommodate myself to your plans than *vice versa*."

Always appreciative of intelligent thinking, Getty was grateful. "The unexpected so often overtakes me," he explained. "I'd no idea that business would catch up with me so extensively here in Europe. Problems one never anticipates occur. And while I delegate authority wherever I feel it's justified, there are moral responsibilities I can't ignore."

The Dutchman was familiar with this sentiment. On rare occasions, Getty spoke of his father and of how much he had always admired—even envied—the latter's brilliant mind and honest diligence. His iron-bound policy, "Moral responsibilities must on no account be side-tracked", and favourite expression, "No man's opinion is any better than his information", were often quoted by his son.

A final visit to the Louvre convinced them that though other "Chancelleries" challenged, none exceeded the beauty of design, colour or weaving of a large tapestry in the ranch museum whose description read:

"*Gobelins Tapestry*. First half of the eighteenth century. Called a 'Chancellerie'. Depicts the arms of France and Navarre, canopied and crowned and represented upon a blue field strewn with gold fleur-de-lis. Woven from a design by G. L. Vernansal and Claude Audran the Younger. Border shows in each corner the arms of Chancellor Chauvelin; and in the centre of the lower border is the cipher or monogram of the Chancellor. The signature of the weaver, Le Blond, appears in the lower right-hand corner. Height eleven feet two inches. Width eight feet eight inches. *Note.* Periodically throughout the eighteenth century, sets of 'Chancelleries' were ordered from the Gobelins Tapestry Manufactury for presentation by the King to his Chancellors."

Another of the ranch museum's treasures invited comparison—a writing table acquired through Botibol's of London. It was French, *circa* 1745-50. Of kingwood, and with gilt-bronze mounts, it was further decorated by bands of guilloche motif. Stamped in several places on the mounts was the letter "C" surmounted by a crown—a tax *poinçon* which was placed upon all ormolu articles during the period 1745-9. This table was notable as one of the very few extant examples showing the introduction of the neo-classic motif—bands of guilloche—prior to 1750.

Both men were surprised when they realized the Louvre museum's weakness in Sèvres plaque furniture of the French eighteenth century.

"I believe there are only two important pieces in the entire collection—'Guerault's Table' and the Gueridon table, by Carlin," Getty commented, and observed also how the white flowers in the lacquered woodwork of 'Guerault's Table' were yellowing with age.

In the Adolphe Rothschild Salon they saw many exquisite examples of the goldsmith's art. These attracted Mueller, but the American remained unaffected by precious metals and precious stones, even while admitting their beauty.

. . . Three invitations were prominent on Getty's desk on

171

this, his last evening in Paris. The opening of the Opera Season, a "gala" charity performance of ballet, and a formal dinner party which was one of the social highlights of the Paris season. In mellow mood he told the Dutchman: "A siege of business conferences leaves me with little desire for the social bright lights. We can hear opera in Italy. I've apologized *re* the dinner party, since I'd scarcely be a credit to any hostess tonight. As for the ballet . . . I only turn into a balletomane when my favourite *prima ballerina*, Markova, is on the stage."

. . . Walking around, enjoying a last view of this beautiful and historic city, the two men found themselves in the Rue de Berri. The address "20 Rue de Berri" was significant; it became a highly fashionable *salon* of the Parisian *élite* in Napoleon's time through Princess Mathilde, daughter of Jerome Bonaparte, who possessed distinguished talents as a hostess.

The art dealer recalled an evening at the Santa Monica Ranch. "It was exciting to find myself sitting on a chair which once belonged to the Empress Josephine. Why, Napoleon himself might have sat on that very same chair!" (This set, comprising a Beauvais tapestry sofa and ten matching chairs, were acquired from the Duc de Trevise's collection in Paris.)

"Do you remember seeing six Empire chairs which I mentioned originally belonged to Madame Jerome Bonaparte? They are graceful little chairs and have Dolphins carved on their gilt frames." Getty went on to relate how these were acquired, together with some rock crystal chandeliers, from his old friend Elsie de Wolff, the late Lady Mendl. Her brilliant taste and flair for furnishings laid the foundation of her fame and fortune. Her wit was memorable and, at the great age of ninety, she had still been an outstanding personality in both Parisian and international society.

Like the Dutch art dealer, Getty indicated that he too was inclined to sentimental dreaming in which he journeyed into the past with some of his art treasures as companions.

"To me my works of art are all vividly alive. They're the embodiment of whoever created them—a mirror of their creator's hopes, dreams and, yes, frustrations too. They've led eventful lives—pampered by aristocracy and pillaged by revolution, courted with ardour and cold-bloodedly abandoned. They've been honoured by drawing-rooms and humbled by attics. So many worlds in their life-span, yet all were transitory! What stories they could tell, what sights they must have seen! Their worlds have long since disintegrated, yet they live on—and for the most part as beautiful as ever. Symbolic, surely?"

He stopped abruptly, embarrassed. "You'd better gag me, Mueller, before my eloquence gets the better of me and I start expounding my pet theories on the inexorable facts of life and death. And of the creations of man's mind, heart and hands which will live on—ageless, timeless—if they don't fall victim to man's lust for destruction and the elements alone are responsible for their destiny."

Mueller, however, had no desire to stop him as, little by little, the American revealed something of his closely guarded inner self.

· V ·

All Roads Lead to Rome

THE Dutch art dealer's life had been mainly dedicated to business, and his travels, while extensive, had been restricted to assignments involving the sale and purchase of works of art.

Unlike the American, Mueller moved in a simple orbit. He was a born bachelor. He had no desire for permanent companionship. Any paternal instincts he may have possessed were satisfied by his sister's numerous children for whom, as the bachelor uncle of more than average means, he accepted a generous share of responsibility.

In typical and stolid Dutch fashion, he was dependable and affable by nature, viewing the world phlegmatically and avoiding the spectacular.

His association with, reputedly, one of the world's richest men inevitably excited comment and gossip. But this did not disconcert him in the slightest, since he had no ulterior motives. As a client, Getty had decided limitations, for his own purchasing field was catholic. Only on a few occasions during their years of acquaintance was the Dutchman in a position to accommodate him. Choice works of art could not be picked up at random.

Looking back over the past months, Mueller realized how his companion's mental vigour stimulated everybody around him. He would be sorry when their European travels ended. Amsterdam, London and Paris had taken on added interest, spiced with a sense of adventure, when he was with the American.

174

His recent visit to the tiny independent Duchy of Liechten-stein—and the sale he attended there—yielded two important paintings of the French School and assorted art objects of decorative value. A small but very rare bronze figure of the Etruscan period was a special "prize". At first considered Greek of the fifth century, it was ultimately identified as Etruscan of Greek influence.

From previous experience the Dutch art dealer knew his client to be a poor correspondent. The American preferred to com-municate by telephone or telegraph. It was therefore a pleasant surprise when a letter from him reached Mueller in Geneva.

While driving to Germany, Getty had detoured in order to see the Magnin Collection at Dijon, former capital of Bur-gundy. "It's really something to see, Mueller! Every wall of every room in the Magnin mansion is covered with paintings, drawings and engravings—literally from floor to ceiling. There are some first-rate things. It's a most impressive collection. But everything is too crowded together, in my opinion."

The Dutchman experienced some difficulty in deciphering his client's sprawling script. It resembled a Continental hand rather than that of a man whose mother tongue was English. The renowned hostelry La Cloche in Dijon, he learned, still boasted some of the best food and wines in France: their venerable chef still ruled in its kitchen. A postscript was added to the letter: "I'm told there's a wonderful bookstore in Geneva named Kundig's, where it might be possible to find some old guide or travel books. If you can find the time to look in there for me, I'd certainly appreciate it. Thanks."

... What an enchanting treasure house Kundig's turned out to be! Mueller was amply rewarded for his visit when, in large, rambling rooms over the store, he discovered some old French books with rare eighteenth-century bindings. They were perfect adjuncts to any furnishings of French eighteenth-century origin, decorative if not readable. He examined an elaborately illustrated almanack designed as a presentation copy for King Louis XIV. It had obviously never been in use. But guide or travel books? In response a partner of the firm of Kundig's reappeared, his arms laden with vellum-bound volumes.

To his delight, the Dutchman unearthed three treasures—an explorer's account of his own *Maiden Voyage to South America*, during which expedition the Straits of Magellan were discovered, in French; *A Voyage to Jerusalem* in Italian; and the report, *A Journey through Italy* in German. The bindings were the original old vellum and exceptionally well preserved. Mueller read a title page.

IL DEVOTISSIMO VIAGGIO DI GERUSALEMME
Fatto e descrito in Sei libri dal Sig' Giouanni Zuallardo, Cavaliero del Santis Sepolcro di N.S. L'anno 1586. Aggiontoni i disegni di varijluoghi di Terra Sante & altri paesi Inagliati da Natale Bonifacio Dalmat.
Con Licenzia di Superiori.
Stampato in Rome, Per F. Zanetti & Gia.
Ruffinelli nell' Anno M.D. LXXXVII.

Underneath this was a small coloured lithograph depicting Biblical characters bearing shields into battle, and the motto in fine lettering:

Non hiero solymis fui/se/sed hierosolymis
bene vixis: se, laudandum est. D. hier Pauli Mon.

It was in antique script. Inside its covers the book contained numerous maps and lithographs.

Possessing a slight knowledge of Italian—plus a smattering of Latin from his student days—the art dealer scanned the pages, convincing himself that his client would likewise consider this volume "collector's choice". He asked the price, thought it reasonable, so bought "A Voyage to Jerusalem".

Written and published in 1617, *A Journey through Italy*

THE LOUIS XVI ROOM, SHOWING SAVONNERIE
CARPET, A "CHANCELLERIE" TAPESTRY, AND
PART OF A SET OF CHAIRS WHICH ONCE BE-
LONGED TO THE EMPRESS JOSEPHINE. ALSO A
ROCK CRYSTAL CHANDELIER

(*Chapter "A Tapestry of Paris"*)

GREEN LACQUER TABLE BY BURB, COMPANION-PIECE
TO "GUERAULT'S TABLE" IN THE LOUVRE

(Chapters "The Ranch" and "A Tapestry of Paris")

THE SÈVRES PLAQUE TOP OF THE TABLE ILLUS-
TRATED OPPOSITE

ONE OF A PAIR OF BLACK LACQUER ENCOIGNUR.
BY DUBOIS

(Chapter "A Tapestry of Paris")

contained woodcuts of Pisa, Florence, Siena, Naples and other cities. More familiar with the German language, Mueller was better able to appreciate this volume. He assured himself that it, also, was worthy of inclusion in the unique guide and travel book library at the Santa Monica Ranch. Completing its purchase, he earmarked his other "finds" as being subject to Getty's approval.

These valuable old travel books, he was told, had been acquired by Kundig's from the Prince of Liechtenstein's private library.

. . . Before the war this famed library and collection of great works of art were kept in the Liechtenstein Palace in Vienna, where the Prince lived for the greater part of the year. Only in the summertime was he in residence in his miniature kingdom of Liechtenstein. Political changes, however, brought changes in social routine. The family now spent most of their time at the castle in Liechtenstein; the palace in Vienna was deserted. Because of limited space and changed circumstances, many of their larger art objects and parts of their extensive library were sold. . . .

The American made no reference to the intervening month, greeting the Dutch art dealer as though they had parted only a day or so before. He volunteered no information whatsoever concerning his prolonged stay in Germany; which cities he had visited; how he had fared. But he looked tired, Mueller observed, and thinner in the face. The skin, stretched taut, accentuated the already prominent bone structure. That almost mask-like coldness of expression Mueller now recognized to be part of Getty's defence mechanism. "Big business" was a jungle of wits; thinking had to be quick and calculated, sensitivity and sentimentality never revealed.

"All roads lead to Rome . . . even if via Switzerland and Amsterdam," the affable Dutchman cut short his companion's apology. "They were two weeks well spent in Amsterdam.

I went there right after your phone call to me in Geneva. And now I am at your disposal without any impediment or business obligation. My partners have a well-stocked art gallery, and I have a clear conscience."

Getty appeared relieved. "I was afraid this trip had disappointed you by comparison with our Looten adventure. Oh, sure, we managed to weave a fantasy of fact and fiction around Gainsborough's 'Christie,' and had the good fortune to see *inside* the Palais Rose. But there's also been confusion. And this letter hardly clarifies it." He handed the Dutchman a letter out of the batch of forwarded mail which had awaited his arrival. "It's from Borovin Anthon, the art restorer. You know him, I believe." He read excerpts, concluding with:

> "*While I was in the Louvre this past summer, I took the opportunity to compare your Rigaud with the identical version there, and I want to say that artistically or qualitatively your picture seems in no way inferior to the one there.*"

Mueller beamed as though Hyacinthe Rigaud's portrait of Louis XIV "Showing a Leg" were his own personal property. Subconsciously he was identifying himself with the ranch museum in almost paternal fashion. "It is good news," he said, "even though it does not provide the answer."

Both men deplored the savagery of war and its wanton destruction of the beautiful city of Munich. Much rebuilding had already taken place, but much that was destroyed was irreplaceable. The Alte Pinakothek, they were told, had buried its treasures underground, so only the structure itself suffered actual bomb damage.

In the cold light of postwar days—his hatred for the perpetrators of this war cooled by time—the Dutchman felt only a weary regret that these fine architectural creations had been subjected to such useless vandalism.

The "Exposition of Old Masters," which opened in Munich on the day of their arrival, was magnificent. "I have seen the finest of exhibitions all over Europe," declared the Dutch art dealer, "but never one to better this."

His statement was justified, Getty realized, as together they saw many of the great treasures which had formerly hung in the Alte Pinakothek, plus famous paintings loaned from prominent collections and museums in various parts of the world. Rubens, Holbein and Memling. Raphael, Botticelli, and Titian. Rembrandt, Hals and Van Dyck. Velásquez, Goya —Old Masters of many nations all proudly competed. There were three or four works by Albrecht Dürer, two of which— full-length companion-pieces of exceptional beauty and quality—evoked admiration from viewers.

The American was less impressed by Munich's much publicized "Exhibition of German Contemporaries". In his opinion, this collection of modern art showed unquestioned decadence, especially in subject-matter. A pair of landscapes, however, unusual in their ultra-modern composition invited discussion.

"This young contemporary artist might conceivably become an Old Master of the future," Mueller predicted thoughtfully. "His technique is precise and his execution vivid." He made a note of the tag and number stuck on to these canvases and afterwards, at the desk, asked the price of the two landscapes.

"They are not what I would call pretty pictures, like the ballet scenes you bought in Paris," he told the American. "Their composition has underlying strength. They are full of character and realistic in essence. Watch this artist, Mr. Getty. I predict we'll be hearing more of him—and of his paintings."

. . . Getty looked up from his copy of Baedeker. "Ludwig's three fabulous castles are all within easy driving distance of here," he said. "We are not travelling on a deadline, so if you won't mind another slight detour on our way to Rome. . . ."

He turned to the Dutchman, with an apologetic smile. "I guess I'm incurable, Mueller! I must have been born with a Baedeker in my hand. Wherever there's anything of interest to see——" He spread his palms out. "Well, can anyone stop an incoming tide?"

"I'm reconciled to the inevitable," said the Dutchman blinking his eyes rapidly as he shook his head. "I'll try to keep pace with you, and hope for the best" had become his almost parrot-like avowal.

They arrived at Herrenchiemsee in time to board the afternoon steamer to the island on Lake Chiemsee where—in 1878—King Ludwig II of Bavaria laid the foundation for his palace which was to be a replica of Louis XIV's Versailles.

Only eighteen rooms of this magnificent edifice were completed and furnished, they learned from the guide. For while the interior of his palace was still under construction, Ludwig had died.

. . . Born on the 25th of August, 1845, in the royal residence in Munich, Ludwig ascended the throne of Bavaria in 1864 on the death of his father King Maximilian II. His reign coincided with an era of European nationalism, struggles, and the unification of the German States which led to the foundation of the German Empire. This latter development forced Ludwig to give up that political independence which his predecessors had won for Bavaria. As an imperial prince, stripped of authority and politically atrophied, he spent the last years of his life, from 1871, in the ever-darkening shadow of his own tragic fate. His delicate soul could not bear the harsh demands of prosaic reality and he perished in consequence. On the 14th of June, 1886, Ludwig II was drowned while boating on lake Starnberg. It is often suggested that he committed suicide. . . .

*

Herrenchiemsee, despite its great splendour of baroque and rococo, was memorable to the American chiefly for its superb crystal chandeliers the like of which, he announced, he had never seen in his life.

From lake edge to castle was approximately a two-mile walk through a natural park on the island, and Mueller figured they must have walked six miles or more by the time they returned to the mainland. He was tired, and more than content to be back in Munich as darkness fell.

The Hotel Vierjahreszeiten, their temporary home, boasted as its main dining room the famed restaurant, Walterspiel.

"This is my idea of the perfect restaurant! Food to satisfy the most discriminating of gourmets, wine to whet the palate of any connoisseur, and impeccable service." Getty, usually indifferent to the gastronomic, became a convert when *Rehrucken mit Preisselbeeren*, followed by the chef's speciality *crêpes*, with an almond filling which melted in the mouth, were put before him. "I wish we could take the Walterspiel along with us," he said to Mueller, enjoying himself with obvious relish.

To see Ludwig's other two castles meant spending a night away from Munich.

Linderhof was their first stop.

Built at the foot of a mountain, the Royal Castle there was less formal a residence than the Palace of Herrenchiemsee. The surrounding scenery was of inspiring beauty, and lovely fountains, sparkling with a rainbow of colours, played in the gardens. An elaborate pergola, built like a Moorish kiosk, had exquisite stained-glass windows shaped to resemble a peacock with tail spread.

Getty read in the guide book: "This 'Moorish Kiosk' was especially designed as a trysting place and tea-house for the King's personal use."

Both he and Mueller were of the opinion that, while beautiful, everything was over ornate. King Ludwig II of Bavaria had evidently possessed the lavish and colourful tastes of an Oriental potentate.

The *pièce de résistance* at Castle Lindenhof proved to be the Blue Grotto. Obviously, it had been no mean engineering feat to dig a tunnel through these extensive grounds and in the centre of that tunnel scoop out an enormous cavern. Inside the cavern an artificial lake of translucent brilliant blue had a stage erected on its farthest bank.

A munificent patron of Richard Wagner, Ludwig II had designed this underground theatre especially to hear Wagner's operas in their proper settings. From an eerie vantage-point high upon a pinnacle among the artificially created stalactites and stalagmites, the King—and possibly members of his court —used to sit and watch the operatic performances.

Two elaborately decorated boats, shaped like swans, which once carried the tenors and sopranos back and forth to the stage, still dotted the blue lake as it shimmered with an iridescent glow in the dank darkness of the cavern.

. . . "The acoustics must be marvellous," declared Getty as they emerged from the Blue Grotto into the contrast of piercing daylight.

"No wonder they called Ludwig II the mad King of Bavaria," shivered Mueller. . . .

It was just starting to drizzle when they set out for the Schloss of Neuschwanstein.

Built on the top of a mountain, Ludwig's hunting lodge, gleaming white with many towers and turrets, resembled a fairy-tale castle.

At the foot of the mountain road the drizzle turned into rain, and with that startling suddenness common in the Bavarian Alps, the heavens seemed to open and release torrents of water on the earth below.

"Well, that's goodbye to Neuschwanstein." The art dealer's voice was devoid of regret. "We can't drive up that steep mountain road in this weather."

"It'll stop as suddenly as it started," the American pleaded. "It always does—in the Bavarian Alps."

The hapless Mueller looked hard at Getty—at his firm set of chin and determination of eye—and submitted to the inevitable. He should have known better, he thought. A few gallons of water would not deter his companion once he had set his mind upon anything, no matter what, where or how.

At the car-park the guide warned them it was unwise to use the narrow motor-road in this deluge. He could, however, offer his horse and *droshky* to make the ascent. It would be absolutely safe, he guaranteed; his horse had trodden this winding path scores of times and could find its way blindfolded.

The Dutchman, clutching on to the seat of the swaying *droshky* as the horse plodded its way up the slippery mountain road, felt he would remember this nightmare ride as long as he lived. The horse was covered with a protecting blanket; the guide-cum-driver had put some sacking over the back of his own head and shoulders; and his two passengers huddled together, side by side, on the open *droshky's* narrow seat—Getty holding the guide's umbrella over their heads as the rain streamed down.

"I'm truly sorry, Mueller! I didn't realize it would be such rough going." His tone was contrite, but his fellow passenger was too miserably uncomfortable to reply.

Later, from a turret window inside the castle, they looked out over a sapphire lake nestling in a ring of snow-capped mountains . . . and beyond.

"Well, wasn't it worthwhile?" Getty demanded. "Have you ever seen anything to equal this?"

Somewhat reluctantly his companion acknowledged the laws of compensation.

The Schloss of Neuschwanstein was spectacular. Oil-painted murals, depicting scenes from Wagner's operas, decorated some of the immense rooms. An indoor aquarium was magically constructed to resemble a cave and served as a passageway between a state reception room and a winter garden. It was all sheer fantasy. The vivid, imaginative mind capable of such ingenuity drew forth admiring exclamations.

The throne room had elaborate wall panels of carved wood covered with solid gold leaf, and floor-length windows opened on to breathtaking views.

That night the two men stayed at a small inn in the picturesque mountain village of Oberammergau.

Comparing these three fabulous castles, it was surprising to find that not one of them contained any important works of art. The Palace of Herrenchiemsee, with its magnificently painted ceilings and multi-coloured marble walls, held immense crystal chandeliers of exceptional beauty, and a very fine eighteenth-century French desk.

The King—according to biographers—had paid forty-five thousand marks for this desk. And his detractors maintained that such extravagance for a mere piece of furniture was proof that Ludwig II was not in his right mind.

"Of course," observed Mueller, "Herrenchiemsee, intended as the King's formal residence and a replica of Versailles, would probably have been filled with art treasures to rival Versailles had Ludwig survived and politics been different."

The Royal Castle of Linderhof contained salons panelled from floor to ceiling with mirrors framed by heavy gold carving. Other rooms had Dresden or Meissen porcelain framing their mirrored panels and boasted unique matching sets of candelabras and chandeliers wrought into floral designs.

The Gobelins Room was of ornate splendour—too ornate even for the American, who so greatly admired French tapestries. All three castles, however, conformed to one pattern in their furnishings. Of heavily carved and gilded woods, some of the furniture was mechanically contrived. The dining rooms each had their "magic table," which used to be lowered into a kitchen below (for the setting and serving of meals) by pressing a button, like a modern hydraulic elevator.

Most of the other furnishings—as in the bedrooms—were elaborately carved, gilded and mirrored, and were permanent fixtures. Embossed silks and damasks, richly embroidered, covered chairs, settees and the matching draperies, all of which looked so new that they invited comment.

A guide informed sightseers that, with the exception of a few days after their completion, the castles and palaces built by Ludwig II had never been occupied.

. . . Extending their detour, the two men included Berchtesgaden and the ruins of its ill-famed "Eagle's Nest," epicentre of one of the most earthquaking chapters in modern history. . . .

On a brief and final visit to the Munich Exposition, Getty succumbed to an impulse which increased his collection of Moderns to a total of six.

"It's about on a par with that water-colour wished on me at Christie's—'A Street Scene of Old London in 1845'. With this one—'Streets of Munich'—they make a pair," he told Mueller.

Like two landscapes the Dutch art dealer had recently purchased, this painting was the work of a comparatively unknown artist. It bore the signature "Hirsch".

"Could be my 'Moderns' are future 'Old Masters'," quipped Getty, catching the Dutchman's quizzical expression.

. . . The annual Wagner Festival at Bayreuth—about four hours' drive from Munich—was too tempting to ignore:

another experience not to be missed. And the challenge that obtaining tickets was only a hundred-to-one chance spurred the American into testing their luck. His gamble yielded them a pair of tickets—last-minute cancellations.

. . . The Opera House at Bayreuth was small and primitive when compared with the great theatres of major cities. Its seats were wooden and of the tip-up variety. But any lack of physical comfort was speedily counter-balanced by the magnificence of *Parsifal*. The theatre's acoustics were faultless, the artists' interpretation of the highest order, and the opera was staged with the utmost fidelity to Richard Wagner's first conception.

In this musical holy of holies, audience appreciation in the orthodox fashion was not encouraged. Quality of performance and superb production were prerequisites of Bayreuth's annual tribute to Wagner, and applause was considered anti-climatic and even sacrilegious.

The performance began at four in the afternoon and concluded just before midnight. Two intervals were provided, during which the audience either left the Festspielhaus, to return later in their evening clothes after dining. Alternatively, a fine restaurant in the gardens of the theatre offered facilities for indoor or outdoor refreshment.

During the first interval Mueller and the American went into the centre of Bayreuth to sightsee Richard Wagner's house, now a "National *Denkmal*". After this exciting day— "An experience I wouldn't have missed for worlds," said Getty —they spent the night at Nuremberg.

On the following morning, at the historic home and studio of Albrecht Dürer—Master among German painters—the Dutch art dealer exclaimed: "This provides greater interest than Rembrandt's house in Amsterdam!"

The comprehensive exhibition of Dürer's technique and

artistry delighted them both. There were few paintings, but a large number of etchings, and some wonderful engravings and drawings. Among these, "The Praying Hands" remained an unsurpassed example of Dürer's genius.

As they were leaving these hallowed portals an old man stepped forward and enquired whether they would be interested to see the Master's grave. One glance at his companion gave the art dealer his answer. A short ride through Nuremberg's "old town" brought them to the cemetery.

. . . A final temptation, within easy driving distance, was the annual Music Festival at Salzburg, now in the closing days of its season.

They arrived on Saturday afternoon, and found Salzburg's quaint, colourful shops already shut for the week-end. Enquiries at the Festspielhaus drew a blank, so they proceeded to the fine Museum of Natural History, of which Salzburg is justly proud. Afterwards, Getty decided to return to the Festspielhaus—"for a final try"—arranging to meet Mueller at the Hotel Goldener Hirsch.

It was only a hundred-to-one chance, but with his extraordinary flair it materialized. At the box office, an acquaintance from New York was in the process of returning one ticket for that evening's performance of *Othello*. A member of his party had unexpectedly returned to Paris, he explained. The American pocketed his prize with unconcealed glee and proceeded to the Hotel Goldener Hirsch.

"We won't see the whole performance," he told Mueller, "but at least we'll see some part of it. Meet me in the foyer during the first interval, and I'll hand you my ticket. I'll take in the first act, you take the second act, and we'll repeat that routine so both of us can share the last act."

In this unorthodox fashion they attended the closing performance of *Othello* at Salzburg's annual music festival.

"It sure had its funny side," Getty said afterwards. "The couple next to me were astonished at finding first one man and then another as their neighbour. And they raised their eyebrows still higher—for neither of us wore the expected dinner jacket."

The Dutchman fully enjoyed their unexpected detour, and his companion now prophesied: "There'll be a stack of business mail waiting to catch up with me in Florence. I can never remain a member of the leisured classes for longer than a couple of weeks."

Delighted with the old travel books Mueller had acquired for him at Kundig's in Geneva, Getty—unpredictable as ever—now deplored losing one treasure he would like to have owned. "If only I'd gone to Scotland when I was invited!" he exclaimed woefully. "Now, that wonderful Burb secretaire is sold, and has disappeared."

Almost without exception, collectors share the same tendency, reflected the art dealer. Offer them a work of art, and no matter how great it is, their first reaction is to shy like a frightened horse. But sweeten the bait by dangling the art object a trifle out of reach and their appetite is whetted.

He was positive that his companion's habit of procrastinating was to blame. The normally placid Mueller was irritated. Adults—even adults of acknowledged scholarship—displayed a lack of intelligent thinking usually associated with inexperienced youth, and expected that money—and money alone—could buy anything and everything, irrespective of the human element and all its puzzling hazards.

. . . Luni, now known as Luna, was their first glimpse of an ancient town which—once Etruscan—later became Roman.

Manœuvring his heavy Cadillac, Getty was reduced to crawling pace in the narrow dirt-track lane where he was forced to follow an ox-cart for about a mile in order to reach Luna's tiny and primitive museum.

The ruins of Luni's amphitheatre proved to be the more impressive. However, none of the city walls remained to protect what had once been a flourishing little seaport before its destruction in the year 1016. The sea had now retreated and was over a mile distant.

The immense marble quarries in the high peaks of the Apuan Alps were their next stop. This marble, discovered by the ancient Romans in about 100 B.C., was then known as Luni marble. In later times the nearby flourishing town of Carrara gave its name to the snow-white stone.

Train loads of sawed blocks of marble stood on the railway sidings—obviously intended for distant places via the neighbouring port. Advertisement posters announced an exhibition of marbles in the vicinity of Carrara.

Although eager to see it, the American decided to forgo this pleasure in order to reach Pisa, and ultimately Florence, before nightfall.

"The beauty of virgin-white Carrara is wasted on me," he declared. "I prefer the warmer tones of Pentelic and Parian marbles."

. . . Pisa, on the River Arno, unique with its city walls and famous monuments grouped in a solitary corner of irresistible charm!

This city is known to the world for its Campanile—its "Leaning Tower". It is also famed as the birthplace of astronomer Galileo Galilei and physicist Antonio Pascinotti—inventor of the electromagnetic ring.

History books record that from the eleventh century Pisa was a powerful maritime republic whose rule extended through Sardinia, Corsica and the Balearic Islands. After the defeat of Meloria (August 6th, 1284), inflicted by the Genoese fleet, she lost her supremacy at sea and had to subject herself to every overlord—including the Viscontis, who ceded her to Florence in 1405.

Romanesque architecture and tradition still persist in Pisa, where sculpture flourished under the influence of Nicolas Pisano, precursor of the Renaissance, and his son, Giovanni. . . .

After parking their car, the American and Mueller went to the Piazza del Duomo. It was there they found that solitary corner of irresistible charm—those monuments the Duomo, the Campanile, the Baptistry and the Camposanto.

The art dealer exclaimed with pleasure at the sight of the Duomo's magnificent bronze door, each panel of which is attributed to a different artist, one of whom was Giambologna. At once he produced a photograph of his client's bronze door and, magnifying glass to eye, commenced a detailed comparison.

Getty, amused, proceeded to the Campanile.

. . . By virtue of its beauty and strange construction, this tower has become one of the wonders of the world. Begun in 1173, its construction was well advanced when a slight land-slide caused it to lean to one side. It was completed in about 1350 by Giovanni di Simone. A cylindrical marble tower, it has six rows of colonnades, each above the other. One can ascend its spiral staircase of two hundred and ninety-four steps to the terrace, and enjoy an unparalleled panorama. . . .

Like the innumerable thousands who see this "masterpiece in white marble lace", Getty speculated on the time when the settling of the foundations would menace the tower and make it dangerous to visit, standing as it did at such a precarious angle.

After investigating the Duomo's interior, with its fine hanging bronze "Lamp of Galileo", he found Mueller outside still comparing carved panels of the bronze door with those of the photograph.

The art dealer made no comment on his findings, so Getty remained discreetly silent. He observed, however, that Mueller appeared to be disappointed.

Leaving Pisa, they detoured a few miles in order to visit the former home of one of Italy's greatest composers, Giacomo Puccini.

. . . Puccini's villa commanded an enchanting view of lake and surrounding hills. In a square facing the villa, a life-sized bronze statue of the composer, wearing hat and coat, stood in silent contemplation.

This monument had once created much controversy. Many pronounced it to be merely a hunk of bronze, ungainly and inartistic, while others commended the naturalness of its costume and pose.

A caretaker showed them around the house with its precious souvenirs—theatre programmes, priceless manuscripts, and behind the composer's beloved piano the room which has now become a crypt and chapel, where both Puccini and his wife lie in final repose.

It was all rather beautiful; sentimentally it seemed right that this brilliant composer should—in death as in life—share honours with his piano.

As they stood respectfully before an effigy of the composer wearing his death-mask, the Dutch art dealer said softly, "Puccini was doubly blessed, for, unlike many others, his talent was recognized and acclaimed during his lifetime."

They reached Florence before nightfall and, as prophesied, a stack of mail and cablegrams had already preceded Getty's arrival at the Hotel Excelsior.

. . . Firenze—Athens of the modern world.

Getty inhaled deeply. "It's thirty years or more since I was here and, if anything, this beautiful city appears to be more beautiful than ever."

That golden patina peculiar to her stonemasonry was still

as golden. But, unhappily, this magic city had suffered the tragedy that is war.

There was evidence of considerable bomb damage. All but one of the fine old bridges across the River Arno were blown up. Only the Ponte Vecchio remained. During those eighteen days of bitter fighting, in August, 1944, when Florence became a battlefield, with Germans occupying the banks of the Arno on one side and the Allies the other, this bridge had been blocked at either end and consequently spared for posterity.

One of the few covered bridges in existence, the Ponte Vecchio, an early fourteenth-century wooden structure, is curved as it spans the river, and, with its roof of wood and glass, resembles an arcade. Lined with quaint little shops, it is mostly the jewellers, goldsmiths and silversmiths who ply their artistic wares and crafts along picturesque Ponte Vecchio.

. . . Florence—or Firenze—once a small Etruscan town, became a Roman city and later a Guelph Commune, during which time she acquired great commercial renown and constantly fought for supremacy in Tuscany. In the fifteenth century, when she passed into the dominion of the Medicis, the Renaissance burst forth in full flower there.

Renaissance—the break with the Middle Ages and the discovery of the classical world—was the beginning of modern history. It started in the fourteenth century and ended in the sixteenth. This period saw the invention of printing, the mariner's compass, gunpowder, the discovery of a new continent and the foundation of the Copernican system of astronomy.

The Renaissance was a development, not a revolutionary cataclysm. An intellectual and literary snowball, it was naturally affected by the temperature of political events.

Florence enjoyed a unique artistic splendour; she was at the heart of every revival of art. The Romanesque, the Gothic, the Renaissance buildings: imposing monuments, paintings

FRAGMENT FROM THE ELGIN MARBLES COLLECTION. SEPULCHRAL RELIEF OF THEOGENIS, NIKODEMOS AND NIKOMACHE

(*Chapter "All Roads Lead to Rome"*)

KORE. FROM THE ELGIN MARBLES COLLECTION

(Chapter "All Roads Lead to Rome")

THE MYTTION. A GREEK FRAGMENT
FROM THE ELGIN MARBLES COLLEC-
TION

(*Chapter "All Roads Lead to Rome"*)

THE GREAT BRONZE DOOR AT THE
RANCH

(*Chapters "The Ranch" and "All Roads Lead to Rome"*)

and sculptures all bestowed upon this city an elegance and character comparable only to Rome. . . .

In a roomy studio overlooking the River Arno the American examined some of Paolo Vaccarino's recent work.

The two men became acquainted when the sculptor visited New York to do a head of His Eminence Cardinal Spellman. Getty had promised vaguely that whenever he was in Florence he might sit for a portrait-bust of himself.

Now, discussing the merits of marble *versus* bronze, the sculptor said that he had not worked in marble for several years. Bronze was preferable because of its weight and was one-third the cost of marble.

He was anxious to make a portrait-bust of Getty, whom he considered a subject full of character, with a remarkably leonine head. Sittings, however, presented a problem. This visit to Florence, he was informed, was scheduled only as a brief interlude for reintroduction to its art galleries and museums. The ancient marbles in the ranch museum were discovered mainly in the vicinity of Rome. Therefore Rome was an important objective and demanded most of whatever time could be spared from business.

Impressed by the bronze figures and heads in Vaccarino's studio, Getty was tempted, but hesitant.

"Give me exactly one week," the sculptor pleaded. "It will mean concentrated sittings—I warn you. However, we shall manage, somehow, in that short space of time."

"I hope you won't think me conceited," the American told Mueller later, a trifle embarrassed, "but the truth is, in a weak moment I promised to provide a painting—or some alternative image of myself—for each of my five sons. To date, I've been painted twice. I'm wondering if a bronze would be acceptable to my family? Also, if it turns out well, whether three copies can be made from the one clay. In that way I'd fulfil my obligation in one fell swoop. Which would surely please me."

"Personally, I prefer portraits-in-sculpture," said the art dealer. "They are less ephemeral than other types of portraiture. But then"—he shrugged his shoulders—"I deal in paintings, so bronzes and marbles are my love. A soldier usually wants to be a sailor—and *vice versa*."

A day or two later the sculptor invited them to lunch at a local *trattoria*, Sostanza. "It's only a primitive little restaurant, but the food . . ." With all the eloquence of the Latin race his dark, flashing eyes completed his unspoken eulogy.

A long, narrow room in a narrow medieval street *trattoria* Sostanza was essentially Florentine. Its clientele ate seated around long wooden tables while Sostanza's owner—who was also its chef—employed his skill at the far end of the room where, sectioned off, was a tiny kitchen.

The two men left the choice of menu to their host, who was obviously an esteemed and regular patron. After this initiation, Sostanza became their accepted rendezvous in Florence.

. . . Once again they found pleasure in Brunelleschi's Gothic-Florentine architecture. The fabulous sculptured works displayed in the Piazza della Signoria and the Loggia dei Lanzi, which form a unique corner animated by figures of marble and bronze, were an even greater joy.

Giambologna's "The Rape of the Sabines" and Cellini's bronze masterpiece, "Perseus", were, in Getty's opinion, superior to all other statuary there. Giambologna's "Hercules and Nessus" was reminiscent of his own statue of Herakles.

Close by, the great Neptune fountain by Ammannati competed with an equestrian statue of Cosimo I by Giambologna. A copy of Michelangelo's "David", and the "Marzocco"—heraldic lion of Florence—a copy of Donatello's original sculpture, invited discussion and comparison with their original versions.

"In my opinion, the only fountain that equals the Neptune

is the Trevi, in Rome," Mueller said as he lovingly admired Ammannati's masterpiece.

His companion stood in silent contemplation by the slab of stone in the centre of the Piazza: the stone which marked the spot where Savonarola was burned to death.

. . . Whenever Getty was occupied sitting for his portrait-bust, Mueller explored the innumerable fountains of Florence in an effort to discover any similarity to the monkey fountain in the ranch courtyard. Familiar with the characteristics, structure and subject-matter of most fountains of renown, he searched for lesser-known monuments by both major and minor sculptors.

When he made enquiries, no one was able to do more than to offer the opinion that a fountain decorated with bronze animals would assuredly be attributed to Tacca or Giambologna. He saw two or three smaller fountains adorned with animal motifs. But none anywhere bore the remotest resemblance to that tall marble pedestal with its three life-sized bronze monkeys seated around the base. . . .

The Palazzo Pitti's unsurpassed variety of paintings had fortunately not suffered any consequences of war.

"Nowhere else in the world are there so many masterpieces of the Old Masters under one roof," the Dutch art dealer explained, "excepting, perhaps, in the Uffizi."

. . . The Galleria degli Uffizi actually holds the most important collection of paintings of any museum in Florence, but specializes mainly in Italian works. It is presumably the richest Italian collection in the world. . . .

The Boboli Gardens adjoining the courtyard of Palazzo Pitti are typically Italian in style, and were designed by Tribolo in 1550. Sunken flower-beds and terraces predominate. One of its distinctive features is a large amphitheatre whose central ornaments are an ancient marble basin and an Egyptian obelisk.

Each terrace is distinguished by some beautiful statue or a fountain, but, climbing as far as its uppermost terrace, neither Mueller nor the American saw anything with which to compare his monkey fountain at the ranch.

"In one of several guide books on Florence I found reference to a 'Fontana delle Scimmie' in the Boboli Gardens," the art dealer said emphatically.

"We've seen their 'Artichoke Fountain', 'Neptune Fountain' and the 'Statue of Abundance', which I've just learned is ascribed to Giambologna and Tacca jointly. Everything that's mentioned in the guide books seems to coincide," commented Getty.

"Except the 'Fontana delle Scimmie'."

"You say this reference was made in one guide book but not in any of the others. Perhaps the 'Fontana delle Scimmie' has been moved out of the Boboli?"

After an hour and a half of exploring, this was their only feasible explanation.

. . . News that an "important American collector" was visiting Florence spread through the art world grapevine, and Mueller volunteered to investigate anything of possible interest while his companion was still partially occupied by daily visits to the sculptor's studio.

Getty exclaimed ruefully: "Had I realized what a tedious chore this would be I'd never have submitted to these sittings! Now, more than ever, I shall appreciate sculptures. Before the days of photography, when the only image obtainable was in marble or bronze, a portrait-bust was the obvious solution. Time was of little consequence and sittings were probably a social pastime. But for anyone who is active . . ." His facial expression spoke volumes.

The Dutchman had seen Vaccarino at work, and, knowing

how restless and therefore difficult his client might prove, was agreeably surprised at the results so quickly taking shape. The sculptor was getting a faithful likeness in which the complex personality of his subject was apparent. Each feature showed its characteristic trait, and there was an overall feeling of sensitivity.

Mueller hoped that the completed clay model would conform with Getty's ideas—which were unequivocal. For the sculptor had indicated from the very commencement that a finished result was always his personal interpretation of a subject; never the subject's idea of how he thought his portrait-bust ought to look.

. . . Although the American evinced but little interest in his monkey fountain, it was unquestionably Italian Renaissance in style. He appreciated the Dutchman's efforts to trace its origin, despite his own indifference, and understood the former's disappointment when T. Crowther & Son—from whom it was purchased—informed them that a written record relating to the marble monkey fountain had once been in their possession. During World War II their premises in London were blitzed, however, and all their business records destroyed.

Wishing to be co-operative—and with that thoroughness which characterized his everyday approach to living—Getty read the many guide books to Florence, including those written in Italian.

Mueller was right, he concluded. Even in Italian there was only one edition which made reference to a "Fontana delle Scimmie". At a bookstore which boasted the most comprehensive library in town, his further enquiries elicited an assurance that the newest guide books were all considered reliable and accurate in detail.

"Did we miss seeing any parts of the Boboli?" he asked the art dealer as they studied an old map showing the Palazzo Pitti and its gardens. An outer garden and a walk running the length of the Boboli atop its furthermost terrace was charted "Il Giardino del Cavaliere".

. . . It was an uncomfortable climb for the Dutchman, with his excessive poundage, and he perspired freely by the time they reached the uppermost terrace of the Boboli Gardens. The American moved with such lithe ease that Mueller envied him.

A *guardia* brought them the large, old-fashioned key. Understanding only Italian, Getty spoke to him in his native language. The Dutchman gathered that the Giardino del Cavaliere was always kept locked, thus restricting sightseers beyond a certain terrace.

The *guardia* unlocked the massive iron gate at the head of a steep flight of stone steps.

"The Monkey Fountain!" Mueller was jubilant, the American incredulous as Tacca's "Fontana delle Scimmie", central ornament in the Giardino del Cavaliere, was revealed upon opening the wrought-iron gate.

"I knew it, my friend. I knew it!" Mueller was no longer the placid Dutchman—nor was he tired and perspiring. His eyes blinked excitedly as he made comparison with a photograph of the ranch fountain. "This bowl seems identical, but the pedestal is different. This pedestal is shorter and has a smoother contour."

Getty still seemed incredulous that an ornament he always regarded as unimportant should have as its companion a creation by Tacca, that great master of Renaissance sculpture.

It was one of those pregnant moments in the life of a collector which brings the imagination into full play and evokes a variety of thoughts. Was this fountain the original one, and his own the copy? Or had the artist created two versions of this unique design? Or had some unknown sculptor been inspired by Tacca's monkey fountain to create a facsimile? Or *vice versa*?

Arousing himself from this reverie, the American used his pocket-sized magnifying glass to scrutinize the bronze monkeys seated around the base of the pedestal. In exact replica to his own fountain, all three sat—feet dangling, grouped and evenly spaced—staring solemnly out at the world.

"There's a difference," he announced finally. "These monkeys have hairy coats and are tailless. Mine have smooth coats and long tails. These are apes; mine are monkeys. Moreover, the artistic quality of the apes is much superior to that of the monkeys. From all appearances my fountain must be a free copy of Tacca's masterpiece."

"I'm not too sure," declared the Dutchman stubbornly. "Perhaps Tacca created two similar works. Or possibly Giambologna made another version 'after Tacca'. We know that many of Giambologna's works are missing from Italy."

"You're an incurable optimist, Mueller."

"An art dealer has to be," came the prompt retort.

The small camera they carried with them proved useless now. The *guardia*, in a stream of excited Italian, protested that it was prohibited to photograph any of the statuary. He would lose his job, he said. The *Signori* must please excuse and understand—the *Sopraintendenti* made these regulations. He deplored the *Sopraintendenti* who enforced such laws—the *Signori* must please excuse . . . He clanged his bunch of keys significantly, anxious no doubt to return to his little *villina* below the terraces.

"I'll cable home and ask for some pictures of the monkeys to be sent here for expertize—just to convince you, Mueller."

"We shall also need photographs of Tacca's fountain—in order to make comparisons," the Dutchman announced.

He stuck to his former interpretation of the "Fontana delle Scimmie"—namely, that these monkeys fashioned in bronze, who sat staring out so solemnly at the world, were the sacred Monkey gods, Thoth, Amen and Khensu.

. . . Thoth, scribe of the Gods, busily recorded all that went on around him. God of intelligence, he was ever inquisitive.

Weirdly, some record even divinely, Thoth parodied the ways of man. Amen, god of creation, was sacred as a guardian of women and children. Khensu, the lunar god, marked the flight of time. With the coming of the dawn their jubilant cries echoed round the world. . . .

Whether sculptured in a distant generation or in the present day, the three monkeys, impervious to time, sat—inscrutable —hearing everything, seeing everything, and saying nothing.

The American's voluminous mail brought information wholly unexpected: Spink's offered, subject to certain conditions, "fragments of fourth- and fifth-century Greek sculptures, parts of a relief or frieze, from the art collection of Lord Elgin in Scotland."

"Yes," Getty answered Mueller's question. "They are part of the Elgin Marbles not in the British Museum."

. . . The celebrated Athenian Parthenon frieze, which cost Lord Elgin seventy thousand pounds and which he sold to the British Museum for thirty-three thousand pounds after long and complicated negotiations, was a major issue of its time. When it was ultimately decided, Lord Elgin retained some few Greek fragments and other sculptured works for his own private collection.

The late Lord Duveen donated—and initially sponsored—a room in the British Museum in which to display these historic marble antiquities. This is now known as the "Elgin Marbles" room. . . .

"Here are photographs of each of the three pieces," said Getty, excitement mounting.

They studied the reproductions, and exclaimed in admiration of the magnificent line and symmetry which puts Greek sculpture beyond all other.

"It's a thrill just to have these offered me."

Never had the Dutchman seen his companion so elated as he declared:

"You're surely my good luck piece, Mueller—as we say in the States! I've waited many years for fourth- or fifth-century Greek sculpture. This is a momentous opportunity."

The descriptions accompanying the photographs read:

MICHAELIS, Supplement in *Journal of Hellenic Studies,* Volume V, 1884.

P. 150. No. 11

LARGE SEPULCHRAL RELIEF OF THEOGENIS, NIKODEMOS AND NIKOMACHE

In the beautiful high relief style of the fourth century

The head of the two females (damaged) entirely detached from the ground. To the right, Nikomache draped as usual, unveiled, is sitting to the left, and gives her hand to the beautiful Theogenis standing opposite her, and draped in the same way; her left hand grasps a corner of the cloak near her breast. In the background between the two females, the bearded Nikodemos stands full face, his breast not covered by the mantle, which falls down from his left shoulder and covers his legs. His right arm is crossed before his stomach; four fingers of his left hand appear, awkwardly attached to the left upper arm; they hold an albaston which hangs from the strip of leather. The lower part of the figures, from beneath the knees, is wanting. Two antæ support an extremely low architrave, with an equally low pediment; on the small cornice which separates them are traces of a painted kymation. On the architrave the names DEFENIE and NIKOAHMOE CONYANO (the omission of the final Y indicates the first part of the fourth century); at the right end of the architrave, the place being wanting for the name of the sitting female, it was written in smaller letters on the horizontal geison of the pediment: NIKOMAXH.

41 in. × 36 in.

P. 148. No. 6

SEPULCHRAL STELE OF MYTTION

The top is entirely plain: it forms a triangle of rather high proportions. Along the two sloping edges, faint traces of a painted kymation are visible; but what is more remarkable, on the horizontal stripe which runs just above the field of the relief is clearly preserved an inscription, the letters of which are not as usually incised, but were painted, and still show a clear smooth surface, easily distinguishable from the surrounding ground which, not having been protected by the colour, is entirely corroded. The letters are MYTTION (distinctly thus, not MYTTLON). Before the M there is a rough spot, but no letter seems to have perished. The name, hitherto unknown, is rather an equivocal one—comp. Hesych. Muttos' Evveos Kai to Yuvokeiov—painted inscriptions on tombstones are not unheard of (comp. Ross, *Arch. Aufs.* i, p. 43)—but rarely do we meet with an example so well preserved as MYTTION. From this analogy I have little doubt that a number of sepulchral reliefs which today appear to be uninscribed, once bore inscriptions in painted letters. The middle part of the stele contains the flat relief, without any border at the sides. A girl is represented, with short curly hair, walking to the right in a very uncommon dress. Over a long ungirdled chiton, she wears a stiff and plain jacket of cafton which goes down to her knees, with long sleeves, exactly like those worn today by the Albanian women. Her right hand, with outstretched index, hangs down; At the lower extremity of the field are some traces of red colour. The lowest part of the stele is but roughly worked, because it was meant to be covered by the ground. The stele, with its very simple shape (comp. No. 16) and the modest treatment of the relief, seems to belong to the fourth century.

28 in.× 9 in.

P. 145. No. 2

FRAGMENT OF ARCHAIC FEMALE FIGURE

Apparently part of a relief, though nothing of the background has been preserved. The sculpture, the real archaic character of which cannot be doubted, shows a draped female of very broad proportions, from the neck down to the knees. She presents herself in full face and rests on the left leg, around which the chiton forms stiff perpendicular folds; the right leg is a little advanced and a portion of chiton was lifted up and grasped by the right hand, according to a scheme of composition very favourite in archaic art. The upper part of the chiton falls down to the waist, forming a stiff mass, almost without folds, in which the bosom is but very slightly marked.

The marble is certainly not Pentelic, but rather Parian, though a little greyish in colour and of a somewhat large grain.

30 in.×13 in.

Without delay, the American sent a cable, and subject to an export permit being secured, these three precious fragments of fourth- and fifth-century Greek sculpture would end their travels in the ranch museum.

"There's another Greek marble in England I'd very much like to acquire," Getty told Mueller. "The 'Petworth Head'. But I'm told the family who own it are most unlikely to sell. Assuming they ever changed their minds, Forrer said the British Museum might claim preference and prohibit its export."

"How about a Greek marble chair?"

"There are only two Athenian marble thrones, or chairs, that I know of. Both are in Scotland. The more important one is at the Earl of Elgin's castle at Broomhall. The other is at Biel, East Lothian, and belongs to Colonel Nisbet Hamilton

Grant. Both are fully described in Michaelis. I've never had the pleasure of seeing either one, and don't believe there's any chance of either ever becoming available."

"You didn't think any of the Elgin Marbles might ever become available," Mueller pointed out. "But with *your* lucky flair . . ." He shook his head in emphasis and left the sentence an unfinished thought.

. . . Sculpture as an art reached maturity earlier than painting. But in ancient Egypt its development was retarded by restrictions imposed by religious and social usage: it was extremely primitive. A group of masterpieces produced under the Middle Kingdom—1700 B.C. approximately—followed a time of political unrest. Another revival under the New Empire, 1690-1580 B.C. approximately, stressed colossal self-portraits.

In Greece, under Mesopotamian and Egyptian influence, a graceful and charming type of sculpture developed at Mycenæ, home of "The Lion Gate" and the "Vaphio Cups".

The foundations of Greek art were laid in about 1400 B.C. (Earlier manifestations were in Ionia and were mingled with Oriental influences.) Eventually the art of sculpture evolved to the great "Apollo" and a growing skill in handling nudes and human roundness. From the primitive, a tolerably naturalistic treatment developed. A prime example is the "Apollo of Piombino" in the Louvre.

The important period of Greek art was typified by Myron, in the first half of the fifth century. His power of handling the human figure in action is unsurpassed. One of his finest examples is the "Discobolus". Pheidias, however, became the master of all fifth-century Greek sculptors. His was the powerful personality behind the sculpture of the Parthenon in Athens; although none of its actual work was ever publicly attributed to him.

Renaissance sculpture centred mostly in Florence. Ghiberti

retained many Gothic characteristics; Donatello combined truly classic treatment with Gothic realism. A prime example is his "Singing Gallery" in the Florence Cathedral.

Lucia Della Robbia, best known for his glazed terra-cotta figures, had produced a companion "Singing Gallery", but it was less vigorous, although full of grace and charm.

Giovanni da Bologna prepared the way for Baroque sculpture of the seventeenth century. Bernini became its most brilliant exponent. His superb technical accomplishment, serving an art both extravagantly dramatic and emotional, aimed at the pictorial rather than sculptural qualities. . . .

The Baptistery in Florence is famed for its three bronze doors. The two men observed that these had recently been cleaned and restored to their original golden patina.

The south door is ascribed to Andrea Pisano, the north door to Ghiberti, and the east door is considered Ghiberti's masterpiece. Each of its ten panels represents a story from the Bible. From the top downwards are: "The Creation of Adam and Eve and Original Sin" . . . "Cain and Abel" . . . "The Sacrifice and the Drunkenness of Noah" . . . "The Angels Appearing to Abraham and the Sacrifice of Isaac" . . . "Esau and Jacob" . . . "Joseph Sold and Recognized by his Brethren" . . . "Moses Receiving the Tablets of Stone upon Mount Sinai" . . . "The Fall of Jericho" . . . "The Battle against the Philistines" . . . and "Solomon Receiving the Queen of Sheba".

The Baptistery dome, faced with wonderful mosaics, similarly depicts stories from both the Old and New Testaments of the Bible.

Their guide book contained information that, according to legend, Michelangelo, upon first sight of the great east door, exclaimed that this assuredly must be the entrance to Paradise, since no entrance could be more wondrous or beautiful.

"So that's why it's called 'The Door of Paradise'," commented Getty.

The art dealer found this masterpiece beyond his descriptive powers; imagination and craftsmanship such as this defied description.

"Don't use it as a yardstick for the ranch specimen," his companion warned. "I have a hunch that my bronze door is, unhappily, only a nineteenth-century copy."

. . . Like collectors the world over, Getty had heard improbable stories of Old Masters coming to light. And, like collectors the world over, he discounted them as colourful fabrications.

At one of the largest galleries in Florence however, he heard one of these improbable stories verified. The head of this, one of the oldest firms of art dealers in Italy, once bought several paintings from the late Lord Duveen, for it was a practised policy for dealers to sell to each other. One canvas caught his skilled and highly perceptive eye.

Despite some ridicule from his family, who declared that were this painting the masterpiece their father imagined it to be, Duveen would certainly never have sold it to him, he had the canvas photographed by X-rays. Underneath the top layers of paint another picture was discovered. When these top layers of paint were removed a work by Botticelli was revealed.

"Duveen must have been fit to be tied," exclaimed Getty, who had listened to the story intently. "Imagine—Duveen of all people losing a Botticelli!"

The young Florentine art dealer laughed.

"My father is fond of telling that story and says Lord Duveen took it in good part. Old paintings are always a gamble. In those days artists were too poor to buy canvases or wood. Unless they recognized a Master's work, they would simply paint over a picture—any picture they could lay their hands on."

206

The gallery had no Greek sculptures to offer. There were, however, several fine paintings among their large and varied collection of works of art.

A picture entitled "The Satyr and the Woman" by Bronzino lacked appeal for Getty only by virtue of its subject-matter. "The Rape of the Sabines" by the Sienese Master, Il Pacchia, was more appealing—reminiscent of his favourite sculpture in the Loggia della Signoria.

Unique for him was a painted panel of Boucher's tapestry, "La Toilette de Psyche".

This painted version, he was informed, would fetch about three hundred thousand lire, whereas its woven counterpart—as he was aware—was valued at fifty times that figure.

A portrait displayed on an easel attracted him. It proved to be Cariani's "The Gentleman with a Sword", at one time attributed to Giorgione.

"We have recently acquired two important works which I would like to show to you," said the dealer. "One is a portrait by Bartolomeo Veneto; the other is a cassone panel of the School of Paolo Uccello. They should arrive at our gallery in a day or so."

That evening the Dutch art dealer said to his companion thoughtfully: "The ranch museum is enviable in French furniture, tapestries, carpets and chandeliers. The classical section is gaining in importance. You have very fine paintings of the Dutch and English Schools. Yet of the Italian School there is only the 'Madonna of Loreto'. And, if I recall correctly, one Primitive."

"And so . . ." Getty pricked up his ears.

"A comprehensive collection needs something of every-thing. A few Italian works will help to round out your collec-tion. The ranch museum is unevenly balanced." Observing the expression on the American's face—reminiscent of their former discourses on paintings—Mueller broke into a broad smile. "A great painting isn't necessarily the work of a great master, Mr. Getty. Great masters did not create masterpieces every time they put their brush to wood or canvas. As an illustration, the painting we saw and liked today, by Cariani, was once attributed to Giorgione. Commercially, a Giorgione is worth untold sums of money, while a Cariani has a more or less ceiling-price value. Yet . . ." The Dutchman's eyes began to blink rapidly as he aired his views and argued his point.

His companion gave little indication of any personal reaction until the following afternoon, when he abruptly suggested: "Let us take another look at the 'Gentleman with a Sword'."

As they stood, admiring the sensitivity of this work, neither man could call to mind any other painting whose subject wore a vivid red beard. And thus Cariani's excellent portrait helped to form the nucleus of Italian paintings at the ranch museum.

. . . Giovanni Busi—known as Cariani—spent the greater part of his life in Venice. His paintings date from 1514 to 1541.

Many of his works were formerly attributed to Bellini, Giorgione, and Palma Vecchio—among others—until careful and extensive research brought to light their true creator.

A painting which hangs in the Louvre, formerly attributed to Gentile Bellini, is now considered by art authorities Crowe and Cavalcaselle as being the work of Cariani.

In Bergamo, the frescoes in the Palace of Podesta, those in the Church of Santa Maria Maggiore and in the Piazza Nuova are all attributed to Cariani.

Listed by Venturi in his book, *Storia dell' Arte Italiana*, the "Gentleman with a Sword" is said to have that same gentle rounding typical of Cariani's modelling and soft colouring, which diffuses light upon the face of the unknown gentleman and the pommel of his gold sword-hilt.

Indexed in *The Venetian Painters*, by Bernard Berenson,

"HE GENTLEMAN WITH THE SWORD." A PORTRAIT
BY CARIANI

(Chapter "All Roads Lead to Rome")

TACCA'S "FONTANA DELLE SCIMMIE" IN THE GIARDIN
DEL CAVALIERE, FLORENCE

(*Chapter "All Roads Lead to Rome"*)

THE MONKEY FOUNTAIN IN THE RANCH COURT-
YARD

(Chapters "*The Ranch*" and "*All Roads Lead to Rome*")

ONE OF THE TWO LARGEST BEAUVAIS BOUCHER TAPESTRIES

Cariani, *circa* 1480-1544, is noted as being the pupil of Giovanni Bellini and of Palma, and influenced by Giorgione, and Carpaccio.

Formerly in the Robert Benson Collection, this painting went to Lord Duveen and later to Count Foresto of Milano.

Among other exhibitions, it was displayed at the New Gallery in London in 1894, at the Royal Academy in 1896 and at the Arts Club in 1914. . . .

Influenced by the Dutch art dealer's logic, the American toyed with the idea of also adding Bronzino's "Little Prince" to his Italian works. A return visit to the gallery, decided him, however, in favour of Il Pacchia's "Rape of the Sabines".

Il Pacchia—born Girolamo del Pacchia in Siena on January 4th, 1477—was not an artist with whom Getty was familiar. But he found that E. Benezit's *Dictionnaire des Peintres et Sculpteurs* provided some data.

. . . Pacchia worked in Florence during the fifteenth century. He went to Rome in the year 1500. Some time later he executed an altar painting for the monastery of Pontignano, a piece which has since been destroyed.

After he returned to his native Siena in 1508, his works were numerous. Among others, his three frescoes in San Bernardino, and the three paintings of Saint Catherine, in the Oratory named after her, brought forth comparisons with Raphael.

Pacchiarotti, with whom Pacchia collaborated a great deal, had the unfortunate idea of persuading him to join the dangerous "club of Bardotti", which was dispersed in 1535.

Thereupon the two painters left for France and entered the service of the King, for whom they painted at the Château of Gaillon.

Cited by Corna in his *Dizionnario della Storia dell' Arte in Italia*, King Francis I of France commanded Pacchia to paint

o

at Fontainebleu because he considered that his works expressed nobility, grace and sentiment.

Bernard Berenson, in his *Paintings without Homes: Fifteenth-century Sienese Painting*, wrote: "Under the guidance of Fra Bartolomeo, Pacchia learned enough of the new 'chiaroscuro' to paint decorations such as the cassone of the 'Rape of the Sabines' that is still in search of a permanent home."

Prior to 1927 this picture was in the famous Achillito Chiesa Collection, upon which eloquent praise has always been bestowed by famous art experts, critics and others. All Italian paintings of the Primitive and Renaissance periods in this collection were authenticated by the late Giacomo di Nicola, who at that time was a Director of the Bargello Museum in Florence. . . .

With the nucleus of a section, "Representative Works of the Italian School by Representative Masters", now established, the American was anxious to locate further paintings of similar quality.

"My intention this trip was to secure ancient marbles—and only ancient marbles. Yet here you have me dabbling in Italian works of art, and getting more and more involved in the fascinating Italian school of painting. You've certainly influenced my thinking, Mueller."

The Dutchman was uncertain whether to regard this as resentment of his influence or as a compliment to himself. "No one who loves art to the extent of making a collection ever stops looking for fine works, consciously or subconsciously," he said. "And no one, Mr. Getty, realizes better than you do yourself that anything you have bought, and are buying, will net a profit any time you care to sell."

"Such is never my intention, Mueller. I admit that I have disposed of one or two things—things I've acquired and later decided were not suitable for my collection. But that is past history. These days, thanks to you, I'm more discriminating. It's good to know you still categorize me as 'a lucky buyer', though."

Next day, the Dutchman followed a lead to a picture authenticated as being by Botticelli. Afterwards he told his client in disgust: "How any responsible person could authenticate that painting as a Botticelli is beyond me! Yet it has been so authenticated, and by a reliable source. At best it's a studio piece . . . if that."

An invitation to a villa, outstanding as a classic example of the Medici, was an opportunity not to be missed. Their Florentine hosts, the genial Bellini family, welcomed them with a spontaneous warmth, and lived up to their reputation for gracious hospitality.

Their magnificent villa situated on the summit of a hill at Marignolle, a few miles outside Florence, was built in the year 1300. In the 1500's, by order of Cosimo dei Medici, it was restored and reconstructed by the renowned Florentine architect, Buontalenti.

At various times in its history the villa was occupied by the families of Medici, Rodolfi and Capponi. The Capponi arms and crest are embossed over its immense entrance doors.

The villa is now a "Monumento Nazionale" and, but for electric lighting, some central heating and additional bathrooms, it has remained unchanged since the days of the Medicis.

He could not remember a more delightful luncheon or such unique surroundings, Getty told his hosts as, below them, in Florence, the Baptistery dome and Giotto's Campanile with its green, pink and white marble façade gleamed in the midday sun.

. . . Further expertize on "The Madonna of Loreto" classified this work as being an early copy—moreover not one of the best—of the famous missing Raphael.

"I told you I couldn't be that lucky," the American said with a wry smile when he conveyed the news to Mueller. In compensation, the high authority who offered this opinion authenticated Getty's Italian Primitive of unclassified origin as the work of an early Sienese master, Girolamo di Benvenuto. . . .

Several clues to representative works of early Italian masters proved fruitless, leading only to second- and third-rate pictures of no importance.

"Most of our great paintings other than those in our national museums and galleries have long since left Italy," one dealer bitterly announced. "Thanks to the late Lord Duveen's salesmanship, and the expert judgment of your Bernard Berenson, many of the finest Italian paintings are now in America."

Like most people who knew the art world, they were familiar with the name Bernard Berenson. This famed American, now an octogenarian, has lived in Italy since graduating from Harvard University in his early twenties. He has long been acknowledged as the foremost authority in the world on Italian art of the Renaissance period.

Getty maintained that Berenson, more than anyone else, made Europe conscious that his fellow nationals could not all be classified as lacking in good taste, without culture, and devoted exclusively to the worship and pursuit of the almighty dollar. For Bernard Berenson was the living antithesis of any such idea. From America he had brought his contribution of a remarkable taste and high intellect to Europe. Both the Old and New Worlds benefited in consequence.

Through Berenson's long lifetime of intensive study and extensive research throughout Europe, parts of Asia Minor and Asia, America—as elsewhere—became increasingly aware of and informed on the Renaissance chapter in both art and history. His books on art and artists of this period have become the bibles of art students. Museums all over the world seek his counsel. He has gained renown as a sage of nimble wit, and carved for himself an enviable niche in literature.

Getty, who worshipped at the shrine of scholarship, disclosed a long-desired hope of meeting this esteemed and legendary figure, familiar in the illustrious world of arts and letters as B.B.

"Yes, Mr. Berenson still lives in Italy—just outside Florence, at Settignano. He's lived in his beautiful villa *I Tatti* for over half a century," the American was told.

. . . A return visit to the Bargello and to the Palazzo Uffizi was, both men decided, a rich reward for venturing out of doors in a strong wind that was gaining in velocity.

"It's abated some," declared Getty. "During the night it sounded like a tornado. Didn't you hear the wind howling round our hotel? It had me scared for a while. It was so fierce that I thought the Excelsior was going to be blown down."

The Dutchman rather sheepishly admitted to being one of those fortunate people who had even slept through the din and explosion of nerve shattering air-raids.

Titian's "Venus", considered to be one of the finest pictures in the world, was of unforgettable beauty.

"The last time I saw this was in 1913, Mueller. It's one of the few paintings that I remember from my youth. To see it is still an inspiration."

There were several excellent Roman copies of Greek originals in the sculpture gallery; the two which impressed them most were "A Scythian Whetting His Knife" and "The Wrestlers". In Greek works of they judged possibly the second or third century B.C., there was a magnificent life-like "Wild Boar" and a "Venus and Satyr".

"I think these are equal to the statuary in the Archæological Museum," the American said. (The Archæological Museum boasted a notable collection of Etruscan, Greek and Roman antiquities. Among the ancient marbles they had seen and admired were the "Idolino" and the "Chimera"—both outstanding Roman copies of Greek originals.)

Much as the art dealer enjoyed being among his beloved

sculptures, he found the dank, musty, stone interior of a centuries-old Palazzo uncomfortable—even physically distressing when there for any length of time. On the contrary Getty never appeared affected, or felt chilled. He would stand around for half an hour at a time studying any work of art which attracted him.

The dank coldness in the Uffizi was penetrating, and Mueller sidled away from the magnificent Greek "Wild Boar", which had an immense fascination for his companion who was examining it in detail.

The Dutchman urged the American to go along for his final sitting to the sculptor.

The wind whipped angrily around them as they walked along a narrow medieval street cutting through to Via Tornabuoni—the most elegant thoroughfare of Florence—and drove them into Doney's well-known tea and pastry shop, where even the American appreciated the temporary respite of a bright interior and some hot tea.

The sitting at Vaccarino's studio was brief, more in the nature of a final check-up.

Standing at a distance, the Dutch art dealer contemplated the finished clay. The likeness was uncanny. Not flattering, but natural, the portrait incorporated Getty's best and worst features as interpreted by the sculptor. An interesting and vital study, it stressed character.

In reply to Mueller's comment, Vaccarino said bluntly:

"No one could call Mr. Getty a tractable sitter. We managed however. And, as you see, my work is completed according to our arrangement. No," he waved aside his sitter's protest, "I have not made your nose too large. Features are always more pronounced in clay and refined down to proportion when cast in bronze. I allow for these adjustments in my measurements. Likewise in the thickness of neck, which also seems to worry you."

. . . Restaurant Buca Lapi was a "must" before leaving Florence, Getty was told, so to Buca Lapi they went.

Entrance to this basement restaurant was through its kitchen, which sparkled with shining copper pots and pans. And there, if one so desired, one could choose the cut of meat for cooking.

"This is where I guarantee you a real American steak," said the sculptor, piloting the visitors to a table.

Travel posters of brilliant hue plastered over ceiling and walls made an effective *décor*. In imagination one could travel the world while eating at Buca Lapi. The *Musica*—that inevitable ensemble in Italy—wandered around and between the tables, singing and playing the accordion. Solo, duo or trio, irrespective of a restaurant's size or capacity, there was always the *Musica*.

A vendor of *frutta di mare* went from table to table offering his appetizing tray of wares—oysters, clams and sea-dates.

Buca Lapi kept its promise of real American steaks, and with the dessert course the sculptor relayed some news.

Bernard Berenson, the celebrated art authority, historian and author, had, through a mutual friend, extended them an invitation to tea at his villa *I Tatti*, presuming that they would still be in Florence on the Tuesday following.

"You bet we'll be here," Getty declared without any hesitation. "This is a pleasure and a privilege. Of course we'll extend our stay! I wouldn't miss an opportunity of meeting Mr. Berenson for worlds."

The intervening week-end was spent in attending to correspondence and preparing for their departure for Rome on the following Wednesday.

In an unusually expansive mood, the American said: "You must certainly visit Greece with me, Mueller. I enjoy your company very much indeed. Of course, I'd prefer to make the trip like some of my acquaintances do—by yacht. I really enjoy

215

yachting, but seldom get enough time for such pleasures."

He had owned a large yacht for a number of years, Mueller now learned. The boat, however, spent nine-tenths of its life at anchor, so he had disposed of it.

"It was fun while it lasted," said Getty reminiscently, "and gave me a *bona fide* excuse to take a navigation course. I never was able to take full advantage of having a boat, though. What a joy it would be to sail—leisurely—to Piræus, and later take in some of the Greek islands. I'm told they're beautiful. Well, who knows? Perhaps some day, when my responsibilities lessen. Right now, as I get older, they seem to increase. Things just don't work out the way we would have them work out, Mueller. Even with the greatest of resources at one's disposal." Then, as though he had been indiscreet, he lapsed into a preoccupied silence.

. . . Bernard Berenson has in his writings referred to his villa *I Tatti* as "My paradise of a house". The American and his two companions felt they could readily endorse the description.

This lovely home on a sheltered Tuscan hillside stood in acres of grounds which in themselves were a work of art.

A series of terraces adorned by discriminately chosen statuary sloped down to a lemon house. "Every Tuscan villa boasts its lemon house," the visitors were informed.

Rose gardens with thick box hedges led to the more informal gardens below. At the far side of the house a wide avenue of tall cypress trees ran the length of the landscaped grounds—and beyond—to where more trees, lush and verdant with leafage and a multitude of flowers, grew in forest-like profusion.

A crystal stream flowed serenely toward a lily pond. Sheltered nooks and arbours appeared with the unexpected offer of a seat—sometimes beside a statue or a fountain—from whence yet another enchanting view unfolded.

And beyond the grounds, among olive-plumed hills some

of whose distant peaks were still snow-crested, nestled Florence, so often declared "The flower of cities".

Getty had heard many descriptions of the villa at Settignano and its lovely gardens. Looking around him now, he realized that none had been exaggerated. "This gentle Tuscan landscape . . . it seems too perfect to be real. It's like looking at a wonderfully realistic painting!" he exclaimed.

"For a man like Mr. Berenson—who has long been a disciple of beauty—this is the perfect setting I envisaged." Mueller spoke with evident satisfaction.

The sculptor drew a breath of silent appreciation.

Their guide, a young woman librarian at *I Tatti*, told them that Bernard Berenson—to whom she alluded affectionately by his initials—walked every day, in rain or shine, either in the hills surrounding his estate or in his own extensive grounds. The avenue of tall cypresses was one of his greatest joys: planted as saplings some fifty years ago, the art historian had watched his trees grow with almost paternal affection. "B.B. finds, and always has found, much of his inspiration in these gardens," their guide concluded. "Sunsets are incredibly lovely here. B.B. seldom misses seeing the sunsets—or the sunrises. Yes." She nodded in reply to Mueller's comment. "It is true, he is a notoriously early riser."

The interior of this gracious dwelling likewise fulfilled all and every expectation. Its *ingresso* (entrance hall), wide, cool and spacious, ran the length of the house from front to back. Upon entering, the first object to attract the visitor's attention was a large black cat. Of bronze, it sat realistically on a Venetian chest set against the wall. Later, Getty acquired a similar *objet d'art* for the ranch museum.

"He—or it might be she—is Egyptian of the Twenty-third Dynasty, in somewhere about 700 B.C.," said the librarian. She offered to show them around until tea-time, and in so doing described some of *I Tatti's* characteristic features, paintings and *objets d'art*.

Further along the *ingresso* was a small Chinese tombstone of the Han period, decorated with a battle-scene.

"It's of an ancient dynasty and is quite rare—like the Egyptian cat." Still further along the hall, she pointed out various paintings which adorned the walls.

A tondo from a chest depicted "The King receiving prisoners" by Domenico Morone. A work by a Flemish follower of the Roman School (sixteenth century) was titled "Hercules and Cacus". Brescianino (a Sienese master in the first half of the sixteenth century) had painted the "Portrait of a Lady in the Figure of Saint Catherine of Alexandria". The fine Venetian painting by Paris Bordone (1500-71), "Rest on the Flight to Egypt", was a composition familiar to them all. A studio work by a Florentine master of the first half of the fifteenth century, Pessellino's "Madonna and Child with Angels playing Music", completed their brief tour of the *ingresso* and brought them to the foot of the *scale* (staircase) and an incense burner in the form of an elephant.

"B.B. always declares—most emphatically—that he does not have an art collection. The paintings and art objects at *I Tatti* are an integral part of his home. They are intended for pleasure and for use, not as collectors' items," their guide smilingly said.

For those who were interested, a catalogue—in Italian and English—describing the paintings and *objets d'art* in each room at *I Tatti*, was conveniently placed in that room for their convenience.

In Berenson's study on the first floor, Getty, absorbed in one of these catalogues and occupied in identifying a printed description with an actual work of art, was jolted back to the immediate present.

"I'm afraid that I won't be able to show you anything

218

further today. Unfortunately, you arrived rather late. It's now almost tea-time."

The American made another quick survey of B.B.'s sanctum —his "holy of holies"—mentally photographing the small kneeling Buddha, a Chinese work of the thirteenth century, and an unusual Chinese Chow bronze vase with handles. Two wooden statuettes of "Virtues" by Vecchietta (Sienese, 1412-80) and two wooden statuettes of angels by Francesco di Giorgio Martini (Sienese, 1439-1502) also fascinated him. Many small *objets d'art* of Chinese, French Romanesque and Mexican origin were placed around the room.

Of the few fastidiously chosen paintings, the beautiful "Madonna and Child" by Domenico Veneziano (Florentine School, 1400-61) was a picture that Getty knew by heart. For a photograph of the art historian taken in his study, seated beneath this—Berenson's favourite painting—had been in an issue of *Life* magazine.

The corridors through which they now passed were also wide and spacious, and lined with crowded bookshelves.

"This is what we call our overflow. *I Tatti's* original library has been extended several times. B.B. just can't resist books, so I expect our overflow will extend likewise. I shall try," their guide volunteered, "if at all possible, to show you the library after tea."

Getty glanced longingly at the fine pictures and art objects adorning both corridors and staircases. But this was not the time to indulge in further scrutiny; other guests had arrived.

Nevertheless, as they descended the main *scale* he paused— as he had done when ascending—to admire the superb full-length painting, "A Franciscan Monk," by Giotto (1266-1336), pioneer in the flowering of artistic genius in both Rome and Tuscany, whose works are now rare and almost priceless.

The *sala di musica* was of expansive proportions and a crackling log fire in a large greystone hearth invited entrance.

Two large fifteenth-to-sixteenth-century Florentine inlaid sideboards held a few carefully chosen art objects of Siamese, Indochinese and Chinese origin.

The long polished table was filled with neatly stacked piles of contemporary magazines, and flowers. An immense vase of flowers stood on the concert-grand piano. A pair of side-tables, each set against a recessed wall on either side of the fireplace, held floral displays. The flowers inside as well as outside *I Tatti* showed the master hand of a gardener with exceptional aptitude for floral arrangement and colour combination.

Two long windows overlooked the terraced gardens. The roomy sofas and armchairs of varying sizes grouped around the fireplace had low tables placed conveniently at hand.

A tea-trolley was set invitingly.

Half a dozen people were already assembled, and introductions were effected by Miss Mariano—Nicky—whose long association with *I Tatti* is almost as legendary as that of its owner.

In response to comment, she explained the origin of an unusual art object which stood, a solitary ornament, upon the hearth.

"It is a French Romanesque stone beast of about the twelfth century, and was once in the cathedral of Conques," she said. "And, like the Egyptian black cat in the hall, it is a great favourite of B.B.'s."

The American was soon deep in conversation with Nicky, and his companions were similarly occupied with fellow guests when, with startling suddenness, all conversation ceased—suspended in mid-air as it were. Bernard Berenson had been observed entering through the door.

All stood to greet this venerable man, famous as a unique personality. And in those few seconds it took to cross the *sala di musica* from door to fireplace Getty's mind registered a photographic impression of the distinguished octogenarian which was to remain vivid in his memory for many years to come.

Bernard Berenson walked across the room sprightly, erect, and with an urbane poise. He bade those present be seated, and then sat down himself.

One corner of the wide settee facing the fireplace, yet within sight of his beloved garden, was always reserved for B.B. Guests were seated on the armchairs at his right and on the sofa at his left—squared off as it were, so that everyone was within vision and hearing.

Berenson's fragile stature belied a still vital energy. In his eighty-ninth year, he looked considerably younger. And despite his great age a certain flamboyance of youth, although subdued, was noticeable.

His mental alertness was stimulating and his presence dominated the room until, skilfully, he manœuvred his visitors —some of whom were strangers to him—into general conversation.

. . . Getty's mind continued to photograph his impressions. The unostentatious luxury, the atmosphere of culture, the prevailing harmony were soul-satisfying. This, indeed, could be "Life in an Ivory Tower". Seated in his favourite corner of that wide settee, Bernard Berenson seemed to become as one with that peaceful room and that gracious house, the soul of its structure; so obviously the core from which *I Tatti*, with all its physical beauty and spiritual inspiration, sprang.

That slightly arrogant set of the head, the chiselled bone-structure of face and those beautiful hands were an artist's delight. His hair and immaculate small pointed beard were snow-white. His fading blue eyes still sparkled with a surprising vigour when he talked.

"His mind is like quicksilver, yet he has all the serenity of the historian," thought the American. Impeccably groomed

221

from head to toe, *Il Bibi*—as the Italian people affectionately call him—looked what he was, an aristocratic scholar. . . .

"Yes—it is true," Berenson spoke in a precise, cultured voice, "*I Tatti*, with its contents and my library, will one day go to my *alma mater*, Harvard University. If you have already been shown around"—his smile became a twinkle—"you will no doubt have observed that my house is really just a library with some living-rooms and bedrooms tacked on to it."

(Later, the three men briefly saw the wing which housed the library.

It comprised some fifteen rooms in all, and contained approximately forty thousand volumes printed in almost every language. Specializing in works relating to art of the Renaissance period, it is acknowledged to be one of the most comprehensive art libraries in existence.

Skilled librarians handled the precious books with meticulous care. The photograph section was extensive and in itself a complete unit. Methodical organization, combined with loving care, was evident everywhere, and the architecture was as beautiful as the rest of *I Tatti*. Lofty ceilings, panelled walls and lovely chandeliers made Berenson's library a place of beauty and repose as well as a unique seat of learning.)

"Mine is what I call a living library," the art historian told his guests. "Much that it contains lived long before my time—and certainly everything it contains will live long after I'm gone. Never fear, though; my ghost will enjoy my library as much as I have done. And *I* intend to be a virile ghost," he pertly warned.

Getty, with others, found himself listening intently.

Berenson confirmed the truth of the story about a treasured painting his late wife once sent to New York.

Cataloguing a famous art collection there, B.B. had accepted the invitation of a man unknown to him, and been a guest at his apartment while the latter was abroad.

Before sailing back to Italy, B.B. wrote to his wife in Florence suggesting that, as a token of his gratitude for this hospitality, she send to his absent host a small painting from his collection at *I Tatti*.

She did so, and the painting was eventually sold by its new owner for about half a million dollars. It now hangs in the National Gallery in Washington, D.C.

"B.B., what on earth did you say to your wife when you discovered she'd given away one of your most valued works of art?" someone asked.

Berenson's blue eyes twinkled with merriment at the recollection. "I just said, 'Oh! Mary.' Didn't I, Nicky? What else was there to say. . . ."

Nicky nodded, smiled wisely and said gently: "You probably said a great deal more than 'Oh, Mary,' B.B., dear. But have the story your own way."

Turning his attention to Getty, who was seated in an armchair at his right, a tea-cup precariously balanced in his hands, Berenson got into conversation with him.

With characteristic curiosity, the art historian asked for details of the ranch museum collection.

"Four objects came from or through the house of Duveen," Getty told him; "a Louis XVI Sèvres plaque secretaire de Carosse, a Louis XVI Riesener commode, a portrait by Romney, and the large Ardabil carpet."

"Tell me something about the Ardabil," commanded B.B. "I know of this carpet, naturally. However, I am not as familiar with it as I am with the Persian carpet in the Poldi Pezzoli Collection in Milan. Do you know that collection at all?"

Getty related his impressions of a visit to Milan and to the Poldi Pezzoli mansion at No. 10 Via Morone, which had been destroyed by air-raids in 1943, but was now reconstructed. The famous sixteenth-century Persian Hunting Carpet there was, in his opinion, his own Ardabil's only rival in importance.

In further reference, he cited an incident which occurred in Paris. Berenson, who was fully conversant with the fabulous Gulbenkian Collection, cocked an ear, enquiringly.

"I was at a luncheon at their Paris home, and Calouste Gulbenkian telephoned from Lisbon. Enquiring from his son-in-law who else was present, he was told: 'The American who owns the Ardabil carpet.' Whereupon Mr. Gulbenkian sent back the message: 'Tell him that I envy him.' "

"It might interest our visitor to have some photographs of his works of art in our library, mightn't it, Nicky?" B.B. turned to his inseparable companion.

Endorsing this idea, Miss Mariano explained how valuable the photograph section of the library was to future students at *I Tatti*. She added that she would likewise welcome the opportunity of seeing photographs of an art collection new to her, since seeing the original was an impossibility.

"I shall order a full set of photographs to be made and sent to you, sir," promised the American, delighted at the interest shown in his collection. "My little museum also boasts a few pieces of fine sculpture—Greek and Roman—including some Greek fourth- and fifth-century examples. I am very proud of them."

"Are you interested in the ancient Greek and Roman civilizations?" the art historian asked with mounting curiosity.

Replying in the affirmative, Getty also disclosed his liking for, and study of, eighteenth-century Europe.

Warming to this stranger, his guest for the first time, Berenson confided how he, too, loved Greek art and the ancient worlds. His devotion to Italian art of the Renaissance period was only rivalled by his appreciation of Greek sculpture.

"You must come and see us again, mustn't he, Nicky? And be sure to bring photographs of all your sculptures with you.

MARBLE HEAD OF AGRIPPINA "THE ELDER"

(Chapters "The Ranch" and "Rome")

THE COTTENHAM RELIEF

(Chapter "Rome")

We can. enjoy them together." B.B. turned his attention back to the room, and conversation became general.

After a while, his vitality seemed to flag. Abruptly he rose from the wide settee, and said: "You must all excuse me now. I have a great deal of work to do before dinner."

He walked out of the *sala di musica*, sprightly, erect, and with an urbane poise. All stood until his venerable figure was out of sight.

. . . Afterwards, back in Florence, the three men compared impressions of an afternoon which each thought memorable.

"If only I could sculpt him!" exclaimed the sculptor. "Many artists have wished to make a portrait-bust of Berenson, but he could never be persuaded to sit. Such a beautiful head! And those sensitive hands . . ." His voice trailed away regretfully.

In his mind's eye, the Dutch art dealer could still see the magnificent tryptich which had faced him on the wall of the *sala di musica* for almost two hours.

Painted by one of the foremost Sienese masters, Sassetta, an artist Berenson is accredited as having helped to discover, the tryptich—three immense panels—depicts St. Francis's assumption into Heaven with Poverty, Charity, Chastity, Avarice, Violence and Vanity. In beautiful pastel tones, it is embellished with gold.

"One of the most beautiful and inspiring paintings I have ever seen," declared Mueller. "What do you think, Mr. Getty?"

It was fully a minute before the American replied with simple sincerity: "*I Tatti* and Bernard Berenson are an event and a privilege I shall always remember. I have never been more impressed in my life."

· VI ·

Rome

THEY drove towards Rome, taking a route which made it possible to visit the picturesque hill-town of San Gimignano.

The American declared that, despite its charm—for San Gimignano, with its numerous towers and strongholds, provided an evocative image of an Italian town in the Middle Ages—it was disappointing when compared with its contemporary, St. Paul de Vence in the Alpes Maritimes, which was less austere and more colourful.

Their second stop, the thirteenth-century walled and tiny hill-town of Monteriggioni, proved of greater interest by virtue of its unchanged medieval way of life and absence of tourists.

In its physical aspect Siena appeared more medieval than Florence. Situated on three hills between the rivers Arbia and Elsa, her narrow, cobbled streets—some only twenty feet wide—wound their way around this unique town, unchanged since the fifteenth century.

In Siena, rich in art and historical interest, they found paintings by Girolamo di Benvenuto, a master whose work "The Nativity" was the first Italian Primitive to find its way into the ranch museum. They admired the works of Benvenuto di Giovanni, likening them to Sassetta for both their composition and delicacy of colouring,

(Later an extremely fine "Nativity" by this master was acquired by Getty for the ranch museum.)

Since purchasing Pacchia's "Rape of the Sabines," the

226

American had become interested in this master's works. Now he studied his fine frescoes in San Bernardino, and his paintings in both the Church of San Cristoforo and the Church of Santo Spirito. His "Annunciation" and "Visitation" were displayed in the Pinacoteca, where Mueller was told that Pacchia had also painted a beautiful fresco at the Villa Radi of Creta. He was familiar with Pacchia's works which hung in the Museum of Budapest, the National Gallery in London and the Pinakothek in Munich.

Commitments in Rome prevented the two men from lingering in fascinating Siena, but they carried away with them indelible memories of its beautiful Cathedral and a Roman sculpture of about seven-eighths life-size, "The Three Graces".

. . . Of exquisitely delicate and life-like beauty the three Graces were attendants of Aphrodite—or Venus—who bestowed the gift of "pleasure in moderation"—a theme preached in the doctrine of the fourth-century philosopher Aristippus. . . .

"My only adverse criticism of Italian paintings is their lack of variety in subject-matter. And especially so in their Primitives," said Getty.

"You have a point there," conceded the Dutchman. "The majority of artistic works created in those days were intended for the Church; hence their religious subjects."

In addition to the two paintings by Pacchia and Cariani respectively, the American, before leaving Florence, had acquired the portrait, "A Lady playing a Guitar", by Bartolomeo Veneto, and the front panel of a cassone (chest). This was painted in the style and tradition known as the School of Paolo Uccello, and was attributed to the Maestro Della Battaglia D'Anghiari.

Much has been written concerning it—and similar works—attributed to this same master. Extracts read:

"Painted in tempera on wood, this cassone-front is forty-four centimetres wide by one metre and sixty-five centimetres long. It represents a battle episode—perhaps of the Trojan War—with reference to the death of Patrocles and of the request of Achilles to participate in the action in order to revenge the death of his friend.

"It is Florentine art of about the middle of the fifteenth century, and is a magnificent example of that decorative art which flourished in Florence in the fifteenth century under the influence of the greatest artists of that period, Paolo Uccello, Pesellino, etc., which has aroused much interest in recent studies, such as those of Weisbach, Venturi, Schubring and Van Marle.

"This panel was an important collection in France before being brought to Florence.

"Its splendid state of preservation is accentuated by the vivacity and expressiveness of its design and the richness and elements of variety which form its composition.

"The figures, architecture, landscape—the beauty of the colouring on this panel—merit the greatest consideration of any intelligent connoisseur who wishes to form an opinion of Florentine painting in the best period of its history, such as can only be appreciated in the vast compositions of mural frescoes.

"In all his work, from the point of view of form and inspiration, the Maestro Della Battaglia D'Anghiari reveals an influence of Paolo Uccello. His technique is, in fact, a step in advance, according to a theory advanced by Weisbach, and it is also influenced by Pesellino, according to a theory advanced by Van Marle.

"This cassone painting was an exhibit in 1951 at the 'Exhibition of Lorenzo the Magnificent' at the Palazzo Strozzi, in Florence. It is of the same period as the 'Battle Scene' in the Museum at Cincinnatti in the United States.

"Two panels also attributed to the 'Master of the Battle of Anghiari' are in the Museum at Pisa.

"Another cassone depicting the 'Battle of Trebizond' (1461) is by this same master.

"In all these cassone-panels of the School of Paolo Uccello the figures are sturdy and muscular, full of activity and nervous movements . . . features which characterize Uccello's works.

"This cassone was formerly in the Bardini Collection."

"The four paintings I acquired in Florence are all interesting in subject-matter—in fact, unusually so—for early Italian works. My ranch museum can thank you, Mueller, for its section 'Representative Paintings of Representative Italian Masters'. It's going to make an exciting addition to my collection," said the American appreciatively.

Gratified that his suggestion had borne fruit and thus far with such satisfying results, the Dutchman beamed. "The Battle of Anghiari was, I understand, painted on a series of panels as a history of the battle. Panels depicting other incidents and phases of that same war are known to exist," he told his companion.

"On this list of cassone-panels attributed to various collections, I see that other battles are also portrayed. For instance, there's 'The Taking of Pisa in 1406', likewise painted by the Master of Anghiari. That one is in the Grenfell Collection in London. There are several interesting panels listed here, but the most exciting, at least to me, are two which depict the same subject as mine—the Battle of Anghiari. The J. A. Bryce Collection in London has them."

There was a gleam in the American's eye which forewarned Mueller.

"I presume you allude to those panels, each of which shows a general entering the town."

"Yes. The generals, by the way, are Niccolo Piccinino and Neri Capponi. Both were in command at Anghiari. It's quite possible that those two panels formed the sides of the cassone to which my large panel formed the front."

Now, the art dealer analysed that gleam in his client's eye. He smiled—the understanding smile of a man who has dealt with collectors for over thirty years—as Getty continued:

"Make a memorandum, Mueller. Some day—*¿quien sabe?*— we might have a complete cassone in the ranch museum: a complete painted history or version of the Battle of Anghiari by the Maestro Della Battaglia D'Anghiari. *¿Quien sabe?*" His half-smile was quizzical.

... According to the list they had seen, various art collections could boast cassone-panels portraying battles.

In the Gallery at Turin, a cassone depicted the Battle of Allia fought between the Romans and Gauls in 350 B.C. The Ashmolean Museum at Oxford had a panel showing the "Flight of the Vestals on the Chariot of Lucius Alpinus". In the Steinmayer Collection in Paris, a panel tells of the Battle of Zama. The "Battle of Pharsalus and the triumph of Caesar" was bequeathed by M. E. Feyre to the Musée des Arts Décoratifs in Paris. Two other representations of the Battle of Pharsalus are known to exist. One is in the Picot Collection in Paris; the other belongs to the Earl of Crawford in London.

In the Spiridon Collection in Paris there is a "Battle Scene with the Triumph of Caesar and the Triumph of Aemilius Paulus, with David killing Goliath" as the centre of an imposing scene of military action depicted on one panel. Two more works by the Master of Anghiari can be found in the Cluny Museum in Paris—"The Battle between the Romans and Gauls outside the Gates of Rome" and "The Entry of Vespasian and Titus into Rome". The latter cassone-front once belonged to Baron Lazzaroni, who loaned it to the Cluny Museum.

Altogether some twenty cassones were ascribed as being by the hand of the Master of Anghiari. ...

Professor Giuseppe Poggi, a Director of the Museums of
Florence, had expertized and praised the cassone-front acquired
by the American, who now told Mueller of his other purchase,
the Bartolomeo Veneto, 'A Lady Playing a Guitar'.

. . . This picture was reputedly painted in 1520, but some
documentary evidence suggests that it was painted in 1492.
The sitter is Cecilia Gallerani, a former sweetheart of Lodovici
il Moro, an important Milanese of those days. He married
her off to the Count of Bergamino. (It might be presumed
that both of these men were her "protectors" at one time
or another.) Cecilia Gallerani was a woman famous for her
beauty, wit, musical knowledge and culture. And she
patronized artists and men of letters, following the custom
of Lodovici il Moro, who later became the Duke of
Milan.

After Lodovici was imprisoned, this portrait of his former
sweetheart was sent to the Certosa at Pavia. (For no one dared
to destroy a work of art, and the funeral monument for
Lodovici had already been set up in the Certosa.)

Because of the painting's allegedly "profane subject-
matter", it was confined to the library and kept out of sight.
In fact it was hung, the only picture without a frame, as an
indoor-shutter of a window. One librarian after another passed
through the Certosa, but the painting remained undiscovered
—or diplomatically ignored.

When Emperor Joseph II took the Certosa di Pavia in 1782,
he authorized the monks to export whatever furniture they
considered suitable. The chaplain of the Noble House of
Frisiani in Piazza S. Ambrogio acquired many of these works
of art. Eventually he went to Milan and left them to his heir,
D. Giovanni Frisiani. In 1843 they passed to Giovanni's sons,
Paolo and Luigi. In 1880 they were inherited by Dr. Carlo,
Luigi's son. And it was he who, in 1881, placed Cecilia
Gallerani's portrait in a suitable frame.

A torn note copied from an inventory made at the Certosa di Pavia in 1784 reads:

"1881—25th June, at the House of Frisiani, Piazza S. Ambrogio 2. This painting is held to be a work by Leonardo da Vinci by commission of Lodovico the Moor, Duke of Milan.

Leonardo da Vinci, born 1452 at Vinci in the Arno Valley
died 1519 at Clouz, near Amboise (France)
This picture was painted in 1492. . . ."

"It is some years since I last saw the Certosa di Pavia," Mueller told Getty, "yet I always maintain that, apart from the difference in size, its stature and beauty compete with St. Peter's in Rome."

. . . Their first weeks in Rome were like those previously spent in Paris and London. Business associates duly arrived to confer with the American; there was some social activity with acquaintances who lived in the city—which included an interesting party at the American Embassy, and they made several visits to museums and historic sites. Then another memorable experience was added to enrich their travels. A special audience was granted to them by His Holiness Pope Pius XII.

Concerning this event, the entry in a small diary which Getty used as a daily log-book of his travels, experiences and opinions read:

"A cherished and momentous occasion never to be forgotten. The Swiss, Roman and Papal guards made a colourful ensemble in their vivid uniforms. The rooms inside the Vatican Palace into which we were shown contained some fine works of art and were richly furnished. The throne room (where we had a photograph taken) was especially impressive. Finally, we were shown into an ante-room. There the six of us waited for His Holiness to be heralded. Several Cardinals wearing brilliant red satin cassocks passed through here. Then, suddenly, without pomp or heraldry and with only one guard wearing red knee-breeches accompanying him, a tall, slender figure dressed in immaculate white robes appeared. As one, we six people of obviously different religions fell upon our knees in homage to one of history's greatest of religious leaders—one of God's representatives on earth. He beckoned us to rise. Then he talked for some minutes with each of us in turn. (Later I discovered that His Holiness speaks some twelve or more languages and therefore greets most everyone in his mother tongue.)

"He was friendly, gracious, and looked well in health for a man aged over seventy-seven who holds one of the most exacting and crucial posts on earth. He presented each of us with a medallion—which he blessed—and then, before leaving, bestowed a farewell blessing upon all assembled in the room.

"It was a spiritually uplifting experience. I shall always treasure my little medallion, which bears a replica of the head of Pius XII, even though I am not a member of the Catholic Church."

. . . The fountain in the Piazza del Pantheon, which is surmounted by an Egyptian obelisk, and the dominating pile of the Pantheon itself—one of the most perfect and best preserved monuments of Roman antiquity—especially inspired the American.

Originally built by Marcus Agrippa, in 27 B.C., the present edifice was reconstructed by the Emperor Hadrian. Dedicated to the seven planetary divinities, it was given the name Pantheon. In 609 it was consecrated as a place of Christian worship dedicated to Santa Maria dei Martiri. Throughout the ages this monument has been an object of wonder and veneration. Several of the Popes restored it. Urban VIII, however, ordered the last of the bronze roof to be removed and melted down to make the columns of the Baldaquin in St. Peter's.

The Pantheon is circular, covered with a superb concrete dome, and has a *pronaos* with sixteen monolith columns in front.

Its interior is equally impressive. The ancient bronze door is the original door, and an incomparable majesty, grandeur and harmony prevail. Around the wall seven recesses alternate with eight shrines (*ædiculæ*), and above, an *entablature* is surmounted by an *attic* with still more shrines. From this *attic* rises the great dome—claimed to be the finest dome in the world—one hundred and forty-two and a half feet in internal diameter and one hundred and forty-two feet in internal height. In five rows of coffers, it diminishes in size toward the circular opening in the centre, which is the building's sole source of interior lighting.

Under the altar is Raphael's tomb. The Pantheon also holds the tomb of King Victor Emmanuel II (first King of Italy) and that of Humbert (second King of Italy) who was assassinated.

Statues have long been removed from the recesses in which they once stood, with the exception of a marble "Virgin" created by Lorenzetto in the sixteenth century.

These bare recesses prompted the American's story.

"Back at the ranch, I believe I told you, Mueller, how—in my imagination—the man who inspired the title of 'The good and wise Marcus Agrippa' might have placed my statue of his daughter Agrippina in one of these niches when he completed this wonderful building."

"You did. And I questioned what became of the rest of her. For there was only her head on a lovely rose marble column. It was in your classical room."

"You've got a memory for detail in addition to a good memory," complimented Getty, gratified as always that the art dealer's interest in his collection was not merely superficial, yet was without personal motive.

. . . Marcus Vipsanius Agrippa, Roman statesman and general, son-in-law of Augustus, was dearly loved by his compatriots. In 41 B.C. he was Prætor, and Consul in the years

234

37 B.C., 28 B.C., and 27 B.C. In 33 B.C. he was Ædile, and from the year 18 B.C. until his death Tribune. He commanded the fleet of Augustus in the Battle of Actium.

To Marcus Vipsanius Agrippa, Rome is indebted for three of her principal aqueducts, several works of public use and ornament, and the Pantheon, which is held to be his greatest monument.

Agrippina "the elder", his daughter, became the wife of Germanicus. A heroic woman of great virtue, she was of the highest character and morality. Tiberius—who also had a daughter bearing the name Agrippina—hated Agrippina "the elder" for her virtues and popularity. His own daughter's life was filled with intrigue and perfidy, and she became the most notorious woman of her time.

Tiberius banished Agrippina "the elder" to the island of Pandataria, where, in the year A.D. 38 she starved herself to death. . . .

"Agrippina's torso lies buried beneath Rome's new subway," said the American dramatically. And he went on to tell Mueller how, when this subway was being cut some years previously, a workman's spade hit against a life-sized marble statue during the excavations.

The workman was unable to move the massive stone by himself, so hastily broke off its head, hid it under his overall, and hurried to a local art dealer whom he knew.

The art dealer, recognizing the head as being an important marble of antiquity, urged the man's immediate return to Rome's subway site in order to secure the body of the statue. He told the man that he was prepared to purchase both head and body.

The workman hastened back to the excavations, but arrived there too late; cement was already poured in, had hardened, and in consequence the remainder of Agrippina's statue was lost for ever.

235

The art dealer kept his promise to the workman and purchased the head of Agrippina from him. Shortly thereafter it became known that this ancient marble was in his possession. Many interested bidders appeared. Among them was a representative of the German *Fuehrer*, Adolf Hitler.

Despite Hitler's highly tempting offer, the Italian art dealer preferred to do business with the United States. So thus the marble head of Agrippina eventually reached the ranch museum in Santa Monica, California.

"It's more or less fact," Getty assured the surprised Dutchman. "Naturally, the sellers wanted to have dollars rather than marks."

He surveyed the Pantheon again—its interior and its exterior —and then said thoughtfully, "What an inspiration this is! Doubtless it's the most remarkable edifice in the world, for it is the only one known to have been in daily use for two thousand years. Michelangelo said that every architect who sees the Pantheon for the first time ought to say a prayer for the soul of the great architect who designed it. It's even fire-proof, and has a natural system of air-conditioning and temperature control. It's a triumph of Greco-Roman science and technique."

. . . Outside air is admitted to the Pantheon only from the floor and the roof. Air rising through the small openings in the floor has travelled through conduits in the earth and has acquired a constant temperature—winter and summer—of about sixty degrees Fahrenheit. . . .

"The Pantheon is one building that has never needed fire insurance, Mueller. Had it been kept insured, the sum represented by insurance premiums with compound interest for two thousand years, would add up to more money than is in the world today."

The art dealer enthusiastically encouraged his companion. The latter, carried away by his subject said:

"Romans always built solidly, but this is the most solid of all their buildings. What remarkable and incomprehensible people they were! People of the Middle Ages seem close to us: they were our ancestors; we understand them. But the Romans elude us. We don't understand them. We don't comprehend them.

"When reading certain letters of Cicero or Pliny, we feel as though a contemporary of ours had written them. Their tone and thought seems modern, and much in contrast to the primitive *ambience* of the Middle Ages. Nevertheless, the gulf between us and the Middle Ages can easily be bridged.

"A hundred years ago some people in Europe still lived the life of the Middle Ages; some of them still live that life. But the gulf between us and Rome is far too wide to be bridged, even in fancy. The Romans were a different race living in a different world. And although we've inherited their civilization, even improved parts of it, I'm afraid we've made some parts of it worse, Mueller."

. . . A comprehensive set of photographs of the ranch museum and its contents arrived shortly afterwards. The two rooms now panelled with the boiseries purchased from Jansen's in Paris looked beautiful.

"What an improvement!" exclaimed the Dutchman. "These are the *right* backgrounds for your magnificent furniture and tapestries," he emphasized. "Even your carpets look finer—if such is possible."

Getty agreed. Appropriate panelling now installed both accentuated and enhanced his art treasures. "Mitchell Samuels —whom I've mentioned to you before as an expert and connoisseur of French eighteenth-century furnishings—visited my ranch a short time ago. The report sent on to me told of his being highly complimentary about almost everything. In the Louis XV room he repeatedly remarked, 'This is the finest room in America.' And that wrought-iron balustrade we got at Jansen's inspired his comment that it was the finest example of its kind he had ever seen."

Both men re-examined the set of photographs. "What an improvement!" Mueller repeated. "What an improvement!"

Thinking out loud—as the Dutch art dealer often laughingly described his talk—he wondered how best to display his client's recently acquired Greek fragments, or reliefs. "I got an idea from seeing the Pantheon," he said. "Niches, set into the walls of the classical room, assuming they can be built large enough and are able to carry heavy weights. That is one suggestion. Failing this, why not mount the marbles on to mahogany bases? They could then be fastened to your walls, and used as panels."

Preferring Mueller's second idea to his first, the American decided to telephone Spink's and ascertain whether such was practicable and, if so, whether it could be put into operation without delay.

Later, he felt increasingly indebted to the Dutchman and his habit of "thinking out loud," for during this telephone conversation he was told that only that very day another important ancient marble fragment had become available. It was the famous "Cottenham Relief".

Familiar with this Greek sculpture, he decided to dispense with the usual formality of having photographs submitted, and effected its purchase there and then.

Mounting marble reliefs on to mahogany bases was both practical and desirable, he was told. The dependable Mr. Forrer promised this work would be carried out swiftly.

Elated by his new acquisition, Getty displayed his photographic memory for data which interested him. He quoted, more or less verbatim, an excerpt from the *Journal of Hellenic Studies*, 1917. It was an article written by the late Professor A. B. Cook and titled "A Pre-Persic Relief from Cottenham":

"Early in the year 1911 a labourer working on the farm of Mr. Arthur Bull at Cottenham near Cambridge struck with his pick the fragmentary relief here published. The fragment came to light at a depth of some eighteen inches below the present surface of the soil and appears to be an isolated relic, thrown out in all probability from a house formerly existing in the neighbourhood. I see from a passage in Lyson's *Magna Britannia* to which my attention was directed by the Rev. Dr. H. P. Stokes that Roger Gale the antiquary (1672-1744) inherited a manor at Cottenham in 1728. His enthusiasm for 'Greek and Roman bustoes' is well known, and it is at least possible that this relief, acquired by him one cannot guess when or where, had at some later date and by some less instructed owner been cast away as a broken and worthless bit of marble.

"It is a piece of white Pentelic marble, and in any case it is of Attic *provenance*. The design shows an *ephebos* leading his horse. The young man appears to be entirely nude, and it cannot at once be assumed that a *chlamys* passing over his shoulders and meeting in front was added in colour. For though we must admit that plastic forms were constantly coloured, that carving was often eked out by colour, and that accessories might be added in colour on a flat background, yet the painting of garments, etc. athwart bodies already existing in relief, constitutes a somewhat different problem. The leader walks on the near side of his horse with the weight of his body thrown back to curb its restive paces. His right arm, stretched out to its full extent, keeps a tight hold on the bridle which, as is indicated by three small holes—two touching the man's hand, one in the angle of the horse's mouth—was added in bronze. His left arm probably held a short stick. The horse tosses its head and champs the bit, impatient of restraint.

"The relief is manifestly archaic in style—witness the isocephalic arrangement of man and horse, the combination of face in profile with body in full view, the updrawn lips, the roundish ear, the absence of all foreshortening. The eye is not clearly marked, the surface of the marble being here damaged. The musculature is on the whole remarkably accurate.

"Another criterion of date may be found in the sculptor's

treatment of the horse's head. The pricked ear, the long bony skull, the soft nose with its inflated nostril, the mobile puckered underlip, the mouth opened just enough to show both rows of teeth and an upcurled tongue—these features together constitute a triumph of naturalistic modelling, and afford a piquant contrast to the conventional lines of mane and broad flat surfaces of cheek and neck. If Kalamis was praised for the 'finish' of his horses, this relief may give us some inkling of his procedure. It should not, however, be forgotten that a detailed rendering of horses' heads was part of the heritage bequeathed to fifth-century sculpture by sixth-century painting. Comparison points to a date *c.* 485 B.C. as that of our relief."

Mueller looked at his companion with unconcealed admiration. Getty continued:

"D. Lysons and S. Lysons. *Magna Britannia*, London, 1808, Vol. II, Pt. L (Cambridgeshire), p. 171. The Cambridge University Library possesses an extra-illustrated copy of this work containing much additional information about Cottenham and its history.

"The 'Reliquiae Galenae'—*Bibliotheca Topographica Britannica*, London, 1781-2, No. II, Pts. 1-3, e.g. M. Collignon, *La Polychromie dans la sculpture Grecque*, Paris, 1898, pp. 43 ff. H. Bulle, *Der Schoene Mensch im Altertum* (2), Muenchen und Leipzig, 1912, p. 444, Pl. 196."

Getty broke into a smile at the expression on Mueller's face. "I'm much better at summarizing passages from printed matter than I am at remembering details of living events, even of recent date," he confessed.

. . . Professor Ludwig Curtius, a distinguished authority and acknowledged expert on ancient Greek and Roman civilizations, director of the German Archæological Institute in Rome, former Professor of Archæology at the University of Heidelberg, was an old friend of Getty's. He unhesitatingly agreed to the suggestion that while the two men were in Rome he might serve as mentor and guide to the city's ancient ruins, museums, galleries and monuments.

"A more learned guide we could never hope for," declared the American with satisfaction. "How lucky we are to find Curtius in town and willing to give us so much of his time!"

The Dutch art dealer smiled knowingly. "I am certain that the learned Professor won't have any cause for regret. Or consider it a waste of time. For, besides all else, he will find us both eager disciples."

The American still devoted many hours of each day to his massive business correspondence, often working far into the early hours of morning.

"There's just no other way I can cope with things, Mueller. For these brief weeks we shall spend part of our mornings and afternoons in the galleries and museums and, weather permitting, take in all we can of Roma Antica between times. So, somewhere along the line I must keep pace with my business."

"But three or four o'clock each morning," the Dutchman reprimanded, "and sometimes even five! It's too much of a strain—even for a person with your abundant and apparently inexhaustible energy." As usual when travelling his companion included the local newspapers in his daily reading. Now he read aloud in Italian, ever-anxious to improve diction and accent.

"Your fluent vocabulary puts me to shame, Mr. Getty. I still find it difficult to understand how any one person can get through such a variety of things in any one day—every day."

"You flatter me, Mueller. I'm hardly the human dynamo you depict. Just a man with lots to do in the course of a day which is, unfortunately, only twenty-four hours long."

... "Yes, I see quite a few changes in Rome." The American spoke in response to Professor Curtius. "Barsanti's antique shop in the Via Sistina has gone. And so has my former dealer, Barsanti. He died some time ago. He was a know-ledgeable man and our business dealings were always amicable. I miss him."

It was many years since Getty had visited Rome. The city's new streamlined railway terminal caused him to exclaim, "It's so enormous and so modern it even competes with our terminal in Los Angeles!"

"There is also our new subway," Professor Curtius reminded him. "Here in Rome we call it the subway to nowhere. It runs round the city, reaches the outskirts, and then abruptly ceases. Few passengers seem to use the Rome subway now. At first it was a novelty. But I fear it is impractical: an unhappy waste of public funds."

"The Corso is as crowded as ever," Mueller commented.

They all agreed that the Santa Maria Maggiori and Lateran Churches were magnificent. And that the Aurelian Wall and, beyond it, the ancient Appian Way inspired dreams of long ago.

. . . Rome, metropolis of Western European civilization, from whence sprang law, art and science, has always been an inspiration to those gifted with imagination. . . .

The American eagerly absorbed every sight. "The changes wrought since I was here some twelve years ago make me realize more than ever how unique a city this is. Relics of every epoch of Rome's three thousand years of history are apparent—from Antiquity through to the Popes, the Middle Ages, the Renaissance and the Baroque."

"The might of the Roman Empire reached its peak during the reign of Trajan. And it is my belief that the decadence of Rome began at the time of Diocletian." It was Professor Curtius who spoke, with all the authority of his seventy-seven years and his deep scholarship, as he accompanied Getty and Mueller around what remains of the Baths of Diocletian.

. . . These were the largest baths in ancient Rome. Even their remains are enormous. Built by Diocletian and Maximian in the year 306, Pope Pius IV later entrusted Michelangelo with the task of putting the structure to some effective use. He transformed part of the baths into a church, and part into a convent. . . .

The American, with his propensity for transporting himself into other realms and eras of time, ventured to reconstruct the original floor-plan of the building in order to comprehend faintly its former grandeur and beauty.

"I doubt whether any modern imagination can visualize the full glory of the Frigidarium façade or of the Great Hall. I'd estimate that twenty per cent. of the original baths is left and eighty per cent. has disappeared into the dust of ages. Thinking back to the Renaissance, I realize that even Michelangelo was a guilty party. His 'Moses' is one of the masterpieces of all time, yet he mutilated these wonderful baths by transforming the Great Hall into a church. Renaissance barbarians I call them! They'd take an ancient statue and cheapen it with inaccurate restoration. And as for ancient buildings—well, words fail me when I realize how they were used as quarries or as a base for some mundane creation, with contemptuous disregard of the superb existing architecture."

Professor Curtius supported Getty's opinion that in sculpture, literature and architecture the ancients surpassed the men of the Renaissance.

"Michelangelo's 'Moses,' wonderful though it is, barely competes with Greek sculpture," he said with quiet authority, and went on to tell his two "disciples" how, after long and detailed research, he had arrived at his recent conclusion that the so-called "Hermes of Praxiteles" at Olympia, was not an original work, but a copy made in Hadrian's time.

"Some scholars persist that the 'Hermes' is Greek but was polished in Hadrian's time. In fact, this little dispute has aroused interesting controversy," Curtius said with a touch of gaiety, as though pleased his investigations had produced a division of opinion. "Argument is healthy," he chuckled;

"and especially so when both sides believe they are presenting indisputable facts."

Through the Professor's scholarship and unquestionable knowledge, they learned that the best Roman copies of Greek sculptures were made in the time dating from Augustus to Claudius. Hadrianic copies were also considered very fine; they were somewhat cold, however, as the result of excessive and over-detailed technique.

Parian marble, they were told, was the most valuable of marbles and had the coarsest grain. Pentelic marble was harder than Parian. Both varieties, however, contained a metallic glint, which accounted for the glittering spectra in them. Carrara marble, pure white and without any glint, was softer than all other varieties and therefore easier to work with, but had little "life" in it. According to Curtius, the making of Roman copies started, on a small scale, in approximately 150 B.C. by Greek sculptors who were then resident in Rome. By the time of Augustus sculpture had developed into an important industry, and it continued to flourish until it reached its apex in the time of Hadrian.

. . . A "Roman" copy can be defined as being a copy of a Greek original of the fifth to second centuries B.C. made in the Roman imperial period from 31 B.C. to the fourth century A.D. Practically all Roman copies were made in the first and second centuries A.D. Many were done at Athens, which boasted a flourishing trade in copies of the great Greek masterpieces.

There never were very many Greek originals in sculpture as compared with the innumerable copies of them made by the Greeks in pre-Roman times. Then came the Romans with their wealth and lavish spending. The Greco-Roman world used marble and bronze statues for the decoration and embellishment of palaces, private homes, parks, gardens, public squares and public buildings.

The number of statues decorating the ancient Greco-Roman world is beyond calculation or modern belief. . . .

"I'm happy that you seem disposed to corroborate my ideas concerning Greek and Roman *versus* Renaissance and eighteenth-century sculpture," Getty told Professor Curtius. "Imagine anyone choosing an Houdon sculpture—at some absurdly high price—if they could secure a Greek work! I echo and endorse Pindar, who said of the Greeks: 'Zeus caused a saffron-coloured cloud to rain down gold upon them, and grey-eyed Athena gave them nimbleness of hand beyond all mortal men.' "

Curtius chuckled as he turned to Mueller. "I have known our mutual friend for a number of years now, and my first impressions of him always remain. For sheer thoroughness I know of no one to equal him. When he becomes interested in any subject, or in any form of the arts, not only does he study it, but everything connected with it. He also enjoys driving a bargain!"

"I certainly hope I'm a discriminating buyer as well as a prudent one," protested the American. "And I always adhere to my father's axiom that no man's opinion is any better than his information. Of course, I also act in accordance with my essential beliefs of what I *want* to do—and what I *can* do," he emphasized. "I like to think I know my own limitations."

. . . In the Museo delle Terme—that section of the Baths of Diocletian which Michelangelo had turned into a convent—two statues, "The Wounded Niobia" (daughter of Niobe), a Greek original dated 460 B.C., and the "Venus of Cyrene" (which had been found in the Baths of Cyrene), impressed them most. According to their learned guide, in the "Little Cloisters" of the Certosa which houses the Ludovisi Collection, the Throne of Aphrodite (or the Ludovisi Throne as this marble is often called), supposedly portraying the birth of

Aphrodite, was the greatest of all treasures. A Greek work of approximately 460 B.C., in Professor Curtius's opinion the Ludovisi Throne was the finest of any ancient marbles still extant in Rome.

(Later, at the Capitoline Museum, Mueller felt inclined to challenge this view on seeing the "Wounded Gaul" and "The Venus".)

The "Mosaic of Doves" from Hadrian's Villa, which was in the Capitoline Museum, evoked comparisons with some excellent mosaics they had seen in the Museo delle Terme.

Curtius explained that both the "Venus of Cyrene" and the "Mosaic of Doves" were Roman copies of the second century A.D. The original mosaic as mentioned by Pliny, famous writer of that time, was in the Royal Palace at Pergamon.

Confirming his old friend's impressions of him, the American quoted excerpts from Pliny's letter, which was written on the very day Vesuvius erupted and destroyed both Pompeii and Herculaneaum. A half-smile lightened his usually serious face as he said: "I merely wanted to reaffirm my interest in the ancient world by some additional evidence. I don't want you to think, Professor, that you're wasting your valuable time on just an idle or capricious sightseer."

. . . The Vatican Museum, unanimously conceded to be the most beautiful of all, with its circular marble stairway and ornate bronze balustrade, boasts the richest and most complete collection of antiquities in the world. It was therefore a surprise when Curtius pointed out that the Vatican Museum possessed only one Greek original—the torso by Apollonius of Athens, of Parian marble and sculptured in approximately 50 B.C.

They admired the sculptures displayed in the Sala a Croce Greca and Sala Rotonda. In the Belvedere "The Apollo", "The Laocoon"—a group discovered in the Baths of Titus—and "The Apoxyomenos" (Scraper) were three works they found most impressive.

It was gratifying to Getty to compare a statue of "Faustina" in the Sala Rotunda with photographs of the "Faustina" he had recently acquired. And, likewise, to be able to discuss their relative merits with so great an authority as Professor Curtius. In the Gabinetto delle Maschere, so-called from the four mosaics depicting theatrical masks which came from Hadrian's Villa, he was also able to discuss and compare mosaics.

Curtius introduced his two "disciples" to his favourite restaurant, Passetto's, which, in his opinion, offered the finest food in Rome. In-between their educational sightseeing, the three men usually lunched or dined there, and discussed the day's activities.

Shown a photograph of Getty's mosaic floor, Professor Curtius pronounced it to be a good example of about the second century A.D. In his opinion, the floor was Roman and came from North Africa. He did not accept Mueller's interpretation that its mosaic design depicted the legend of Bacchus, God of Wine.

"This is the story of Orpheus with his animals, my friend." He held a photograph of the mosaic floor in one hand and with the other traced its characteristics for his eager audience. "Look carefully and you will recognize how this central medallion shows Orpheus and his animals. If you recall the fable, Orpheus loved animals and used to tame them: after which they grew to love him. You will also observe that in each of these four corners surrounding the central medallion there is a goddess. Each goddess represents one of the four seasons." He indicated: "Spring . . . summer . . . autumn . . . winter. And beyond each of these four corners there is a bird, also significant of each of the four seasons. These birds relate to the goddess, thus confirming each particular season."

When one was familiar with various types of mosaics, it was simple to trace the regions from which they came. The story or message implicit in art created in those regions was reflected in their designs, the Professor smilingly told them.

"Interpretations appear such a simple matter because you are fully cognisant with your subject," said Mueller with respect. "There is no substitute for scholarship, Professor Curtius."

"Scholarship yields a rich reward, my friend, as long as one does not measure it by a financial yardstick."

The Professor had a robust appetite and "knew" good food and good wines. It was an education just to be in his company, both men agreed.

The American spoke of Florence and of their memorable afternoon spent at the villa *I Tatti*.

"I am a great admirer of Bernard Berenson," said Curtius. "Not only is he one of the most respected authorities in his field and a distinguished scholar, but he is also one of the kindest men I have been privileged to know. Oh, yes, I have known Mr. Berenson for some thirty years or more! He is unique in more ways than one, believe me. He is that rare example of a scholar whose scholarship has yielded him many rewards. Please convey my warmest regards if you should be writing to him or speaking to him on the telephone."

"Certainly," Getty promised. "It will be by letter, though. Miss Mariano—Nicky—told me that B.B.'s pet idiosyncrasy is his dislike of telephones. He has stubbornly refused to use that instrument for forty years or more, whether for business or social purposes." Catching the Dutchman's eye, he continued: "Not like me, Professor—as our friend here can testify. Any time I'm within reach of a 'phone it seems to ring automatically. My ear is constantly in demand."

"And from all over the world—or so it seems," his companion corroborated.

. . . Mueller had expressed his appreciation to the American for the privilege of such scholarly guidance around the galleries, museums and ancient remains of Rome.

248

"In addition to being a true scholar of the classical world, Curtius is also a man of exceptional intellectual integrity. I'd back his opinions against anyone in the world of archæology. Just as Bernard Berenson is the highest accepted authority on paintings of the Italian Renaissance, so Ludwig Curtius, in my opinion, can make a similar claim in his own sphere. But although he's well known and has written several important books, he isn't an outstanding personality like B.B.," said Getty.

"The Professor seems to lean more to the technical and less to the artistic, as compared with Mr. Berenson," rejoined Mueller. "It has been a great privilege to meet them."

"I'm surprised to find such little change in Curtius," observed Getty. "I haven't seen him since pre-war days and apart from his use of a walking stick—which I've noticed he leans on rather heavily—he seems as active as ever. Scholars must have the secret of longevity, Mueller. The Professor, at almost seventy-eight, stands as erect as I do myself. He keeps going for hours at a time without showing any sign of fatigue. And, as for eyesight—he certainly has it all over me! I can't read for long these days without using spectacles. Yet he's able to rely upon natural vision a good deal of the time. Mentally and physically, he seems to be as alert as in the old days."

. . . Of above average height and of proportionate build, Professor Curtius, with almost white hair and beard, had the distinguished appearance of the typical gentleman and scholar. These tours of Rome's ancient monuments and archæological remains—of which he possessed an intimate knowledge—never palled, for his two companions proved eager listeners. He was, in fact, rather enjoying this opportunity of propounding his own views and theories, in addition to imparting knowledge to two who so avidly welcomed it. . . .

"I shall indeed be regretful when you decide to leave Rome.

However, before the arrival of that unhappy day, I hope to show you something of Ostia Antica. They have done a great deal of new excavating since you were there last." Professor Curtius, as always, spoke precisely. His punctilious phrasing betrayed the fact that when speaking in any language other than in his native German, he was automatically translating.

The former Temple of Antoninus and Faustina faced them as they approached the end of the Via Sacra.

. . . Dedicated by the Senate to the memory of the Empress Faustina in 141, this temple was later consecrated to the memory of her husband, the Emperor Antoninus Pius, after his death in 161. Now transformed into the Church of San Lorenzo in Miranda, its baroque façade dates from the year 1602.

It has an imposing portico of ten Corinthian columns, six in front and two at each side: monoliths of Euboean cipolino, they still support part of the *entablature*. The *cella*, built of peperino, still preserves its frieze of griffins, candelabra and vases, and is considered to be one of the finest examples of Roman decorative art.

Below the temple lies an archaic Necropolis, a cemetery of the ancient inhabitants of the Esquiline—or of the original settlement on the Palatine—which dates back to the ninth and seventh centuries B.C. . . .

"Could be my 'Faustina' once lived here," observed the American. "If you can recall to mind my statue, Professor, it's larger than life-size and depicts the Empress when she was Consort. I've been unable to secure any information beyond the fact of the immediate previous owner. But a companion-piece exists. It's in the Dresden Museum. You are doubtless familiar with it as 'The Matron from Herculaneum', supposedly created for the Temple of Antoninus and Faustina. Could be mine was also."

"Could be . . . !" The Professor surprised them and mimicked: "Could be! It is not impossible that your Empress

Faustina was sculptured as a decoration for this temple. In ancient times marble portraits were generally of life-size when made for individuals. They were, however, larger when sculptured as monuments. And your statue is considerably larger than life-size. It is indeed unfortunate that so few documents are available to help us. So much of the ancient world is shrouded in the mists of time. Historical data is sparse and often inaccurate. So much is, alas! idle conjecture."

"If only my 'Faustina' could turn into flesh for long enough to confirm where she lived, in all her glory, in Imperial Rome. My 'Leda and the Swan' lived at the Villa Magnani on the Palatine, in 1775. I know little about that marble group, either. Only the name of its immediate previous owner."

The Dutchman suggested that it might be safely assumed Getty's "Empress Faustina" had once reigned in the temple—for who could authoritatively dispute such theory.

. . . The façade of the Palazzo Poli frames the Fontana di Trevi, in the centre of which are two enormous Tritons drawing a winged chariot bearing a triumphant Neptune. Commissioned by Clement XII, it is the largest and most imposing fountain in Rome—a city of fountains. Tradition insists that any traveller who throws a coin into the basin of the Fontana di Trevi will return to the Eternal City. . . .

Comparisons with fountains made the Dutch art dealer self-conscious. He said to Professor Curtius, "I still have a feeling that the ranch monkey fountain is important. But unhappily no one appears to agree with me. The latest report confirms that it's Italian—in the style of the Renaissance period. And that is all. My interpretation of the mosaic floor proved hopelessly wrong. I suppose the bronze door will be classed as 'A nineteenth-century copy—of no significance.' From here on, I'd better confine myself to Dutch works of art. Sometimes my evaluation of them turns out right."

The American hastened to reassure the chagrined Mueller. "You have more than a merely superficial knowledge of ancient marbles, and can claim real authority in your own sphere—which is an achievement in itself. No one can be right all the time."

Rome yielded little, if anything, by way of good works of art for purchase.

"Nothing spectacular has come into the possession of any dealers here during recent years," Professor Curtius told Getty. "As is usually the case, you will find the best Roman statues for sale anywhere but in Rome. You were very fortunate to secure such fine Italian paintings in Florence."

They did, however, succeed in locating two sculptured works classified as being of what Curtius termed artistic merit. The fine "Republican Senator's Head" was a distinctive marble and full of character. The "Lion's Head" was uncannily realistic and virile. They saw some mosaics, but nothing comparable to the floor in the ranch museum.

Professor Curtius said some of the best mosaics came from Serbia and Macedonia. Often, they were part of the interior walls of mosques or churches, and throughout the centuries had been vandalized by a covering of paint or whitewash. He cited the cases of some unique examples being uncovered and concluded:

"The 'Orpheus Motif', as portrayed in your mosaic floor, was highly popular. Many adaptations of it have been found. Another popular motif was one showing Christ within a circle of sheep."

He went on to relate how, in the earliest of mosaics, classical influence and treatment predominated. In his view, the finest mosaics were produced between the fourth and eighth centuries A.D. Afterwards their quality declined, until a revival took place in Italy.

Attributing particular development in mosaics to the

Byzantine Empire, the Professor also stated that Salonica once boasted exceptionally fine examples of this craft. In conclusion, he asked whether either of his listeners was familiar with the wonderful mosaics in Ravenna and Venice.

. . . It was customary for a dealer from whom a work of art was purchased to arrange for its crating, packing and dispatch. The small dealer in Rome was apparently unfamiliar with this procedure, and the marble heads of the "Republican Senator" and the "Lion" were delivered to Getty at the Hotel Excelsior.

"I'll have to get Amexco—the American Express Company —to ship them for me," he told Mueller as, together, they re-examined and admired his recent acquisitions of Roman sculpture. . . .

Later, at Rome's Zoological Gardens, the unpredictable Getty apologized to the art dealer: "Forgive me for rushing you down here, but the 'Lion's Head' made me homesick for Teresa. I really miss my animal kingdom when I'm abroad for any length of time."

Mueller vividly remembered his first encounter with Teresa, the lioness at the ranch in Santa Monica. He enquired whether there were any recent additions to the American's zoo family.

"I haven't bought any more stock for myself, but I did buy a chimpanzee for our County Zoo."

The County Zoo, apparently, was minus chimpanzees, and the youngsters who visited there had long clamoured for these favourites.

Getty went on to say that he was a Director of the Los Angeles Zoological Society and, when time and place permitted, enjoyed participating in its activities. "Though I'm sorry to have to admit that I'm a shockingly inactive member."

All the animals in Rome's Zoological Gardens were kept in their natural habitat, or as close to it as possible, and were often separated from the public by ditches only.

As on previous occasions, the art dealer expressed astonishment at his companion's sensitive understanding of, and feeling for, these wild creatures. Some sort of communion appeared to exist between them. The great beasts purred, or roared out their greeting, as the American approached.

The roar of a lion reverberated, and caused the Dutchman to jump back. His eyes began to blink at an increased speed, and Getty could barely refrain from laughter. A second roar was even longer and louder.

"It's remarkable how these great beasts can sense if a human is familiar with their kind. I'll bet this handsome fellow can smell Teresa—even though she's six thousand miles away." The lion shook his handsome mane and roared once again. "Isn't he magnificent?" Getty turned round only to discover that he was talking to himself. His companion had sidled away, as far as possible out of earshot of the massive lung-power of this king of the jungle, and was standing somewhat sheepishly, nervously mopping his brow with a handkerchief.

The House of Livia on the Palatine recalled to their minds a portrait-bust of the Empress which was in the ranch museum.

Exploring what remained of this house, Professor Curtius smilingly enquired whether his American friend held any preconceived theories relative to his own sculptured head of Livia.

"I have. But I shall reserve Livia's story for some other time."

. . . The House of Livia is a rich dwelling with elegant mural paintings. On the right, a *triclinium* opens on to a square court. At the back are some large rooms, the centre one being a *tablinum*, decorated in late Pompeiian style. Of two side rooms (*alae*), the one on the left has a yellow frieze representing small scenes which are very fine examples of Alexandrian art. In the middle room a fresco represents the myth of Io and Argus. . . .

"Augustus was both loved and respected," agreed the

Professor. "Not only in Italy, but also to the north and south."

"I saw the magnificent 'Trophy of Augustus' at La Turbie in the Alpes Maritimes some years ago," Getty told him. "It's still in an interesting state of preservation."

"I am very sorry that you never visit Rome during the summer months," said Curtius. "To describe the beauty of opera as it is staged in the ruins of the Baths of Caracalla is beyond my descriptive powers. No," he replied to Mueller, "the Caracalla Baths were, of course, smaller than the Baths of Diocletian, although they surpassed them in magnificence. You must both make an effort to hear Italian opera performed in such a setting. If you are ever fortunate enough to see *Mephistopheles*, you will never forget it. Even La Scala in Milan does not stage it any better, if as well, or as dramatically. The natural scenery of these high, jagged ruins of Caracalla, with their background and interlacing patterns of tall cypress trees, makes such a sight unforgettable. And at that time of year there is often a full moon in a cloudless sky to enhance its fairy-tale setting. You should certainly make an effort to visit Rome in the summer months."

. . . Under the Capitoline Hill they recalled the legendary origins of Rome as the she-wolf stalked moodily around her cage.

Entries in Getty's diary were numerous these days:

"Borghese Gallery . . . marvellous sculptures and paintings. Colonna Gallery . . . wonderful marble-floored *salon*, fine pictures and sculptures. Piazza Navona—changed times . . . the former Massimi Palace is now an apartment house. Visited the Villa Julia.

"Am convinced, from my recent reading, that Greek sculpture had not died out in Greece even in the time of Herodes Atticus, the greatest of all patrons of Greek artists, who lived in the reigns of Hadrian, Antoninus Pius and Marcus Aurelius.

"Professor Curtius says he expects to go to Greece. If only it were possible to time my prospective visit with his! What an education to be in Greece with him as a guide. I'm sure that Mueller would be equally appreciative.

"Drove along the Via Cassia—a lonely road through typical Campagna scenery—to Via Flaminia and Prima Porta. Climbed the hill and visited the Villa of Livia and Augustus. This was their summer home, and it commands a fine view of the winding Tiber and the Campagna. With almost uncanny clarity, my mind was transported to the ancient world. I could see my young Herakles, my Venus (before she had been mutilated) and my portrait-bust of Livia. Maybe it was fantasy; maybe it was fact. Who is to deny it one way or another? Some day I would like to try my hand at writing their stories. Some day, if I ever have enough time.

"Yesterday, we went to Ostia."

. . . Ostia Antica—formerly known as Ostium (taken from the *ostium*—or mouth—of the Tiber) was founded, according to legend, by Ancius Marcius. However the surviving ruins do not date from earlier than the fourth century B.C. Ostia was once the great commercial port of Rome. It began to decline under Constantine, and became progressively more deserted owing to the ravages of the malarial mosquito which infested the port. . . .

The American had not visited Ostia since 1939, and he was much impressed by the new excavations there. The city itself was now half-excavated, about eighty-two acres being accounted for.

Later, he made an entry in his diary:

"Was thrilled to walk the ancient streets and enter the homes and public buildings of people who vanished so long ago. Was impressed by the modern look of the city, and its

SECTION OF CASSONE-FRONT. SCHOOL OF PAOLO
UCCELLO, AND ATTRIBUTED TO THE MASTER OF
ANGHIARI

(*Chapter "Rome"*)

MOSAIC FLOOR IN THE CLASSICAL ROOM

(Chapters "The Ranch" and "Rome")

conveniences and comforts, which are well up to present-day standards.

. . . The ruins of Hadrian's Villa are vast, and excavations are taking place in several of its various neighbourhoods. Professor Curtius showed his two "disciples" the best vantage point from which to survey the villa—on a hill behind the Serapeum.

When building this, his favourite residence, Hadrian's objective was to recall to memory those places which had most impressed him during his extensive travels in the Empire. He attempted to reproduce them in his own home . . . the Lyceum, the Academia, the Prytaneum and the Stoa Poikile of Athens; the Canopus of the Egyptian Delta; and the Vale of Tempe in Thessaly.

The Greek Theatre, one hundred and eighteen feet in diameter, still retains its original form. A cypress avenue leads to the Poikile—once a fascimile of the renowned arcade in Athens. Hadrian's reproduction of this arcade was a peristyle in the middle of which was a large pool. Its surrounding area was probably a racecourse. Its substructure—a wall with three rows of small chambers—was apparently once occupied by the Prætorians. A rectangular building with an apse, attributed as being the ruins of the Philosopher's Hall, contained numerous niches for statuary.

Here Getty's lively imagination came into play. Professor Curtius suggested that his friend's statue of the young "Herakles" would probably have stood in the vicinity of the Temple of Serapis.

Critically, the American surveyed the Canopus, which proved to be an elongated hollow designed in imitation of a sanctuary consecrated to Serapis, the original of which stood in the neighbourhood of Alexandria in Egypt. At the head of this sanctuary was the Temple of Serapis.

Ruins of the Stadium, the Small Baths, the Great Baths

R

and of an immense swimming pool bounded by a Crypto-porticus which lead to a Prætorium, were equally impressive and stimulating to the imagination.

Ruins of the Imperial Palace itself comprised several build-ings grouped around four peristyles. The Piazzo D'oro, the Doric Atrium, the Great Peristyle and the Court of the Libraries were all still in evidence and could be imaginatively reconstructed. The Great Peristyle was formed by sixty columns and, alongside, one of its series of rooms contained vacant niches formerly occupied by statues.

"Here, I think," Professor Curtius indicated, pointing with his walking stick, "is another place where your 'Herakles' might have stood. It is also quite possible that marbles adorned the main chambers in the Court of Libraries—perhaps in the Greek Library or in the Latin Library."

Mueller made an observation that marble statuary, generally limited to portrait-busts of medium size, or bronzes were the customary library embellishments.

"I'm inclined to believe my 'Herakles' occupied a niche in one of these rooms alongside the Great Peristyle which was part of the Imperial Palace itself," said Getty. "As you'll doubtless recall, Professor, all the statuary discovered in and around the Temple of Serapis was Egyptian. Most of it is now in the Capitoline and the Vatican Museums."

Professor Curtius lapsed into a thoughtful silence. "Your theory is more logical than mine," he said finally. "I am not adept at reconstructing how or where a marble statue would stand—only at how or where buildings have stood, and their relation to and with ancient life as indicated by archæological survey."

It was evident to both Mueller and Curtius that the American was unusually preoccupied. His mind seemed to be dwelling on things far away from this scene.

Was he—once again—mentally traversing those distant horizons of civilization's distant eras?

Simultaneously this thought must have occurred to both men. They exchanged an understanding glance.

. . . Anzio, Antium in ancient times, revealed no sign of Nero's Villa, in front of which the seven-eighths life-sized marble torso of "Venus with the Looking-glass" or "Aphrodite", as she is perhaps better known (now in the ranch museum), was recovered from the sea. But concrete "Pillboxes"—remnants of World War II—and much evidence of bombings were grim reminders that the beaches at Anzio had been major battlefronts.

To compensate for this sacrilege, the rather primitive villages had now evolved into little modern towns. Square white buildings, neon lighting, drug-stores with soda fountains and gleaming, chromium-plated fittings, news-stands bedecked with gaily-covered magazines—all were now part of the scenic pattern.

As they critically surveyed one such scene, Getty observed: "It isn't picturesque or colourful as it was before, but I'll bet it's a whole lot more comfortable to live in. A slice of pure Americana—twentieth-century edition—sandwiched between Italian Renaissance and the remains of the medieval and ancient worlds. It's a strange sandwich! Could be it's a significant one. Could be," he mused.

. . . At several points, later, they were to encounter other replicas of small towns such as one might find in any part of the United States, now replacing some former Italian village which had suffered extensive bomb damage during World War II. . . .

It was always a pleasure to study photographs of works of art in his ranch museum—a pleasure enhanced when shared with such a distinguished authority as Professor Curtius, who showed a lively interest in all matters concerning art.

Discussing a photograph of a handsome blue Sèvres vase

decorated with gilt mounts by Gouthière, the American explained how this had been a favourite *objet d'art* of Marie Antoinette—its original owner—and was always greatly admired by her close friend, Countess Lubomirska. In 1793, during the French Revolution, when certain contents of the Palace of Versailles were being auctioned, Countess Lubomirska made the long journey to Versailles from her estate at Landshut in Poland for the special purpose of purchasing this vase. Acquiring it, she took it back to Poland with her. Count Alfred Potocki, her great-great grandson, eventually inherited the estate at Landshut, where he lived until Germany invaded Poland in 1939. It was he who sold Marie Antoinette's favourite blue Sèvres vase to Getty.

These photographs revived a temporarily discarded plan to catalogue the ranch museum art collection. The upshot of this conversation was that Professor Curtius undertook to catalogue the marble antiquities and suggested Mueller might do the same for the paintings.

The Dutch art dealer protested that he was not qualified for such a task: an authority in or adviser to a museum would be a more desirable choice. Curtius was an eminent official at the German Archæological Institute in Rome, and Mueller maintained that cataloguing miscellaneous paintings demanded someone of similar stature—for example, Dr. Valentiner of the Los Angeles Museum. Also an authority from the Louvre in Paris—if someone were available—would be the logical person to catalogue the French furniture, tapestries and carpets.

"I am merely an art dealer. I make no claim to being an authority," Mueller declined with a broad smile and—with what was rare for the always accommodating Dutchman—an unexpected firmness.

. . . No matter how late the hour, Getty always jotted down before retiring "events and comments of the day" in his little diary or log-book. Some new additions read:

"In my opinion, Mueller under-estimates his own ability."

"Curtius has agreed to catalogue my marble antiquities, so tonight have cabled home for large photographs of every marble in my collection."

"Also wrote Dr. Valentiner *re* cataloguing my paintings."

"A call from Paris. Rosenberg and Stiebel have accepted my offer for the Duke's secretaire. As always, luck—or chance—plays a part in the affairs of man. Even in building an art collection. . . ."

Next day when discussing the ranch museum's latest acquisition and speculating on the strange and diverse route by which an art treasure ultimately joins a collection, Getty related:

"It's well over a year ago. I was lunching at White's Club in London with a friend of mine—a Duke of Scottish descent. When the conversation turned to art, he told me that his ancestors had bequeathed to him the more or less usual quota of uninteresting paintings and unimportant French furniture.

"He had never considered selling his works of art. If I were seriously interested in any he owned—well, he might change his mind. I was invited to spend that week-end at his castle in the Scottish Highlands, his family seat. A few pieces of eighteenth-century French furniture were there, the finest being a large secretaire acquired by a certain Lady Elizabeth— the Duke's ancestress—on a visit to Paris way back in 1760.

"He was so modest about his possessions that I imagined he owned nothing beyond run-of-the-mill art objects! I'd like to have accepted his invitation, but had too many calls on my time.

"Strange as Fate, right after luncheon I met a friend, a famous connoisseur of French furniture. Most important examples in private collections, museums, or belonging to British nobility are known to him. He couldn't recollect anything outstanding in the Duke's family. However, he was going to Scotland in the near future, so I suggested that he look in at the castle, on my behalf. If he saw anything of

261

importance, he could advise me—subject, of course, to the Duke's approval.

"I was in Italy when, a couple of months later, he reported that much to his surprise a superb example of eighteenth-century French furniture was in the castle. Yes; it was the large secretaire which the Duke's ancestress, the Lady Elizabeth, had acquired in Paris in 1760." Getty forestalled Mueller's eager questioning and continued: "I was advised to purchase it, so began negotiations. But on realizing its importance and value, the Duke accepted an immediate offer. The secretaire my friend expertized as being by Burb, and one of Burb's greatest examples, was already sold."

Getty went on to describe his efforts to trace the new owner of this treasure, who was said to be in London, and of how all knowledge of its purchase was denied. Enquiries at a name and address in New York where the desk was said to have been shipped, drew a blank. Any knowledge of this piece was disclaimed.

"Sure, I was sore at losing a treasure I felt I'd virtually uncovered. But I could do nothing except resign myself to the fact that one great example of eighteenth-century French furniture was lost to me. I kicked myself for not having accepted the Duke's invitation."

Many rumours as to new ownership and the whereabouts of the secretaire floated around, vague and unconfirmed. Finally, the American gave up all idea of acquiring it. The Burb desk seemed to have disappeared.

A year later, in Paris, a casual mention that the Galeries Charpentier were selling some important paintings took Getty to the sale. There he met Stiebel, whom he imagined to be in New York.

As usual Stiebel acted as his guide, pointing out the most important works in the Galeries. During this "instruction", the American recalled that, among others, his firm were rumoured as having acquired the Duke's secretaire.

At first Stiebel declined to speak about it, but eventually admitted that this precious piece of furniture was in their possession in New York. His firm had acquired it as a private investment—not for resale—hence the secrecy surrounding its mysterious purchaser.

"Well, should you ever decide to sell, here is my firm offer," the American quoted an attractive figure. . . .

Now, he told Mueller, "Late last night Stiebel called me from Paris. Apparently he's just returned from New York. A chance remark about a sale of paintings—a chance meeting —and the mystery was solved. And now this magnificent example by Burb is mine."

Getty went on: "Stiebel, who's probably seen more French furniture than anyone else from Gatchina in Russia to San Francisco in the U.S.A., is an excellent judge. I asked him which, in his opinion, were the dozen most important master-pieces of eighteenth-century French furniture in both public and private collections at the present time. He listed them thus:

"Number one is my newest treasure, the large secretaire by Burb. Two is the Metternich bureau plat, for which Baron Edmond de Rothschild reputedly paid one million gold francs to Count Metternich in 1900: it's at Maurice de Rothschild's home at Pregny, near Geneva. Number three is a Sèvres plaque commode, also at Pregny. Four is the bureau du roi, by Oeben, in the Louvre. Number five is a black lacquer commode in the Vienna Museum. Six is a Dubois cornerpiece, the property of Baron de Rothschild. Number seven is my own little green lacquer table by Burb. Eight and nine are a pair of bonheurs-de-jour in the Hillingdon Collection. Number ten is a bonheur-de-jour in the Camondo Collection. Eleven is a Sèvres plaque table in the Wallace Collection. And number twelve is a Cressent medailler owned by Calouste Gulbenkian, which is in the National Gallery in Washington."

The Dutch art dealer displayed his evident satisfaction. "So your collection can now boast two out of the twelve most important examples of eighteenth-century French furniture known to exist. Even to the number one piece. . . ."

"Yes, thanks to your persistent effort to impress upon me that only the best is good enough. And that a fine work of art can never be gauged by its price-tag. For, as a fine work of art, it is virtually beyond price."

Mueller beamed and said: "Your ranch museum and myself have an affinity. Its trial and error have become almost a personal challenge."

Suddenly all sightseeing came to an abrupt halt.

"I am a businessman before all else," Getty told the Dutchman. "Business letters, business reports, business conferences, business problems make up the greatest part of my life. And if the midnight oil has to be burned, well it *is* burned, until my desk is clear, and I can go to bed with a clear conscience."

. . . The Church of Loreto evoked the legend of the missing Raphael.

"Imagine, Professor, how Mueller whetted my imagination with visions of my 'Madonna of Loreto' turning out to be the original! But the highest of authorities recently declared it to be only a copy—and not even one of the best," Getty said ruefully.

Later on the mysterious disappearance of great works of art provided a topic of conversation over the luncheon table at Passetto's.

"Sometimes, though, they reappeared," said the Dutch art dealer with authority. He cited the case of Rembrandt's "Marten Looten," which was lost from sight for so long before being discovered among the possessions of Cardinal Fesch, then French Ambassador to the Vatican.

"What a stimulating experience it would be," announced Professor Curtius, "to pursue a work of art—say, an ancient

Greek marble—from its conception to its creation and throughout its life history."

The American's eyes widened, alert with interest. "After a fashion, that is what I have tried to do by delving into backgrounds of my treasures. The idea—in theory—was provocative. In practice, however, it yielded little."

"Ah," said Curtius, "you evidently kept your imagination in check. Facts often prove disappointing. One must liven them with fiction. Let me assure you that even our archæological surveys are coloured by imagination. True, our objective is to be factual, but we try to avoid the drabness which often accompanies factuality. Reconstructing other eras of life on this planet stimulates the imagination." His voice took on a note of urgency. "Please colour your facts—without distorting them. Let your imaginative mind embellish whatever facts you unearth, and salve your conscience with the thought that author's licence is not only permissible—it is universally practised and accepted."

Conversation turned to Greece. Professor Curtius insisted that Latin and Greek authors were hard to read. Their thinking was different. He said it took him approximately two hours to read twenty pages. Church Latin, he maintained, was simple. It was similar to street Latin of the fourth and fifth centuries. Xenophon, the Greek author, he found easy to follow. But Plato, Thucydides and Æschylus were all difficult for a modern mind to understand: there were always differences of opinion relative to the interpretation of many passages in their works.

Mueller took no part in this discussion; it was a subject of which he possessed little knowledge beyond the smattering of Latin he remembered from his college days. On the contrary, the American appeared as familiar with Greek authors and ancient languages as the learned Professor himself.

"How I love Rome," Getty observed as they emerged from Passetto's and walked along the street. "For me, this city has

265

everything Paris has to offer . . . plus." He drew a deep, appreciative breath.

. . . Roma, old Roma and Roma Antica—three cities in one. The Rome of today, with its fashionable salons, lovely villas, plush hotels, movie theatres—as cosmopolitan as any city to be found in Europe. The Rome of yesterday, with its alley-like winding streets, as medieval as any existing in Italy. And, thirty feet below ground level, buried by dust of the centuries, ancient Rome.

Where excavations had already taken place, the ancient city was exposed. Standing on a street in old Rome, surrounded by monuments of modern Rome, one looked down on remnants of streets, forums and buildings constructed two thousand years before. Now they were once again visible to the human eye. . . .

This unique combination was a sight of which Getty never wearied. "How I love this city!" he repeated.

Of Rome's many wonderful churches, St. Paul's, with its row upon row of ancient stone columns, was his favourite. "Although I agree there is no other edifice in the world to compare with St. Peter's for splendour."

. . . St. Paul's was austere where St. Peter's was ornate. Its avenues of antique columns, rising from the floor to the immense vaulted ceiling, cast intriguing criss-cross shadows as shafts of sunlight pierced the windows. . . .

They found it difficult to tear themselves away from Rome and its enchantment. The American deplored the fact that time was an element only a fortunate few could afford to ignore, and that he was not one of those fortunate few.

"Personally, I'd enjoy staying here for months. My urge to learn more about the ancient world is irresistible. Those earlier civilizations set the pattern for ours today. And I'm not so sure that people then were not wiser than we are. Our present-day statesmen and politicians could take lessons from the

Greeks and early Romans. The future of this planet we call our world is shaped by past events. Who was it coined the phrase that 'history always repeats itself'?"

By dint of good management their visit to Greece was fixed to coincide with that of Professor Curtius, who was to attend a meeting in Athens.

"This trip has certainly been momentous," Getty told his companion. "Mueller, in the parlance of America, I repeat that you surely are my good luck piece! I hope you've enjoyed these travels as much as I have."

. . . Despite a chill in the evening air, the sidewalk tables outside Doney's were filling up with their regular clientele of internationals. From the terrace of his hotel room, which also commanded a view of the distant Colosseum and the glistening white marble dome of St. Peter's, the American exclaimed: "Via Veneto has become a conglomeration of all the Bond Streets, Rues de la Paix and Champs Elysees of Europe!"

Mueller, whom he addressed, was reflecting on aspects of Rome relatively unimportant to Getty. Like most Dutchmen, Mueller ate for pleasure and enjoyment, not merely as a necessity. "Passetto's" . . . where the cuisine pandered to his palate . . . *Fettucini* at "Alfredo's, where the *maestro* initiated newcomers by personally mixing the gleaming noodles, butter and cheese with a golden fork and spoon. Who, anywhere, could compete with the fat, genial Alfredo, whose elaborate presentation of simple *fettucini* made one feel an honoured guest? He recalled the plush, sophisticated Open Gate Club . . . the American, presumably occupied in business conferences, was already watching the floor-show when the Dutchman and a "friend" arrived there. Both Getty and himself diplomatically refrained from making any reference to that evening and its embarrassing head-on collision. . . .

Numerous *trattorie* and their recommended local wine or

wines of the district gratified his palate. He inherited a taste for ambrosia, a full-bodied red wine, rich in bouquet. So many and such varied memories of these memorable travels! Professor Curtius—his precise manner, unexpectedly bluff laugh and good-natured tolerance of the two "disciples" who so eagerly took advantage of his scholarly guidance. It was going to be difficult to adjust himself to a more prosaic way of life when these travels ended.

"I guess we'll have to change into dinner jackets for the opera," the American interrupted Mueller's reverie.

... To hear Puccini's work performed in his native land was an opportunity not to be missed, declared Getty, who invited both Mueller and Curtius to the opera season's opening performance, which coincided with their last night in Rome. . . .

Between acts, the foyer of Rome's beautiful Opera House presented a glittering social scene.

"Ah, yes," Professor Curtius said, contentedly puffing on his cigar, "the women of Rome have always been famous for their elegance."

"Their looks, too, I'd say." His host appraised the fashionably dressed and jewelled women and their conventionally attired "black-tied" escorts.

The Dutch art dealer made no comment, but his eyes blinked with increasing rapidity as one lovely lady after another brushed past him on her way through the crowded foyer.

"Wagner as performed in Bayreuth and Puccini as performed in Italy are memorable experiences for us, aren't they, Mueller?" said Getty.

They made an interesting trio . . . the corpulent little Dutchman in an obviously new dinner jacket, his accessories all fastidiously correct; the dignified elderly Professor in old-fashioned evening dress, distinguished, his beard freshly trimmed and a gold-knobbed walking stick to aid his gait;

268

the tall American with his characteristic easy poise and lean face of almost mask-like coldness, until he smiled.

The Professor nodded greetings to a few acquaintances, and Prince Vittorio Massimo, who knew him but slightly, was sufficiently intrigued by the trio to proffer a personal salutation.

Introductions were effected and the Prince, a lively young Roman patrician, said that he had heard of the American's fine art collection.

"I've heard of you, too," replied Getty, returning the compliment. And he repeated an anecdote of how, when Napoleon once asked a member of the distinguished Massimo family whether there was any truth in the statement that they were descendants of the Emperor Maximus, the reply was: "I do not know, Sire, but it has been a rumour in our family for some two thousand years."

With a flash of white teeth, the Prince retorted: "We believe it to be true, of course. We are a very old Roman family and until recently, like my ancestors, I served as a member of the Papal Bodyguard."

Prince Vittorio Massimo possessed a notable collection of Etruscan art. "Some of which I dug up myself," he said, and invited them to see the latest additions to his treasures.

"Let me drive you out to Capena—it's only thirty kilometers from Rome—and show you some recent discoveries. We can start early, be back in time for lunch at my home, see my modest collection, and you will still be able to leave for Naples in the early afternoon."

It was never difficult to tempt the American, with his avidly enquiring mind: the Dutchman was, as ever, amenable: and Curtius was intrigued.

"You are a surprising young man," he told the Prince, and went on to explain to his two companions how Prince Vittorio and his elder brother, both students of Etruscan art

269

and therefore interested in archæology, spent their leisure time excavating for ancient remains.

"This time, sir, we turned our findings over to the authorities. These excavations are of real importance—not merely Etruscan objects such as we have often unearthed for our own collection," said the Prince.

. . . Next day at the old *castello* belonging to the Massimo family, Prince Vittorio showed his guests hundreds of small terra-cotta objects and fragments which had been discovered in the vicinity of Capena. He related how he came upon a mound of freshly-dug earth and a broken statue on a hill hitherto untouched.

"A workman, digging for treasure, evidently found the broken statue, considered it worthless and left it on the hill. I started to investigate and began digging there. For some time it appeared a fruitless task, but eventually a number of terra-cotta objects came to light. I recognized them as being votive offerings—which indicated something important existed deeper down. But deep excavation needs Government sponsorship. It took me some time to convince the authorities. Now across those fields you will see the results of my discovery."

. . . "It's a miniature Ostia," said Getty with delight.

Professor Curtius made no comment, but walked slowly around the excavated area critically examining earth, stone and structure.

"Only archæologists who are actually employed on this site know any of the details of these excavations," explained the Prince. "The authorities preferred to wait for a while before issuing a public report on our findings."

Curtius was in his element; it was difficult to pry him away. "I am deeply indebted to you for showing me these diggings. I cannot imagine why I have not heard of them before. It seems incredible that I should have been ignorant of such important developments so close to home."

Later, it was equally difficult to pry him away from Massimo's private collection of Etruscan art objects, which, according to Professor Curtius, contained many pieces of major importance.

So ended what the American pronounced to be his most stimulating stay in Rome. Previous visits suffered by comparison. True, he had departed from his original intention to explore the backgrounds of his art treasures. Yet some of his activities were directly or indirectly related to art, he maintained. And what an educational *festa* it had been!

. . . Relaxed, as always, when behind the wheel of his Cadillac, Getty steered the car through Rome's traffic maze, *en route* for Naples. In about ten days' time they would board ship for Piræus. Greece excited his imagination. What a soul-satisfying finale to these travels. He glanced at his companion. But Mueller was absorbed in the notes which Prince Vittorio Massimo had thoughtfully provided for inclusion in the American's "log book of comments and events":

COLONIA JULIA FELIX LUCO FERONIENSE

"This little military town, discovered in 1952, is now being excavated. It is located about thirty kilometres from Rome on Via Tiberina, in the territory of the village of Capena near the castle of Scorano.

"The town was developed in the immediate vicinity of a pre-existing religious centre dedicated to the cult of the goddess Feronia. She was strictly an Italic goddess, venerated mainly by farmers and by freed slaves.

"A little path on the left-hand side of the hill leads to the

excavations where a forum is being uncovered. The fundaments and trunks of several columns have been found. Also
excavated were fundaments of statues bearing inscriptions
from the second century B.C. Along the traces of this forum
several shops were discovered.

"On the right-hand side of the little path, a stipes was
excavated. This contained a great number of votive objects in
terra-cotta, pertaining to the temple of the goddess Feronia. It
is supposed that the precise location of this temple was between
the stipes and the forum, which is exactly where the path
crosses. The objects found in this stipes might date from the
fifth century B.C. onwards. This indicates that the temple of
Feronia was greatly venerated even after being looted and
destroyed by Hannibal during his Italian campaign.

All inscriptions found in this zone refer to the cult of the
goddess Feronia. It may therefore be concluded that the famous
Attic temple existed in this zone.

"A LADY PLAYING A GUITAR" BY BARTOLOMEO
VENETO

(*Chapter "Rome"*)

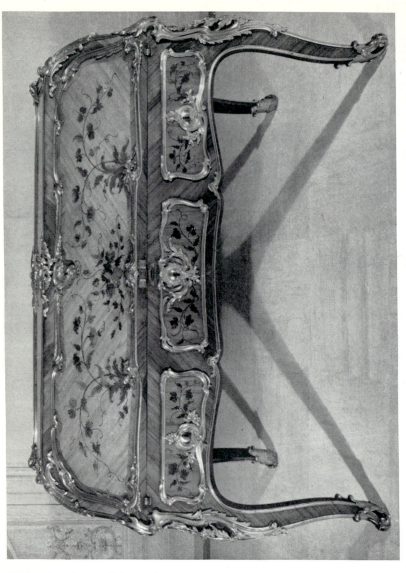

WRITING DESK BY BURB WHICH IS CON-
SIDERED ONE OF THE FINEST EXAMPLES OF
FRENCH FURNITURE

(*Chapter "Rome"*)

CORNER OF THE BURB DESK SHOWING DETAILS OF
ITS INLAID WOODWORK AND ORMOLU MOUNTS

(*Chapter "Rome"*)

MARBLE PORTRAIT-BUST OF LIVIA. ONE OF THE FEW
STILL EXTANT WHICH SHOWS HER AS A YOUNG
WOMAN

(Chapters "The Ranch," "Rome" and "The Emperor's Birthday")

· VII ·

Prelude to Greece

AS they drove from Rome to Naples, Mueller observed the American's vigilant study of the landscape. The latter explained: "It's a habit of mine, dating back to the time I started in business. Finding oil has been one of my major occupations. I've studied petroleum geology and oil-finding long enough to realize that oil is where you find it. A 'nose for oil' is essential! The territory around here is sedimentary, and could be productive given the right kind of structure. Such structures are often visible to the trained eye. To me, every trip through possible oil territory is a journey of reconnaissance."

Not only through oil territory, the Dutchman thought. He recalled occasions when, driving past a factory, his companion had stopped the car in order to find out what kind of plant it was, what sort of goods were manufactured there, and so on. A furniture factory had proved of special interest; and permission was obtained to view its assembly line—for what purpose, Mueller could only guess. Another time it was a factory making aircraft parts. Getty was denied entrance—it was a Government property—but the day watchman took him on a tour of its outer buildings.

. . . Naples, spreading fan-wise above one of the world's most beautiful bays, situated at the foot of the Phlegræan Fields and opposite Vesuvius, is still the intellectual and commercial centre of southern Italy. Apart from the beauty of her natural surroundings, she is gay, noisy, exuberant—

s

typically Mediterranean in character. Rich in works of art of the thirteenth-century, Renaissance and seventeenth-century periods, her Museo Nazionale also boasts unparalleled treasures from the excavated towns of Herculaneum and Pompeii—both of which were buried by the Vesuvius eruption of A.D. 79. . . .

The beauty of the fabulous Bay of Naples inspired exclamations—and certain reservations: absence of the familiar funnel of smoke rising from the mouth of Vesuvius had caused the scene to lose some of its former magic.

"Such a beautiful spot, Napoli. But talk about living on the edge of a volcano!" The American's facial expression was eloquent.

. . . The Museo Nazionale (National Museum), housed in a vast palace, is one of the world's richest in antique sculptures and materials for study of the civilization and art of Magna Græcia.

"Only in Greece itself can one find sculptures to surpass some of these. As for mosaics—can any surpass them?" The Dutch art dealer was in his element, as he contrasted the antique marble group of "Antiope" with its woven version as portrayed in a Beauvais tapestry panel in the ranch museum, one of the famous "Loves of the Gods" series designed by François Boucher. Forthwith he related the legend of Antiope, refreshing his companion's memories of Greek mythology.

. . . Antiope was a great beauty and the Satyr, Zeus, also known as Jupiter, took her by force. She ran away, and her father, in order to avenge this act, killed himself. In revenge, Antiope's brother Lyceus killed her husband and then, finding the truant Antiope, imprisoned her. She escaped from prison and on the Plains bore twin sons, Amphian and Zethus, who were brought up by the local herdsmen.

Dirce, the wife of Lyceus, was insanely jealous of Antiope's beauty and made constant trouble for her. When Antiope's twin sons grew to maturity, they killed Lyceus in order to avenge their mother's suffering, and then bound their jealous aunt to the horns of a mad bull.

Dionysus, also known as Bacchus, god of wine, made Antiope mad and caused her to wander restlessly all over Greece until she became cured. Afterwards, Antiope married Phocus of Tithorea on Mount Parnassus. And there they were both ultimately buried in one grave. . . .

Getty's sightseeing lust was apparently still insatiable. "We'll see their grave if the dust of ages hasn't scavenged it beyond recognition," he said to Mueller hopefully.

. . . The environs of Naples enchanted them. Nisida, which they entered through a causeway, Pozzuoli and Posillipo. Numerous craters of the volcanic region of Campi Flegrei have resulted in the formation of picturesque hills, and they saw remains of Cape Miseno and Mount Procida, which Homer and Virgil used as settings for some of their poetry. Baia, fashionable bathing resort of Romans in the early days of their Empire, now only offered ruins of its once-luxurious villas and remains of three so-called temples.

They found the richness of these environs, steeped in mythology and legend, the perfect prelude to a visit to Greece, and saw Porto di Miseno—the antique Misenum—built by Marcus Agrippa as a refuge for the Tyrrhenian fleet. Misenus, trumpeter to Æneas, is said to be buried there.

The Amphitheatre at Pozzuoli was completed in the reign of Vespasian; its substructure amazed them. The series of rooms were in such excellent preservation that it was a simple matter to visualize them as dens housing wild beasts, and the adjoining rooms as containing complicated stage machinery to hoist the animals up into the arena.

At Cumæ—now known as Cuma and which as Kyme was one of the oldest Greek colonies in the West—they found the Acropolis surrounded by ramparts of the fifth century B.C.

Imposing ruins of these walls were still visible. On the acropolis, temples of Apollo and of Jupiter had long been transformed into Christian churches. At its foot there was the
trapezoidal Cave of the Cumæn Sybil.

. . . Of that subterranean cave, Getty's journal recorded:
"It is a marvel in acoustics. The Sybil was in effect a fortune-
teller, and faithful believers in her powers were legion. She
became almost a religion. When asking questions to solve their
problems, her followers remained at one end of the distant
corridor, and the Sybil's voice as she answered reverberated
in mystic fashion from her temple high on the hill. In the time
of Augustus her believers were decreasing in numbers and
considered highly credulous by the sophisticated.

"What a beautiful site for a city had Cuma! I left it with
regret as darkness fell."

The Greek Temples at Pæstum were likewise noted in his
journal. "Pæstum is a romantic ruin midst the silent plain of
the Sele. Its wonderfully preserved Doric temples produce an
incomparable effect of majesty and grandeur. As Poseidonia
(the city of Neptune), it was founded by Greeks from Sybaris
in the sixth century B.C. I learned that the Temple of Neptune
ranks with the Theseion at Athens and with the Temple of
Concord at Agrigento as being one of the best-preserved
Greek temples in all of Europe."

And a later addition read: "Find myself much impressed
by Italians' passionate love for their children. Noticed it many
times, and especially yesterday at Nola.

. . . Nola, birthplace of Augustus, had little else to offer of
historic or artistic merit, and a mystified Mueller asked the
reason for his companion's keenness to visit the place.

"Some day, maybe, you'll find there was a reason," the
American said, a far-away look in his eyes. "Some day,
maybe."

Nola's inhabitants were out in full force, for it was a *festa,* one of the innumerable Saints' days observed as religious holidays in Italy.

Their sightseeing attempts yielded little beyond muddy shoes and they found themselves standing in line at the one and only shoe-shine stand in Nola's main square.

Ahead of them a man wearing patched clothes tightly held the hand of his little girl, aged about four. Despite evident poverty, the child wore a pretty white dress. When their turn came, it was her little shoes which received attention, not those of her father, who obviously could not spare the precious thirty lire for his own use. But for his *bambina*——!!!

Her tiny white shoes were cleaned as carefully as if they were the fabled golden slippers, and a grateful father held out the necessary thirty lire.

"Today is *festa,*" said the shoe-cleaner. "I make a present to the *bambina.*" He watched the little girl, beaming, as she paraded in her now spotless white shoes before her father, whose eloquent brown eyes were aglow with that love the simplest Italian has for all *bambini.* . . .

This item, in Getty's journal concluded with: "The incident was human and touching. I gave the shoe-cleaner a little extra, to compensate. He was a man of simple dignity."

No business associates appeared in Naples; there were no conferences, but the American still spent many hours on his business reports and still, Mueller discovered, found time to study.

Adhering to his formula for improving his accent and increasing his vocabulary in foreign languages by reading aloud whenever possible, Greek was now the challenge. "I'm woefully out of practice," Getty said. "Oh, I know that speaking the language of a country isn't strictly necessary. But it's certainly an advantage. Haven't you found it so?"

The Dutchman readily admitted that his companion's

fluent Italian had added to his own pleasure and convenience.

"Of course, my knowledge of Greek is very limited. I'm far better at reading ancient Greek than speaking the modern language."

Talking about his collection and the future of the ranch museum, he expressed appreciation for the sincerity of Mueller's interest and expert guidance.

"I really don't know how to thank you for so generously giving me your time, and so graciously putting up with my erratic way of life. You're an indulgent travelling companion, Mueller."

On occasion, however, the latter found it difficult to keep pace with Getty's restless energy, so diplomatically retired whenever a long period of strenuous activity threatened. Professor Curtius, despite his seventy-seven years, had displayed remarkable agility and endurance when Mueller felt taxed beyond his physical resources. Now the American's plan to see the crater of Vesuvius was far from enticing, yet the Dutchman felt morally obligated to accompany him.

. . . The lower slopes of Mount Vesuvius, one of the most active volcanoes in the world, were once planted with vineyards, and a belt of woods just above them was famous for its wild boars. In A.D. 63 a violent earthquake caused serious damage to Pompeii, Herculaneum and Naples; in A.D. 79 the eruption of Vesuvius buried Pompeii, Herculaneum and Stabiæ. Subsequent eruptions occurred, but after the upheaval in 1500 a period of absolute quiescence set in for a hundred and thirty-one years. On December 16th, 1631, another violent eruption destroyed all towns at the foot of the mountain, and lava reached to the sea. Of several subsequent upheavals, the most terrible one occurred in 1871-2. Another in 1906 was

278

almost as violent. A new eruption in 1929 destroyed some fifty houses at Terzigno. The last eruption of Vesuvius was in March, 1944. . . .

The two men drove up the mountain road as far as the Observatory, where they stopped for lunch. Then they proceeded past the Atrio del Cavallo and Valle dell' Inferno to where the road ended, and parked the car. Vesuvius consists of a truncated cone called Mount Somma, on the summit of which is a crater from whose centre rises a small cone which is the properly so-called Vesuvius.

It was that twenty-five-minute climb, on foot, to its crater on the summit which Mueller found so distressing.

A spectacular panorama spread before them. The crater itself—an awe-inspiring sight—was many hundreds of feet deep with vertical walls. It was quite safe to look into the bowels of the crater, but no one was permitted to descend, the guide warned them. The volcano—now inactive—still menaced. The American's eager questioning elicited the fact that there was a very small discharge of steam near the southeast rim of the crater.

The Dutchman—as usual—envied his companion's lithe gait. He appeared to be exhilarated by their steep climb, while he himself was perspiring and experiencing some difficulty in breathing.

During the return journey to Naples, Mueller was noticeably quiet, and on arrival at the Hotel Excelsior declared his intention to rest for a while.

Complete absorption in his own activities and interests made Getty unobservant of others, and consequently rather thoughtless. It never for one moment occurred to him that what was easy for him taxed others heavily. "Fine, I'll see you around eight," he said to Mueller unconcernedly. "If it stays warm, we can eat at Zi Teresa's."

They dined in the open air and at the water's edge.

Zi Teresa's, a famous water-front restaurant, bustled with activity and was alive with diners, waiters, flower-sellers and the inevitable *musica*.

Getty talked of recent days spent at Pompeii. "Walking along the Via dell' Abbondanza to the Amphitheatre, I imagined myself back in those far-off days. That election propaganda we saw written on the walls, and the announcement of the Amphitheatre, seemed to be contemporary." He quoted: *Pompa Venatio Athletai*. And in response to Mueller's request interpreted: "A colourful procession would be covered by the word *Pompa*. Wild beast hunts would make *Venatio*, and *Athletai* would presumably be the gladiators."

The Great Palæstra, with its immense swimming pool, graduated in depth as are modern swimming pools of today, and Pompeii's fine homes made one realize the amenities of life in those days, said the art dealer. "Their plumbing of practically two thousand years ago is so obviously the pattern of ours of today."

"I found myself thinking of those boys who were around the swimming pool on that fatal August morning in the year 79. The excavations surely take us back in vivid fashion to that far-off Golden Age of Imperial Rome! I got the feeling that Pompeii's inhabitants had only recently evacuated their city—instead of nineteen centuries ago.

"And who could ever doubt that their *Thermæ Stabianæ* is the blueprint for what we now call 'Turkish Baths'?"

. . . The frescoes and paintings on some of the walls and villas of Pompeii are a miracle of preservation, and, after studying them, Mueller and the American were able to distinguish four periods in art. In the first (Samnite) period, the stucco ornamentation imitated marble panelling of Greek or Roman mansions, with no human figures visible. In the second period (first century B.C.), marble decoration was imitated in painting, and figures were introduced. In the third period (first half of the first century of the Roman Empire), figures became more numerous. In the fourth period, figures were accompanied by bizarre architectural design.

The stretch of Pompeii's city wall between the Porta Vesuvio and the Porta Salinensis, and the atrium of the "House of the Silver Wedding", had excited their interest. Getty discovered an entrance to the Amphitheatre which was rarely, if ever, used by tourists. Here roots of giant plane trees planted around the Palæstra had been recently excavated. Cement filling these roots had assisted the experts to date the age of the trees and forecast the date of the Palæstra itself.

The huge plane trees were about a hundred years old when Pompeii was buried in the year 79. Thus the Palæstra was built in about 21 B.C.

. . . Less than forty-eight hours before their scheduled departure for Piræus, Mueller became ill. Even Getty, with his usual preoccupation, could not fail to notice a change in his companion. The Dutchman's bland face became creased with pain, despite all effort to disguise his suffering.

He was a victim of recurrent sciatica. In the intervals between attacks he was surprisingly free of pain. Now it was evident that over-activity had brought on a bad attack, the most acute the art dealer could recall.

Dismayed, Getty hastened to assure him that it would be a simple matter to postpone their visit to Greece.

"You must go as arranged," the art dealer insisted. "A chance to see Greece with someone like Professor Curtius is the opportunity of a lifetime. You must go as arranged."

Disappointed and concerned, the American sought the best medical advice available. The consensus of opinion was unanimous. Mueller was near Ischia, where curative treatment was obtainable. Ischia, an island situated in volcanic terrain, is a three hours' boat trip from Naples and has gained renown as a curative spa for inflammatory diseases. The doctors recommended both its radioactive mud and its mineral springs. Alternatively, similar treatment could be obtained at the close by Terme di Agnano. Agnano itself was actually situated in the crater of a former volcano. For quick and beneficial results in this instance, however, Ischia was strongly recommended.

The easy-going, affable Dutchman proved obstinate.

"Warmth, rest and quiet" was the treatment usually prescribed for his sciatica attacks, and "warmth, rest and quiet" would again prove an effective palliative, if not a cure, he stubbornly maintained.

His own three weeks' trip to Greece could coincide with Mueller's three weeks' course of treatment at Ischia, Getty pointed out sympathetically. "It's certainly tough luck for you and disappointing for both of us. But if you had to get an attack of sciatica, it's just as well it happened right here in Naples. Ischia might prove to be that permanent cure you obviously haven't found elsewhere."

Pain and physical discomfort ultimately convinced the reluctant sufferer. "What is your decision concerning this?" he asked.

"This" was a photograph of an Italian painting selected from several recently submitted. Through the grapevine known only to art dealers, news had spread that the American was now interested in works of the Italian School, and numerous photographs had been forwarded with his recent mail.

This portrait of a youngish woman was attributed to Moretto da Breschia. It was a large painting, and the lady wore a fashionable velvet gown of the period, with enormous ruffled sleeves. An air of serenity pervaded and characterized the work.

Critically, the American re-examined the photograph through his pocket magnifying-glass. "It isn't a picture that excites my imagination—in fact, quite the contrary. Yet I find it strangely soothing. I believe I'll wire and ask for an option until I get back from Greece. What do you think?" He handed the photograph to Mueller, who scrutinized it long and seriously.

"Whoever painted it, this work has great merit. Your 'Italian Painting Section' can only be enriched by a picture of this fine quality. It is first-class," the Dutchman concluded with authority.

On the day fixed for his departure, Getty saw his companion safely aboard an early morning boat to Ischia. The art dealer, though still in pain, was able to walk unaided.

"I'll meet you back here in about three weeks' time, Mueller," he said, shaking hands. "*Arrivaderci*, my friend. I shall certainly miss you."

. . . Later, in retrospect, Mueller would have sworn on oath that his unpredictable companion's eyes had blurred with emotion as he turned and walked away. He saw him reach the dock below, and waved to him from the rails. But the American did not look back. . . .

Sailing time for Greece was nine that evening, so Getty spent the intervening hours in another visit to the Museo Nazionale and a drive to Caserta.

Built by the Bourbons, the Palazzo Reale at Caserta was begun in 1752 and completed in 1774 from designs by Vanvitelli. It held some magnificent tapestries and paintings. The American enjoyed comparing them with his own treasures. He was told how this beautiful palace had been the Mediterranean Allied Headquarters during World War II. It was here also that the German forces in Italy had surrendered on April 29th, 1945. The royal gardens at Caserta—an immense park—were famous for their fountains and ornamental waterworks, which were embellished by groups of marble statuary.

Driving back to Naples, Getty felt very much "alone"

without the Dutchman's affable company. He would unquestionably have cancelled his prospective visit to Greece were it not for the fact that Professor Curtius had already announced his arrival in Athens.

With his precious copy of Pausanias (in its Greek original) under his arm for safety, the American was at the reception desk checking out, when he caught sight of Bernard Berenson and his inseparable companion, Miss Mariano—Nicky.

Their greetings were cordial. Berenson said they had arrived in Naples only a few hours previously, and were proceeding to Sicily within a few days. He repeated the thanks previously expressed in his written note for the interesting set of photographs Getty had recently sent to *I Tatti* for inclusion in the photograph library there.

Delighted at this chance meeting, the latter noted that in physical appearance the fabulous B.B. still brazenly flouted his venerable years. Spry and dressed with his customary meticulous care and elegance, the eminent art historian appeared to be as nimble of mind and of wit as ever.

"So you are just off to Greece," he observed with the characteristic bird-like tilt of his head. "It will indeed be interesting to have a tycoon's reaction to ancient Greece—won't it, Nicky?" Berenson's eyes twinkled gleefully at the thought. "You must not fail to see us on your return and give us a first-hand account of it—mustn't he, Nicky?"

Nicky laughed. "Don't, for goodness sake, take B.B. seriously. He loves to tease people, and today he is in one of his incorrigible moods. Actually, he is envious of you. For you are going to one of his most favourite of all countries."

"Indeed I am," corroborated Berenson. "Greece and its islands are heaven itself to an art-lover. To visit them is an inspiration for all time." He turned his attention to Miss Mariano. "My favourite biped," he said, "we must not detain our friend with idle chatter else he might miss his ship." And, with a handshake which was surprisingly vigorous, he said to the American: "*Bon voyage. My blessings are with you. We must meet again—and soon.*"

Getty sat out on deck as the ship plied across the Bay of Naples to begin her journey to Greece. "It's been a long time since I was last in Greece," he thought. "I had the impression then that I was arriving late—two thousand and fifty-nine years late. Now I'm two thousand and ninety-eight years late. Two thousand and ninety-eight years since the destruction of Corinth! Supposing I had arrived there before the city fell. What would it have been like in those days?" A sensation that he was being transported to worlds long past swept over the American, and his recently acquired statue of the young "Herakles" became vivid in his mind. He mused: "As I make this classic pilgrimage, I wonder if I can bring to life—in words—a story that lives in my imagination. It tells of a journey from Corinth. . . ."

PART TWO

By J. Paul Getty

· I ·

A Journey from Corinth

THE dark blue of the water in the Gulf of Corinth rivalled the darker blue of the Greek sky. A glorious union of colour, light and shadow heralded another sunset. The marble and bronze in the magnificent agora—or civic centre—of Corinth seemed to challenge in beauty the matchless hues of sea and sky. The Peirene Fountain at the eastern end of the Agora next to a pentelic marble statue of Herakles was a favourite trysting place for lovers. The Peirene water was believed by the Greeks to give wisdom and knowledge to those who drank it. There were comfortable seats around the Fountain, and at almost any time in the late afternoon or early evening one or more couples could be seen talking together oblivious of the splendour around them.

An observer might perhaps have noted with special interest one such couple. The girl, about twenty-three years of age, was of striking brunette beauty. She was dressed in white, and a thin white veil covered her face from below her eyes. Her companion, a finely-built man in his early thirties, was dressed in the ordinary tunic as worn in those days—147 B.C. He bore no sign of rank or of his particular occupation, which was that of a landscape architect. The girl's voice was light and musical. She spoke rapidly to the man, whose deep bass could be heard in reply:

"Tell me, Glaucus, do you seriously think Corinth is in danger? You propose moving to somewhere round the Bay of Neapolis (Naples), and ask me to go with you. Don't you think it's all a bit far-fetched? How can anything happen to Corinth? Our city has been here for hundreds of years."

"I doubt whether even the Romans could capture Corinth's citadel," the young man replied gently, "except through treachery or famine. Yet should our city below ever be destroyed, what good would our citadel be? The wall round our lower city is as strong as any in Greece. But the walls of Carthage are also strong, and the Romans, no doubt, will succeed in breaching them.

"I don't wish to alarm you, or others, Daphne. It may well be that in a hundred years from now Corinth will be standing just as she is today, and her people will have come to no harm other than the normal lot of mankind. In fact, I think, dear one, the odds favour this.

"Our Council and principal citizens are not so reckless of their lives and property as to engage in a trial of strength with Rome! Unfortunately, Corinth, politically, is in the hands of reckless men who are supported by the mob. The Romans are hated by the mob because Rome protects the rule of the propertied classes, doubtless because she deems them less likely to take risks and cause trouble. The fanatical demagogues who lead the mob are willing, in their blind hatred, to involve Corinth in a war with the greatest power in the world—the Roman legions.

"Carthage was far mightier than all Greece put together; she had the best General since Alexander, and she was defeated by the Romans! We also know what happened to Macedonia; she waged war with Rome, and as a result has ceased to exist."

Daphne looked at Glaucus fondly. She was proud of his knowledge and always encouraged his oratory.

"In spite of these object lessons," he continued, "the Achæan

287

League—under the leadership of Corinth—attacked Sparta three years ago, and knowingly incurred the grave displeasure of Rome by this breach of the peace. Rome has been patient with us since then: she's tried to negotiate a peaceful settlement with us. But will she succeed?

"The reckless demagogues in our city seem set on defying Rome. They have a following among the less intelligent in our democracy and are gaining strength from day to day. Truly, I smell danger. Wise counsels might not prevail, and sooner or later Corinth and her people might feel the power of the Roman fist.

"The Romans, in their harsh treatment of Macedonia, showed how they intended this as an object lesson for any Greek states which revolted against their authority. Doubtless due to their struggle with Carthage, they have been most conciliatory in their relations with the Greek states.

"If Corinth revolts, Roman fury and indignation will know no bounds. They will probably determine to teach the Greeks a lesson to last for all time. They might—Heaven forbid!— capture our city, raze it to the ground, and kill or enslave our people. If such a time comes, I don't want either of us to be here, my dear one."

"It's good of you to worry about my safety, dearest," said Daphne. "Don't you think we would have ample notice of any threatened danger? If such danger appeared, we could then carry out your plan and go to Neapolis together."

Glaucus shook his head. "Any warning of impending trouble might be short—too short. Others would have the same idea of flight; travelling would be difficult, if not impossible. Neither you nor I have any strong reasons for remaining here; our parents are no longer living.

"Your sister and her husband are welcome to come with us if they will. But since your brother-in-law's business is well established in Corinth, I doubt if he could be induced to move elsewhere. As for my uncle, with whom I live; when I

STATUE OF THE ELDER FAUSTINA

(*Chapter "Rome"*)

THE "CROUCHING VENUS", ROMAN REPLICA OF
GREEK ORIGINAL (FOURTH CENTURY B.C.). UNLIK[
STATUES OF THIS SAME SUBJECT IN THE LOUVRE, TH[
METROPOLITAN AND THE TERME, THIS PARIA[
MARBLE FIGURE IS COMPLETE WITH ITS OWN HEAD

(*Acquired 1955*)

mentioned the matter to him, he laughed at me. So, dear one, if we leave we must go by ourselves."

Daphne looked serious. "If you think it best for us to go to this far-away land, I'm willing to go with you, Glaucus," she said softly. "I know you must have considered it all very carefully, in your usual methodical way. I trust your judgment. I can have my things ready in a fortnight. We can be married then—if you will have me as your wife so soon."

"The sooner the better, my darling. Any delay to our marriage will never be due to me."

A fortnight later Glaucus and Daphne were married at the home of her sister, and Glaucus soon completed preparations for their early departure.

Their friends and relations found it difficult to understand the young couple's desire to leave the pleasant and prosperous city of Corinth for a distant town in a strange country. True, the inhabitants of Neapolis were Greek in race and speech, but they were not in close touch with the Greek people in Greece, and there was very little travel between Neapolis and Greece.

Glaucus had never made a long sea journey, so he thought it well to take advice from an experienced traveller before engaging passage. Theo, an acquaintance in Corinth, had made several sea voyages, and Glaucus sought him out.

"So you are thinking about a trip to Italy?" Theo mused aloud. "You will naturally travel by boat rather than take the long, dangerous road round the Adriatic. There is also the practical choice of going to Brundisium and thence by land to Neapolis. Or you could go by boat all the way. There is a good road from Brundisium to Neapolis; the distance is some two hundred miles. You could complete the journey within a week. If you go by boat all the way, you might make the journey as quickly; but if there are contrary winds, it might take a month. If there's good weather and a favourable wind,

T   289 a boat trip would be a great pleasure, and you would save money as compared with a trip by land of some two hundred miles.

"Taking it all in all, if I were you I should go by boat. You are not urgently required in Neapolis. It might be as well to spare yourself the extra expense and inconveniences of a long land journey.

"Now as to boats: I can offer some advice. Get the largest boat there is, one that has not made too many voyages. Select a captain who is experienced, skilful, and of good reputation. Otherwise you may be fleeced of your money and property, or suffer many annoyances. It's common practice for an unscrupulous captain to take a passenger's money and luggage and then, after he has gone ashore, suddenly hoist sail and depart without him! And some captains say they are sailing in two days when they know full well it will be in two weeks.

"You must take your own supplies along, and look after yourself on board ship. It isn't necessary, however, or advisable to take a cask of water. There is always the ship's supply. If for any reason it ran short, you wouldn't feel comfortable being the only one on board who had fresh water. You would have to share it with the others, so one cask more or less would make little difference.

"You'll each need a mattress. Be sure it's the right length. And, of course, enough food to last for thirty days—dried goods and salt meat. It might be possible to buy fresh food on the way. But don't rely on it. You won't need any charcoal for cooking; there is plenty available in the ship's galley, which is the only place where you are allowed to build a fire. However, you must take your own cooking utensils."

"Is there any danger of pirates?" interrupted Glaucus.

"Very little on such a trip," Theo assured him. "You won't be getting into Cretan or Asiatic waters, so you shouldn't meet any pirates. No guarantees are ever given, however. One must always accept that slight risk.

"The principal danger will be off the southern coast of Italy. Your captain will probably hug the land pretty closely, though, so you could escape to the shore if pursued. As long as your boat has wind, you are not likely to be taken by pirates—unless they have two boats and box you in from each side. If they're astern, and your captain maintains a good look-out, he should be able to keep ahead of them until dark, and then lose them. If he is negligent and allows pirates to draw close before he takes alarm, you might be run down before darkness could save you.

"Usually the principal danger is when lying becalmed within sight of shore. If someone hastened to notify a nearby pirate, within a few hours a heavily manned ship might row up alongside you. Smoke signals along the shore usually indicate an attack.

"If your boat stops at various ports and carries local passengers, be careful of your money-bag or you might be relieved of it.

"You'll have suitable clothes for your journey. A traveller should be plainly and simply dressed, and make no show of wealth. Sailors themselves are often untrustworthy; they wouldn't hesitate to plunder a passenger who shows signs of affluence.

"In any event, the sailors will get some of your money. A tip to each one of them is obligatory. You will enjoy no peace unless you donate at least two drachmæ to each sailor before quitting the ship at Neapolis."

Glaucus listened carefully as his friend Theo continued:

"If you go ashore, be careful of chance acquaintances who suggest leading you to an out-of-the-way place to see some interesting sight. You might find yourself robbed, or kidnapped and sold into slavery.

"Avoid arguments and political discussions is also my well-meant advice, Glaucus. Remember that you are not on your own territory; therefore it's best to be prudent." He said this with a smile, knowing his listener's reputation for verbosity.

"Eat the food you are accustomed to; try strange dishes sparingly. Avoid water unless you know it's pure. Take care of your health.

"A happy journey from Corinth. God-speed to you and Daphne," he concluded warmly.

Glaucus learned that there were two or three sailings a week from Corinth to Brundisium and other east-coast Italian ports, but only two or three sailings a month to Neapolis. The *Bellerophon*, a Greek sailing vessel, which was due to leave for Neapolis in a week's time, was now loading cargo. Going down to the harbour, he soon located her and spoke to her Captain.

"Yes. I can carry two more passengers. The fare will be two hundred drachmæ each. My ship supplies charcoal for cooking and water for drinking. Passengers supply their own food, cooking utensils, dishes and, of course, their own mattresses and blankets. Don't take candles or oil lamps on board. They are a fire hazard. I don't allow my passengers to use them. Anyway, you'll find yourself going to bed when it gets dark.

"There's room for your mattresses below deck. Or, if you prefer, you can sleep on deck when the weather is good.

"I think you will like the *Bellerophon*, if you care for sailing at all. I have served in one capacity or another on a score of ships, and she's the best of them. She's only five years old, and her owners have enabled me to keep her in first-class condition. She's one of the largest ships calling at Corinth. Her length is a hundred and twenty feet by forty feet beam, and she can carry three hundred tons of cargo."

"What sort of cargo do you usually carry?" enquired Glaucus with interest.

"Whatever offers," replied the Captain. "Business hasn't been brisk in the Greece-to-Italy trade. Both countries have plenty of olive oil and wine. Both countries are importers of wheat.

"One of Greece's principal exports is marble. We have plenty of good marble, and so far Italy has none. All of the worked marble for export to the west is shipped from here. It's too valuable to be shipped from eastern Greece around Cape Malea—that home of storms and a graveyard for ships. The money value of ships lost off Cape Malea in the last century would pay for a ship-canal through the Isthmus of Corinth several times. But Greece is poor and divided politically, so the ship-canal is just a dream."

. . . Raw marble was shipped by boat from Piræus and Paros, around Cape Malea to Italy. If a boat was lost, it was bad for the crew and her owners. But the raw marble could easily be replaced. Sculptures in marble from the studios in Athens and Argos were shipped by water to the Corinth Peninsula. There they were unloaded, transported by wagon across the four miles of peninsula, and reloaded on to another ship for transport to Italy.

If the ship was small, it could be set on rollers and pulled across. This unloading—transporting four miles—and reloading, cost as much as the rest of the voyage did. It was only practicable with valuable cargo. . . .

"You see these boxes here?" said the Captain, "they contain marble statues from Athens destined for Rome. I'll unload them on to barges in the harbour of Ostia, and the barges will then deliver them to Rome, fourteen miles up the Tiber River. So, when you see Greek marble sculptures in Italy, you may be sure they've come from Corinth or across its peninsula."

"Unless the Greek marble was worked into a statue in Italy," said Glaucus.

"Theoretically, that's true. But practically it's a fact that all Greek marble sculptures are made in Greece—unless they are portraits of local people in other countries. No one would go to the expense of shipping raw Greek marble to Italy to have it botched by stone-cutters there."

A few Greek sculptors were practising in Italy, but their

work was confined to portraits and reliefs. A copy of a Greek masterpiece made in Italy from Greek marble would have cost more and would have had less prestige value than one made in Greece.

"Rome is noted for her roads, and we are noted for our statues!" continued the Captain. "In addition to marble statues, I generally carry a good cargo of our famous Corinthian bronzes of all subjects and sizes. Corinth never amounted to much in the making of marble statues. We are not well located for it, being too far removed from the quarries. But in bronzes we have almost a monopoly. My ship carries its fair share.

"So, if you sail with me, young man, you'll be accompanied by many works of art," concluded the Captain with a broad smile.

Impressed by the efficient look of the ship and its Captain's friendly manner, Glaucus forthwith purchased two passages to Neapolis.

. . . On the day appointed for the *Bellerophon's* departure, the young couple were on board early. The vessel was not due to sail until the third hour. The Captain had warned them previously that if the breeze was fair, he might leave earlier to take advantage of it. Glaucus had packed his belongings in one chest, which was not overfull. Daphne, however, had experienced difficulty in getting her things in four chests, each larger than the single one of her husband.

"Don't scold me, dearest," she said. "If we were going away for a short visit I could have managed with one chest. Since we are leaving with little intention of returning, I have had to bring all my possessions with me."

Although the hour was early, some of their friends had already gathered to wish them a safe journey and bid them a last farewell. More continued to arrive, until finally the Captain approached Glaucus and said: "I'm glad to welcome anyone aboard my ship, but we're busy with last-minute preparations. My crew are being hampered in their work by your friends standing round the deck. So, if you will do me a favour, please ask them to say goodbye to you now. We are about to sail and require all deck-space free so that we can handle our sails."

. . . Glaucus and Daphne felt a deep emotion as they said their goodbyes to relatives and friends. Neither had travelled much before, nor had they ever crossed the sea. The thought of leaving Corinth and all it held dear to them seemed, suddenly, to be an almost indescribable tragedy. Greeks were very much attached to their homes, and banishment was one of their severest penalties.

Under the influence of a fair breeze, the *Bellerophon* gradually drew away from the quay. Voices and faces of their dear ones became fainter. The harbour was a small one; in less than ten minutes they were in the open Gulf of Corinth. The month was March, and all on board hoped that winter storms were over, that the ship would get fair winds and avoid gales and calms.

Ships' captains in those days were rather uncertain of their navigation and of the seaworthiness of their ships, so they preferred sailing near the coast. The Captain had a book of sailing directions giving a description of every mile of the Greek and Italian coastlines, and of the islands.

As the *Bellerophon* sailed north-west along the Peloponnesian coast, about two miles offshore, the young couple looked with rapture at the glorious view of Corinth and its mighty citadel, surely one of the fairest views on earth. Its principal buildings and numerous colonnades were all of marble. They were clean and dazzling in the sunlight, even those that were centuries old. There was no coal-dust to grime and befoul them. Twenty miles away, on the northern side of the Gulf, Mount Helikon reared its white head. A few miles further to the north-west, mighty Parnassus dominated the whole Gulf.

Daphne burst into tears. "How can we leave all this beauty; all that Corinth means to us? It's like going into exile. We have done no wrong."

Glaucus put his arm about her comfortingly. "I am sad, too. But remember, dear one, if our fears are not realized and the trouble blows over, we can come back. If the worst ever happens and we cannot return, how lucky we shall be to have been away from here."

She dried her eyes, and they talked of Greece, of its glories and its tragedies. Both were well-educated. Glaucus had studied for four years at Carneades' New Academy in Athens, and Daphne had graduated from a renowned girls' school in Corinth. In conversation, they forgot much of their sorrow.

Corinth, and the tiny white dot which was Daphne's home, gradually disappeared. Long after the city itself was invisible, its mighty citadel could still be seen.

"Why must there always be war, or threat of war!" exclaimed Daphne, vehemently.

"I wish I knew," said her husband. "I suppose an organized and universal world state could end foreign wars. Rebellion and civil wars would still, however, be possible. Such a world state could reduce the amount of warfare by at least two-thirds—possibly three-fourths—since there would be long intervals of peace. Some of those peaceful intervals might even last for centuries." He lapsed into a thoughtful silence. Daphne urged him on.

"The superficial reasons for war," he told her, "are well-known, but the basic reason lies in human nature. Mankind is predatory and litigious. War is the source of booty and the last court of appeal.

"Nations are born and die in war. Maybe in future generations some other way of settling differences between sovereign states will be found. But I doubt it. We who are living in this generation must make the best of it, for we cannot change from one generation to another."

"If we could change generations, dearest, which one would you choose?"

"That is not an easy question," Glaucus replied, smiling. "But, then, you never ask easy questions," he teased. "I think, though, I'd choose the age of Pericles. We Greeks were at our best then.

"There may have been greater heroes with Agamemnon on the field of Troy, and no one since has equalled Homer. But in the time of Pericles we didn't depend on a small band of heroes, nor on one great poet. We were supreme in every field: the ablest generation of the ablest race that ever lived." He said this without any thought that it might appear boastful. A Greek knew his worth, and took it for granted that he was superior to other races in everything, except in the ability to harmonize differences and create a broad political union of all Greeks. Only Alexander the Great accomplished this, and his Utopia ended with his life.

"Do you think we shall ever see Greece again? Or is this our last view of our homeland?" Suddenly Daphne's voice trembled again.

Glaucus closed his hand comfortingly over hers. "We're both young. Should times get worse, they might get better later. Why shouldn't we return some day?"

"I hope we will," she said, tearfully. "I so hope we will. Somehow I'm afraid times will never get any better for Greece. We both know that conditions have gone from bad to worse. And so far no one has found a remedy."

"I must admit the future isn't bright for Greece. World history hardly offers another example of such a swift fall from power as our country suffered. I suppose it's due to the fact that, fundamentally, we've never had a basis as a world power.

"Our land is small, our population scanty. The few Greeks who exist are divided politically. Even had we been twice as numerous, and united politically, we still would have been too few to hold world leadership for long."

"What do you think the future of Greece will be, Glaucus? I love to hear your opinions."

"I don't know, dear one. Our future does not depend upon us Greeks. The Romans will probably continue Greece as a protectorate: sooner or later they will absorb our whole country into their world state. Greece is important today only for her glorious past. Like a dead city, she will not change. Her past will then be further away, and probably more glorious and legendary than it is even to us.

"The history of Greece can be compared with a day which begins with a beautiful sunrise, is followed an hour later by a thunderstorm, and then drizzling rain which lasts until night falls."

"When do you think our night will fall, dearest?"

"Ah, that's a question only time can answer. Greece, as a glorious memory, and an insignificant present, may last much as she is now for another hundred generations. Unhappily, we can be sure of one thing—our country will never again be a world leader. I may be too positive in this statement. I mustn't forget the words of my teacher, Carneades: 'Nothing is sure; it's only probable or improbable when we speculate about things.' So I had better say it's improbable that Greece will ever be a world leader again."

"Perhaps not in politics or economics. How about our future in art?" Daphne asked.

"Your question is well put, dear one. We Greeks have rivals and superiors; but not in art. Our leadership has lasted so long and with so little challenge, that it seems certain it will last as long as our civilization.

"The world of today is half-civilized and half-barbarian. Ultimately the barbarians must be civilized. When this

298

happens, it will doubtless result in a new and somewhat different civilization from ours.

"This new civilization may bring forth new standards in art, and new artists, different from ours. Whether they will surpass the Greeks must be left to the judgment of posterity.

"It will be interesting to see the artistic works of the next two or three millennia and compare them with our own. But I fear I shall no longer be here when that time comes," he said with a smile.

"Do you regret that human lives are so short, Glaucus?"

"Frankly, *I* do," he emphasized. "But since Providence has willed it so, we must assume Providence knows best. Life itself should last a very long time, due to the unending cycle of the generations. The sun rose this morning, and I expect there will be millions of other sunrises. The present generation is here today. The world is full of young people today. It was full of young people two thousand years ago, and it will be full of young people two thousand years from now. We two, are among the young people of today. We were not here to be numbered among the young people of two thousand years ago. And even though my name be on the military rolls two thousand years from now, I shall not step forward when my name is called."

The *Bellerophon* gradually drew nearer to mighty Mount Parnassus. "It's a superb mountain!" exclaimed Daphne. "So grand and so dignified. In every way worthy of Homer's heroes. Ulysses hunted there, and it's the home of the Muses. What will we do when we can no longer go to our theatre at Delphi to listen to the voices and music amplified and softened by the protective cliffs of Mount Parnassus?"

"There will be theatres in Italy," her husband comforted. "Although none like Delphi. No theatre in Greece can compare with it, except Epidauris.

"I recall with pleasure my many happy trips to Delphi.

Now I, too, am seeing it for the last time! The first time I ever attended our theatre at Delphi I was fifteen—just old enough to be admitted. We left Corinth at daybreak but our boat was delayed, so I reached the theatre at the tenth hour, just before they began *Prometheus Bound*. I was never more impressed. The great theatre was packed with people from all over Greece as well as from foreign countries. As the noble lines of Æschylus were spoken by our best actors, their voices resounded from the towering cliffs along one side of the theatre. One who has not heard it, cannot imagine what power and resonance it gives a voice! Soon a chorus of beautiful maidens dressed in yellow skirts—some with pale blue jackets and some with beige jackets—came on to the stage. Some of their skirts had black horizontal stripes. And they all wore blonde wigs. The men were dressed in yellow, gold and red. The performance was awe-inspiring to most of us there. I, for one, shall never forget it."

It was now time for lunch, which the passengers prepared for themselves. The wind held fair, by evening they were in the Strait of Patras, where the Peloponnesus and northern shore of the Gulf of Corinth are only two miles apart. Daylight was nearly gone. As the Captain had no intention of sailing through narrow seas in the dark, the *Bellerophon* was anchored fifty feet away from shore.

A ship's dory landed passengers for a short walk to stretch their legs, and then brought them back for the night; it was safer to be on board than to camp on shore.

At dawn, the ship was on its course west. Mount Parnassus was no longer visible and by noon the Greek mainland was well to the east.

Towards sunset, anchorage for the night was made in a small cove on the eastern side of the island of Ithica, formerly the home of Ulysses.

The crew, some fifteen in number, were all Greek. Glaucus and Daphne enjoyed listening to the stories of adventure and hardship that one of the older sailors related as they sat round the fire after their evening meal.

"We were three ships," the old sailor began; "the largest carried thirty men and our two others were not much smaller, when we sailed through the Pillars of Hercules bound for the far north, where we were to get as much tin as our ships could hold. We sailed along the coasts of Hispania and Lusitania for three weeks. Then the coast trended east so we followed it for another three weeks until it trended north again. Finally, we reached the Land of Tin. There was no trouble in getting all the tin we could carry in exchange for the money and goods we'd brought from Greece, and within three months of the time we'd sailed through the Pillars of Hercules we headed back towards it. It seemed as if everything had gone smoothly. Occasional foul winds, occasional calms, occasional storms— but the storms and calms didn't last very long. Although, mind you, the season of year was daily getting more unfavourable, for we were well into autumn and big storms were expected.

"Our boats were heavily laden. There was not much shelter along that shore. The land everywhere was east of us, and we would be sure to get the full force of any westerly gale that came at us from the far reaches of the ocean. Still, the weather remained surprisingly good. Wind was fair part of the time. When it wasn't, we tacked against it, and every day brought us that much nearer. We weren't more than twenty miles from the Pillars when a sudden severe storm broke. In ten minutes there was so much spray whipped up by the wind that we could hardly see twenty feet ahead of us! The wind was north-west. Our Captain made every effort to avoid being blown ashore, so whether it was due to this or to a slight change in the wind's direction I don't know. But we escaped the shore and continued on, in a welter of foam and spray midst waves as high as our masts, for four days and four nights. Then the wind left us, the sea went down and we laid becalmed.

"For a week there was no wind, and we started to get short

of water. We began to wonder if we'd been saved from that tempest only to die of thirst. Then one day a breeze sprang up and within another day our Captain navigated within sight of land. He'd lost his reckoning during the storm; he'd no idea where we were, but reasoned that this land must be the coast of Africa. His sailing directions didn't run more than two hundred miles south of the Pillars. We soon saw the coastline —maybe it was four or five miles long—and off one end of it a small island, not more than half a mile along. There were very few trees along that coast. Prospects of water didn't seem any too favourable. The point of land and the island, however, would provide shelter from the wind from almost any direction.

"We gradually drew in towards shore and anchored in shallow water, a quarter of a mile off the island. We got our boat out, rowed to the island, but found no water on it. Our Captain signalled us to return to his ship, which we did. We upped anchor and made along the coast for three or four miles. Then the Captain sent our boat ashore again. I was in charge and as soon as we got ashore I started looking for water. We kept close together, I can tell you. Our bows and spears ready for use. No telling who might be lurking round, or what sort of reception waited for us! We went along, near to the sea, for half a mile or so, but there was no sign of fresh water, so we decided to look inland. Half an hour later we found a spring not more than a mile from shore, so we started to fill the water-casks we'd brought along.

"Hardly had we done this and set off on our return journey when a shrill whistle came from behind some rocks above us. This was answered by whistles from all directions. We were surrounded. The whistling stopped and for a short while there was an eerie silence. We stood our ground firmly, each man holding his bow and spear, ready and willing to use them if required. Within a few minutes a creature appeared from behind a rock and walked our way. It looked like a man, naked, but with a body covered with hair. He came up and spoke in some strange language none of us understood. Realizing that we didn't understand, he made signs for us to throw down our arms. This, of course, we refused to do. An angry look came over his face, or, rather, into his eyes; we couldn't see much of his face because it was covered with hair. He spoke again. It was some sort of speech, although it sounded more like an animal growl and rumbling. His hair was so long and thick on his head—in fact, all over his body—that it was hard to determine what shape of man or creature he was.

"I looked at his head closely as he spoke, and was horror-struck to find a little horn growing from the top of his head; or rather from the top of each side of his forehead. These horns were almost hidden by hair. I said nothing to the others, hoping they hadn't noticed. No use making them more nervous than they already were! The man-creature gestured savagely for us to throw down our weapons. He pointed to the surrounding rocks in an evident gesture of warning as to what would happen if we refused and he called upon his followers to attack us. I decided that matters had gone far enough. It was more than time to get back to our ship. As quick as a flash, I pressed the point of my spear against the creature's heart, and called my men to press their spears against his body—but not to hurt him unless he attempted to fight. Holding him—surrounded by our spears—we made our way back to the sea-shore.

"When he realized that we were holding him hostage—instead of the reverse—he called out to his followers. In what seemed a split second some forty or fifty of these man-creatures jumped out from behind rocks and followed us at a distance. They were all shaggy fellows, looking not unlike ape-men, and on many the horns stood out clearly. When we reached shore we got into our boat, keeping our hostage with us. We'd seen no weapon among his followers. But for all we knew they might have carried an unknown type of weapon, something

303

small enough to be hidden upon their person. No use taking chances. We soon reached our ship, and tried to take our captive aboard. None of us had any rope to bind him with, so the ship's mate threw down some rope; our captive might prove a slippery customer to take aboard unless bound securely. Our Captain and crew were mightily interested in what went on in our boat below I can tell you! A length of rope was soon dropped, and with it plenty of advice. As we started to run the rope round this man-creature he broke loose with a display of terrific strength. He dived overboard, and for a moment we could see him swimming strongly under water. We tried to follow, but lost him almost immediately. There was just enough wind to ruffle the water and make it hard to see where he was. Some of the men on ship fitted arrows to their bows and watched for his head to appear above water—but nothing more of him was ever seen. All this time his followers were running back and forth along the shore. None of them had ventured into the water to follow him or try to save him.

"Our Captain thought it wisest to leave such a place without delay. We'd managed to lug a couple of casks of water along, so sail was hoisted and in a few minutes we drew away from that island with its man-creature inhabitants and headed northwards. Four days later we reached the first landmark in our sailing instructions. We stopped for water next day, but had no further adventures. Three days later we were in the harbour at the Pillars of Hercules, none the worse for our strange experience."

. . . Later on, when they were alone, Daphne eagerly asked Glaucus: "Do you believe the old sailor's story—especially his part about a man with horns?"

Glaucus laughed. "Sailors are famous for their tall tales, and this is no doubt one of them. I don't believe any men or man-like creatures with horns exist. I think the old sailor was just spinning a yarn. And what is more, thoroughly enjoying hearing himself talk."

Next day the ship remained at anchor. A wind was blowing strongly and the sea was covered with white-caps. The Captain said: "I prefer to wait until this wind blows itself out. If it doesn't get any stronger, we could go out to sea and be confident of handling the waves safely, although it might be uncomfortable. By the time we got three or four miles from shore those waves would be fifteen feet high, and breaking with plenty of force. Still, we could manage safely, but there's no guarantee that the wind wouldn't increase. Then we might have a dangerous time of it. I'm in no haste. We'll just wait here and take things easy for a day or two."

Next morning, at daybreak, the Captain worked out a weather forecast for the following two days. The strong wind had spent itself, only a gentle breeze was blowing, and the sea no longer looked angry. He said: "Now is a good time to get across; we've just had a storm, and it's unlikely we'll have another for a day or two." He ordered the anchor hoisted. In a few minutes they were away from the island and heading directly west towards the coast of Italy.

"It's a hundred and eighty miles across the Ionian Sea; we'll have no shelter for that distance. We should be across by tomorrow evening. If the weather didn't seem so settled, I would have sailed north along the islands to a point about forty miles north of Corcyra. From this point it's only forty miles to Italy! This is the route Æneas took on his famous voyage to Italy. Like him, I prefer forty miles of open sea to a hundred and eighty miles of open sea. But I have a better boat than Æneas had; we should get across safely and save three or four days in time as well. Once we get across, we are all right. There's hardly a stretch of fifteen miles without some shelter."

In a few hours they were out of sight of land. The Captain

held his course by reference to the sun. Glaucus asked how he managed when the sky was covered with cloud. "Holding a course without markers along the coast, with no view of the sun or stars, is difficult. The best of us are apt to go astray. That's why I like to keep in sight of the coast and anchor when we can't see markers. Of course, in a narrow sea like this, even if the sky were completely obscured, there wouldn't be much trouble in making enough westing to reach the Italian coast."

"Wouldn't it be possible," said Glaucus, "to fix your location every day at noon? The height of the sun would give you your latitude—or your position north and south—and the time of day would give you your position east and west."

"Well, I suppose," the Captain mused, "our scientists and learned men will reason that problem out eventually. First, we must find some way to measure accurately the altitude of the sun at noon on board a ship. Then we must make a clock which keeps absolutely accurate time. Our finest clocks are as yet not accurate within three or four minutes of sun-time as determined by a correctly constructed sundial. And a sundial on a boat wouldn't be practical.

"For a good many years to come we'll navigate as we've always done. It's a risky profession! That we must follow the coast in order to know our position and be able to take shelter from storms has the disadvantage of giving ships but little sea-room. There's a danger they could be blown ashore in any onshore gale. Lost with all hands! If our ships were more sea-worthy, the farther from shore the safer they would be—unless they were in snug harbour."

In the late afternoon of next day mountains could be seen far ahead, and the Captain announced: "There's Italy. If the wind holds we'll be off her coast in another few hours."

. . . The following morning Glaucus and Daphne were on deck early. The *Bellerophon* was headed south along the coast of Italy, some three miles distant. This was the first foreign land the young couple had ever seen, and they looked at it with eager interest.

"Well, dear one, we've crossed the sea in safety. Now all we have to do is to sail along the coast till we reach Neapolis." Protectively he put his arm round Daphne's waist, and she leaned against him.

"How far is it, dearest?"

"Our Captain told me it was eight hundred miles from Greece to Neapolis. Of this, five hundred miles would be along the coast of Italy. He said if there was favourable weather we should make the journey from Corinth in about ten days."

All day the *Bellerophon* proceeded along the coast, sometimes eight or ten miles from the nearest shore, sometimes only a mile or two from some projecting point. The sky was blue with a few fleecy clouds, and the Captain seemed well content with its appearance.

Two days later they were "off the toe of the Italian boot". For three hours they sailed almost due west—directly against the setting sun. Just south of the sun Mount Etna gradually grew nearer. At sunset, they turned almost due north and entered the Strait between Italy and Sicily. The Captain had no intention of sailing his ship through any narrow strait in the dark, so anchored near the Italian shore for the night.

Assembling his passengers, he said: "You will have observed land ahead of us on both sides, and doubtless know the land to our left is Sicily. The strait we are about to enter is that of Rhegium. It's only two miles wide at its narrowest point, and you'll see some specially fine scenery as we pass through it."

At daybreak their voyage was resumed. The Strait of Rhegium gradually narrowed, giving beautiful views of both shores. When they were in its narrowest part, the Captain pointed out a rock on the Sicilian shore and another rock on the Italian shore, approximately opposite each other. He

307

explained that the rock in Italy was the home of Scylla, and the rock in Sicily was the home of Charybdis—about which so much has been heard.

"Where are they now?" Daphne asked eagerly. "Some say they were only a fable."

"Well, I suppose, like all fables, there had to be some origin, and this origin was based to a certain extent on fact."

. . . Scylla and Charybdis has long been a favourite legend. Poets adopted it, and the story became more and more fanciful until, finally, it was about five per cent. fact and ninety-five per cent. fiction. Its original meaning and significance, nevertheless, remains. According to the story in Homer, Scylla is a fearsome sea monster with six heads, twelve feet and a voice like a puppy's yelp. She lives in a cave in a high rock, and sticks her heads out occasionally to fish for marine creatures, and to snatch unwary seamen out of passing ships. Within bow-shot is another rock, under which lives another fearsome monster name Charybdis, who, thrice a day, sucks in and spouts out sea water. When Ulysses sailed between these two rocks, Scylla snatched six hapless men out of his ship. . . .

"None knows better than I do," said the Captain in all seriousness, "that there's some real basis for this story. It's told there's always a danger to ships which seek to pass through these narrow waters. Either one shore or the other may see the vessel driven on to it by winds and currents. This Strait, as you see, is very narrow. Winds and currents are often strong and changeable. It's possible for even the most careful and skilful of captains to find his ship in the grip of wind and current, inextricably drawn to those shores to be dashed to pieces on their rocks. Every time I go through here, I say a prayer to all the gods."

By the eighth hour of that day they were through the Strait; at the fifth hour of that night they were a mile west of

Stromboli and had a wonderful view of the active volcano. The sea was calm, and the dark night lighted only by a burning mountain was an unforgettable experience. All the passengers stayed on deck until they could no longer see Stromboli's flames licking the pitch-black sky. Four days later the south face of the island of Capri was ahead of them. And within a few hours they were in the Bay of Neapolis.

As soon as his ship was alongside her quay, the *Bellerophon's* Captain told all passengers they were free to go ashore.

Daphne and Glaucus thanked him for his courtesy during their voyage, and declared that if they ever made another journey by sea, they hoped it would be under his command.

A number of porters were standing on the quayside. It needed four of them to carry the young couple's luggage to the Customs House. Here, after a search of their effects had been made, Customs duties of some seven hundred sesterces was demanded.

Glaucus protested in vain against what he considered to be an imposition. After he had paid this amount, his purse was considerably lighter.

The Captain had recommended a certain inn as being the best in Neapolis, and before long they arrived there, more than ready to sit down to their first shore-cooked meal in ten days.

. . . Neapolis in the year 147 B.C. was a pleasant city of some fifty thousand inhabitants. The centre of Greek civilization in Italy, none of its buildings—either public or private—was particularly noteworthy. The importance of Neapolis was due to her location on the matchless Bay. . . .

Without the street-map in their guide book and the frequent questioning of passers-by, Glaucus and Daphne would not have been able to find their way round this city with its hilly,

narrow and winding streets. Speaking no language other than
Greek, they were thankful that, even though abroad, they
were still on Greek territory. Pronunciation differed from that
in Corinth, but not enough to make any real difficulty.

Their next few days were occupied sightseeing in a hired
carriage. Far from wealthy, both nevertheless felt such an
extravagance justifiable in order to learn something of their
new home. Their joint capital consisted of personal belongings
of no great intrinsic value and about five thousand drachmæ
in cash which Glaucus had deposited with a Greek banker in
the city.

"Well, dear one, what do you think of Neapolis, its Bay
and the surrounding country we have seen?" Glaucus asked
somewhat anxiously.

Daphne thought for a moment before replying. "I don't
like Neapolis as well as Corinth; it's not nearly so beautiful.
People here seem rather abrupt, sometimes almost discourteous.
I hope we won't have to live here, Glaucus. Oh, the surrounding country is lovely, I admit—almost as lovely as our surroundings at home. But I prefer the smaller places, like
Pompeii and Herculaneum. Maybe you can find some work
there, dearest."

A landscape architect by profession, Glaucus, just at the
beginning of his career, had left few clients behind. The
urgent tone of his wife's voice disturbed him. Was she unhappy so soon?

"Daphne, I more or less agree with what you say; I too
think we will be happier away from here. I'll talk to Leurides—
the banker with whom I've deposited our money. Possibly he
can advise me about finding some clients, about a home.
It isn't very comfortable for you at the inn. The sooner we are
out of there the better."

Early that evening Glaucus sought out Leurides, who
listened attentively to his problems and then said bluntly:

"Young man, it is a good thing you have some capital. If you stick to your own profession, you are not likely to be able to support yourself for some time to come. You have no reputation here as a landscape architect. And from what you tell me you have none in your home town, having only just started to practise. My advice is: try to find employment with the owner of a large villa. Someone might be able to use your services, and in return provide a monthly salary and a cottage for you and your wife. In this way you could prove your ability as a landscape architect. Later on, should you desire to leave your employer and set up in business as a consultant, you will by then know many people. Also you will have accomplished some work to which to refer possible clients. Then there's the prestige of having been employed by a rich man. I will make some enquiries for you, if you wish me to do so," he concluded kindly.

Glaucus thanked him for his constructive advice, and agreed that this seemed the best plan to adopt.

A couple of days later Leurides announced an interview was arranged with a wealthy Roman owning a large villa and estate at Herculaneum, Calpurnius Piso.

. . . At the appointed time Glaucus was admitted into the presence of Calpurnius Piso, a pleasant-looking Roman in his late thirties, although a trifle pompous in manner. He took careful stock of his applicant, and after a few minutes of questioning announced bluntly: "I like your face and your manner; you appear to know the theory of landscape architecture, even though you are too young to have had much practice. I'm without a landscape architect at present. I dismissed my former one because he had rigid ideas and I couldn't agree with him. I have ideas of my own. And since this is my land, and I intend to live here, it must be improved in my own way in landscaping and not in someone else's way.

"You seem to have a flexible mind. If you understand that I mean to have my own way in landscaping, and you wish to act as my assistant and further my efforts, instead of trying to thwart them, you and I should get along very well.

"There's a small cottage where you and your wife can live. It's on the grounds and therefore convenient for your work. I will pay you one thousand sesterces a month, and provide the cottage rent free for as long as you are in my employ. If you were an older man, I would pay a higher salary. But, after all, you have only just finished your studies and are without any practical experience."

Unhesitatingly, Glaucus accepted this offer, and assured Calpurnius Piso that he would do his best to assist with the landscape gardening in whatever manner preferred. He offered to report for work as soon as the cottage should be ready for occupation. Both he and his wife were anxious to leave Neapolis and the inn where they were staying.

The cottage would be ready next day. Glaucus could report for work immediately after he and his wife were settled in their new home, he was informed.

. . . Calpurnius Piso owned one of the largest villas in that part of Italy. Its buildings covered some ten acres, and its gardens extended along the sea-coast for over half a mile. Piso was born in Rome, the only child of a very rich father who was now Consul. He had hoped to make a career for himself in politics, but after a brief experience decided that he possessed little political ability; and since he was a man of great wealth, would be better out of political life than in it. Subsequently, he left Rome, bought some two hundred acres of land on the Bay of Naples—adjoining the little village of Herculaneum— and in recent years occupied his time building this great villa. The work had progressed well. Only some of its gardens remained to be completed. . . .

Glaucus proved himself an able assistant and a pleasing one to Calpurnius Piso, who in turn was a generous employer. One month later he said to the Greek: "We have made more progress in the last month than I made with my former landscape architect in three months. And, more important still, I have not had to use up my nervous energy in arguments."

Daphne soon settled down, happy once again, and her husband was much relieved that she so readily adapted herself to this new environment.

Their cottage was half a mile from the main villa. Unpretentious but comfortable, it was on higher ground than the villa itself, and had an even finer view of the Bay of Naples. They were permitted the use of a small vegetable garden and supplied with all the milk and fruit they desired. They seldom had reason to leave the estate; apart from occasional long walks, they preferred being in their own little home together when Glaucus was not working.

One Sunday they decided to visit Pompeii. The distance was only nine miles, and there had not been sufficient time to see its sights when driving through the city on their first visit. They went leisurely along the sea-shore and within a couple of hours' time were passing through the Salt-Makers' Gate.

Glaucus became acquainted with two prominent citizens of Pompeii when they visited Calpurnius Piso and he was asked to show them round the estate. He received an invitation to visit them whenever in Pompeii, and now asked Daphne if she would care to call on either one.

At first she demurred. Rather a shy young woman, she was never anxious for any company other than that of her husband. Strangers made her nervous.

"Dear one, I'm a professional man with our living to earn. Some day I expect to set up as a consultant and shall need clients. If we live like hermits, we'll find it harder to

313

attract the attention of prospective clients; or of their friends. Nobilior, who gave us this invitation, may not need any land-scaping done now. But he knows many people. Some of them, some time, might require the services of a landscape architect. When they do, I hope they'll remember my name."

The wife looked at her husband and smiled. "How wise you are, dearest," she said. "And how silly I am."

Before long they were knocking on the door of Nobilior's house in the Vicus Tocosa. A porter opened the heavy entrance door, Glaucus gave their names and the object of their visit, and he assigned a page to take the couple to Nobilior.

It was the first town house on a large scale that the young couple had seen in Italy, and they looked around with eager curiosity as they passed through it.

Nobilior was relaxing on a couch at one end of the *peristylium*, reading a book, when they entered. He rose and greeted them warmly: "Welcome to my house, Glaucus. I suppose this lovely creature with you is your wife, whom I am now to have the pleasure of meeting?" After their introduction, he asked: "And how do you like Pompeii? We are a strange mixture here—Samnite, Greek and Roman. My house, as you can see, is not pure Greek either in architecture or decoration. It's more or less a mixture or adaptation of all three styles. In Rome you will see many pure Latin houses, in Capua purely Samnite houses; while in Syracuse you can see houses that are practically identical with those in Greece. Here we are on the borderline, with Romans and Samnites to the north of us and Greeks to the south."

"Who are the Samnites?" asked Glaucus. "I have heard about them, but I don't know whether my information is authentic."

"The Samnites," Nobilior explained, "are a warlike tribe who inhabit the mountainous centre of southern Italy. They speak Oscan, a dialect of Latin. They are related to the Latins."

Nobilior's house, they discovered, contained many works of art. To the practiced eye of Glaucus these were of good quality, and he complimented his host's taste. The two men soon became engaged in a discussion.

"It is surprising," said Nobilior, "that Calpurnius Piso, certainly one of the richest men in Italy, takes such little interest in collecting objects of art. He seems to have no thought for anything except architecture and landscaping. To my mind, a really great villa such as his needs to be adorned with great works of art."

"Piso, being a Roman, is more concerned with directing building and in laying out gardens and roads than in collecting statues and paintings," said Glaucus. "As I understand it, Romans are never particularly concerned with works of art; although I believe in the last few years some small collections have been formed. The average Roman today is aware of the value of a work of art even if he has no desire to possess such a thing. They are always conscious of ancestry. Many Roman patricians own one or more portrait-busts of their ancestors done in wood, plaster, earth, bronze or marble. From a portrait to a fully-fledged statue is only a short step, as you will doubtless agree."

"What do your artistic circles in Corinth think about art and artists nowadays?" Nobilior questioned.

"We-ell—you can divide them into schools of thought," Glaucus replied after a moment. "One school says everything new and modern has great artistic value, and everything done in past generations is more or less inferior. The other school, equally numerous, says that modern art is completely degenerate and of no artistic value or significance. The one school more or less says there were never any artists before the present generation, and the other school insists that the last good artist was born three hundred years ago."

"What is your personal opinion?" His host smiled.

"I try to strike a happy medium. I believe art is a continuous process and that no particular generation of artists has a creative monopoly.

"An archaic artist cannot project himself forward through several generations and create work of the Golden Age. Nor can any artist born generations after the Golden Age recapture its spirit and technique. The difficult question, of course, is how to date these periods.

"Everyone agrees the Archaic Period ended before the Parthenon was built. Our artists who created that architectual masterpiece might have marked the beginning of the Golden Age in Greek art. How long does a Golden Age last? From what we know of Egyptian art, they may still be in their Silver Age after thousands of years."

"I don't believe," said Nobilior thoughtfully, "that Egyptian art is significant for the development of Greek art. It was held in a rut by religious and governmental influence, whereas Greek art was free. And your art may change more in one century than that of the Egyptians in a millennium. How would you, yourself, date these periods? Do you think Greek artists are still in their Golden Age?" He drew the younger man out.

"I often ask myself that question. Some of our modern artists and critics believe that our art today equals or surpasses anything of the past. The Temple of Diana at Ephesus is, in its present form, an achievement of the last one hundred and fifty years. Nearly everybody claims it far surpasses the Parthenon. Our best modern sculptors inject more life and meaning into marble or bronze than artists did at the time of the Parthenon. Still, I suppose there is no gain without some loss.

"I readily admit our best sculptors and painters of today do not have the same nobility of expression or matchless simplicity as their predecessors. Possibly they are too far away from the

316

Archaic Period. They are weak where the Archaic artist was strong, and strong where he was weak.

"Modern artists have reached a mastery of technique, but in doing so have lost some of the majesty and simplicity of those who went before them."

Eloquence and clearly defined opinions in so young a man as Glaucus appeared to amuse Nobilior, who said, smiling broadly: "By this time you must both be ready for your lunch."

After an excellent meal, they all observed the accepted routine of an hour's siesta. Nobilior then showed them some of Pompeii's sights.

At the Forum, the civic centre, he explained the history and significance of the various buildings, shrines, and statues which embellished it.

"I cannot make claim," he said, "to anything outstanding; nevertheless, its total effect is pleasing. And if we consider the size of this city—twenty thousand inhabitants—it's indeed a creditable effort for a little place like Pompeii. As you will notice, our Forum is about a hundred and twenty feet wide, about five hundred feet in length, and runs exactly north and south. It's completely surrounded by this portico with its columns of travertine, on which, as you see, there's a loggia composed of smaller columns.

"On the south side of this square are bronze and marble statues of the most civic-minded of our citizens of both this and past generations. On the west side, is our Tribune for those orators who wish to address the citizens. This portico and loggia, I believe, add greatly to the beauty of our square. But there is one drawback—to some extent they hide the buildings fronting on it.

"If you look around you can see the Temple of Jove, and, just beyond it, Vesuvius rears its head menacingly even though its flanks are covered with beautiful forests of chestnuts.

"That building straight ahead of you is the Curia, our town hall. Pompeii is a compact little city. No part of it is more than fifteen minutes walk from where we stand.

"Our Forum—here in front of us—is the centre of our religious, civil, political and economic life. Nearly all our principal buildings are located here. Most of them are of rather recent construction. The Temple of Jove was only completed some three or four years ago.

"We can boast many well-to-do citizens, but no one possessing a great fortune. I have no doubt that Calpurnius Piso has more money than have all the residents of Pompeii put together!

"Our citizens make a fair profit on the not inconsiderable trade which flows through here. A well-known fish sauce invented locally, the monopoly of Pompeii, has also brought us some prosperity. We cannot complain about hard times here, and for that I'm grateful.

"If you would care to see our theatre, it's only a few minutes' walk."

The young couple found their host instructive and interesting and were pleased indeed to see Pompeii under such expert guidance. Its theatre, of Hellenistic design, was similar to the one in Corinth, but not as beautiful. It had seating for about five thousand spectators. Seats were all in the open; in case of rain a canvas cover was stretched across the entire theatre.

Later, whilst driving back to Herculaneum, Daphne asked: "Dearest, of what nationality or, rather, of what race is Nobilior?"

"Greek," replied Glaucus.

"I thought so!" she exclaimed. "His Greek sounded too good for any Roman. Yet I understood he was a Roman." Her husband patiently explained. "Yes, dear one; he is a Roman and also a Greek. He's Greek by race and Roman, politically. There's an interesting story about him, and I think it's true. He was once the slave of a certain Roman patrician, Nobilius by name, who lives in Rome. Nobilior, by means of his intelligence, hard work and fidelity, rose to the position of business manager for Nobilius. He became well-to-do himself, and eventually purchased his freedom. Preferring Pompeii to Rome, Nobilior bought a house here—the one he now lives in—and settled down to the life of a gentleman of leisure. The 'or' at the end of his name indicates his connection with Nobilius."

"He's a fine man," declared Daphne. "His house is very different from any average house in Corinth. It's impressive and quite luxurious inside. But our Corinthian houses are much nicer; they haven't that shut-in look. Its outside walls are starkly bare—without any windows. And inside, everything was built round the small courtyard and the big courtyard."

A few weeks later Glaucus came to his wife with an unusually grave expression on his face. "Have you heard from home lately?" he asked.

"No; I haven't," she replied. "Is anything wrong?" He turned his head to hide his sudden tears.

. . . The impossible had happened. Corinth was captured and sacked. The Romans, maddened by the opposition offered and believing that Corinth's citizens were to blame, showed no mercy. They decided to make an object lesson of Corinth to show the rest of Greece what would happen, if and when they dared to thwart the will of Rome.

Corinth's inhabitants were killed or sold into slavery; their works of art were carefully catalogued and removed; their beautiful city was given to the flames. The works of art were shipped to Rome, with the exception of a few sculptures, which were distributed to certain Greek allies of the Romans.

Mummius—the Roman General—was granted a triumph by the Senate. In his procession many of Corinth's works of art were paraded through the streets of Rome. Among these was the statue of Herakles, from the Peirene Fountain, which had been a silent witness to the courtship of Daphne and Glaucus.

After the triumph, these works of art were disposed of. A few were retained by the Government, but most were sold at auction for the benefit of the Army treasury. Among them, the statue of the young Herakles. . . .

. . . For some time Glaucus had been trying to awaken an interest in Greek art in the mind of his employer. Calpurnius Piso came to agree that works of art were a necessary part of a fine home. But he possessed none.

Together, they paid one or two visits to art dealers in Neapolis. When Glaucus informed him that few, if any, of the objects displayed were, in his opinion, first rank, Piso decided to await better opportunities.

News of the "Sale at Auction of Works of Art from Corinth" was a splendid opportunity to build an important collection. The Greek told his employer such a chance might come only once in a lifetime, and persuaded him to attend the auction in Rome with a view to acquiring some of the items offered for sale. Piso, however, would not consider buying any work of art without the Greek's opinion as to its quality and suitability. So the two of them prepared to leave for Rome.

Daphne, when told of the impending journey, begged to be taken along.

At first Glaucus demurred. But Piso, a kind-hearted individual always ready to give happiness, said: "If you don't mind a hard non-stop journey, you will be welcome. We shall ride to Rome, and plan to reach there within three and a half days. I hope you are at home on horse-back?"

"I have ridden a good deal," Daphne assured him. "I'm

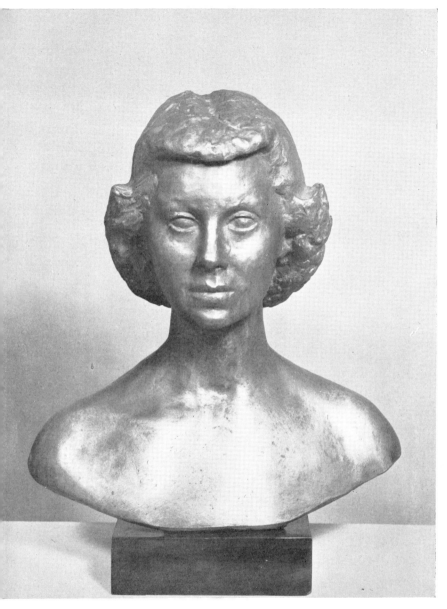

BRONZE PORTRAIT-BUST OF ETHEL LE VANE (1953)
NOW IN RANCH MUSEUM

"LEDA AND THE SWAN"

(Chapter "England: a Gainsborough—and a Roman Statue")

certain I shall be able to keep up with you." She looked appealingly at her husband.

A few days later they were at Piso's town house in Rome.

. . . Many art objects were to be sold at the auction, which was due to start an hour after daybreak and continue until sunset.

On the first day Piso bought several bronze statues. He and Glaucus were both surprised at the number of people present and the active bidding. Many items he bid for were lost to competitors who continued bidding after Glaucus decided the price was high enough.

Before the beginning of the auction the Greek advised his employer to set a limit on each item. If others desired to bid above this limit they were welcome to do so. "It's bad psychology," Glaucus told him, "to keep bidding in a flurry of competition. Most works of art are not priceless. There's no point in paying more than a fair price merely because some uninstructed or stubborn person bids more than it's worth. If we come across any original works by any of the great masters of three centuries ago, I shall advise that you forget about price and buy it—no matter how high. These bronzes—in fact, everything we have seen or bought today—are modern copies and should be valued as such. Some of the bidders here will have a rude awakening if they ever try to re-sell their acquisitions."

The auction was scheduled to continue for an entire week. Each day Calpurnius Piso and his landscape architect arrived at its opening and stayed until it closed; and each day their list of acquisitions grew longer.

Bronze statues were sold during the first three days, marble statues and miscellaneous items during the latter three days.

Daphne went to the sale on its opening day and intended to be present when marble statues were being offered. She said to her husband: "If our Herakles is auctioned, promise me you'll persuade your employer to buy it. The thought of our city's treasures being dispersed among strangers saddens me. When I think of what has happened to our relatives and friends . . . " She burst into tears.

Glaucus, trying to console her, had to fight down the emotion which had shaken him, day after day, as he saw the art glories of his native city brought to the auction block.

On the final day of the sale, the statue of Herakles was one of the first works to be offered. Bidding was brisk and Glaucus, representing his employer, did not enter the contest till only two or three bidders were left. Its price was already up to ten thousand sesterces. A few more offers brought it up to fifteen thousand. Piso's bid was successful at fifteen thousand five hundred. Two or three other purchases were concluded during that day, and thus the sale ended. Corinth's art treasures were scattered to the four winds.

. . . "Well—how do you like our purchases?" Piso asked Glaucus as they walked through the narrow streets of Rome on their way back to his town house.

"I think you now have a good nucleus for a collection. Everything is of first-rate quality. True, they are modern: it was disappointing to find none of the original works of the old masters being disposed of. I suppose the Government, acting on expert advice, is retaining them all. We have seen some active bidding this week, but it is nothing to what would have taken place had there been an original work by Phideas or Polycletus. A sculpture by either one of these masters would have fetched a million sesterces."

Daphne was delighted to find that their old friend the Herakles now belonged to Piso, and would be set up with other statues on his estate at Herculaneum.

"Just think," she said; "once Herakles is standing in the gardens we can sit beside him again—like we used to do in Corinth. I don't know whether I'm glad or sad! In a way I'm glad he's come to join us, but at the same time I'm sad he isn't home in Corinth with everything just the way it used to be. Do you think we'll ever know what has happened to our friends and families, Glaucus?"

"I doubt it, my dear one. Unless we meet an eyewitness. I still find it difficult to understand why I had such a strong presentiment to leave Corinth. Certainly it was due to Providence rather than to any logical thinking."

. . . A month later the Pentelic marble statue of Herakles stood on a terrace beside a fountain, and overlooking the sea. Purposely, Glaucus set him as closely as possible to the way he had stood at Corinth. Nearly every afternoon, as the sun was setting he and Daphne met to sit a while beside their friend.

"I wonder what Herakles is thinking," she said happily one day. "He looks at us so steadily and good-humoured—there's something friendly about him. He appears so competent—capable of performing the things he's said to have done."

Glaucus smiled, and tightened his arm around his wife's slender waist. "He looks about thirty years old, and I suppose that is his actual age. It must be about thirty years ago when he was fresh from the sculptor's studio and set up in our Forum at Corinth. I'm just about his age, I wish I could hope to hold my strength and figure as long as Herakles will hold his! We cannot guess the future: maybe we shall outlive him, but it's much more likely that he will outlive us. And he'll still be looking, with those kind and steadfast eyes, at people both young and old of distant generations. What strange sights Herakles may see, and what new and different languages he may hear, we cannot even guess. All we know, my dear one, is that at this particular moment in time we three are contemporaries."

. . . Within a few years' time Glaucus set up in business for himself. As a landscape architect and contractor he enjoyed a modest success.

Daphne and he lived simply and happily together. And to the end of their lives never regretted making that momentous journey from Corinth.

. . . Successive generations of Pisos were born, grew old, and were eventually gathered to their fathers. But the Herakles never seemed to grow old. In Herculaneum he still stood on the terrace, beside the fountain and looking toward the sea—a strong young man carrying a club and wearing a lion skin. . . .

In the years to come a Roman Emperor, Nero, a friend of art if not of man, paid a visit to the luxurious villa of his friend, the young Calpurnius Piso of Herculaneum.

He was welcomed cordially, entertained to lunch, and after their siesta his host showed him round the estate

Piso remembered a story told by his ancestors: a love story of a young couple named Glaucus and Daphne, and how the Herakles standing upon his terrace once stood in the Forum of Corinth, a silent witness to their romance and courtship.

Now, approaching the terrace, he entertained the Emperor with this story.

Nero, who prided himself upon his knowledge and love of Greek art, examined the statue carefully. "It is a good work," he proclaimed, "and almost old enough now to be called an antique. I admire it far more than the older 'Bearded Herakles'. There is a calm confidence in this young man that I find quite inspiring."

Calpurnius Piso was no diplomat, but he rose to the hint. "I would consider it a favour, Cæsar"—he bowed—"if you would accept this statue as a slight token of my regard and esteem. Both for you personally, for all you have done for art, and as a tribute to your own great artistry."

His gift was accepted without further ado, and within a few days the Herakles was once again on its road to Rome.

. . . Nero's new palace, at that time being built in Rome, was shortly afterward completed. When the Emperor moved in he announced: "Now I am housed as a man should be."

Piso's gift was set up in the palace gardens among other works of Greek art.

For some unknown reason, Nero took a great fancy to the young Herakles, and used this young man of marble as his audience when rehearsing roles he was going to play in the theatre. To his friends the Emperor explained: "Herakles inspires me. He overcame great difficulties successfully, and so will I. We appear to be about the same age, and I can claim that our figures are somewhat similar. Like me, he bears a good-humoured expression. We could almost be brothers."

. . . Within a few short years Nero was no longer Emperor. His palace was dismantled, his gardens became the site of new buildings and streets.

The statue of Herakles was moved once again, this time to the Campus Martius. There the young Herakles observed Roman youths at their play and martial exercise. Time passed; many Emperors rose to power, ruled wisely or badly, and then made way for their successors.

And now Hadrian occupied the throne of the Cæsars. Hadrian, the great traveller, had come to a time of life when the inconveniences of ancient travel made him loath to take long journeys. He was an enthusiastic builder, and near Tibur, or Tivoli, began to build a country villa. One day the statue of the young Herakles was moved there.

Romans were noted as builders of homes, from simple country houses to the most ornate, extensive and palatial country homes. Many generations of rich Romans vied with each other in adorning the landscape of their ancient world with villas. Some of these—such as the Villa of the Papyruses at Herculaneum—were so grand and extensive, and held so many art treasures, that it is difficult for anyone of later generations to imagine such wealth and splendour.

Hadrian set his mind upon building a villa to surpass everything ever created before. The site was well-chosen and covered some one hundred and eighty acres, about sixteen miles east of Rome. For a number of years the resources of Hadrian—richest of Roman Emperors—were devoted to this work until completed.

The results staggered the imagination of his contemporaries. Even the "Golden House of Nero" seemed a cottage by comparison. The villa was so splendid and on such a vast scale that no Emperor or Roman millionaire could afford to live there. After Hadrian's death, it was maintained as a show-place until the dissolution of the Roman Empire.

Of Hadrian the traveller, Spartian relates: "He created in his villa at Tivoli a marvel of architecture and landscape gardening. To its different parts he assigned the names of celebrated buildings and localities, such as the Lyceum, the Academy, the Prytaneum, Canopus, the Stoa Poikile, the Tempe; while, in order that nothing should be wanting, he even constructed a representation of Tartarus."

The edifice was truly on a gigantic scale; its largest room was one thousand and twenty feet long and three hundred and thirty feet wide. To walk through the villa itself took over an hour. It was, nevertheless, a quiet and restful place for the Imperial traveller, who was weary of long journeys.

Its Latin and Greek libraries testified to its master's love of literature; the vast collection of statues, paintings and other works of art to his taste and energy as a collector. Here were gathered more collector's items than were ever assembled before or since.

. . . Some sixteen centuries later the greatest King of a great people built the largest and finest of modern palaces. If one has visited Versailles and Hadrian's Villa at Tivoli, one may reach the conclusion that, great as was the achievement of Louis XIV, it was surpassed both in grandeur and in artistic quality by the villa of "The Little Greek". After all, the King of France was only a King; his resources in money and in art could never match those of Hadrian. Yet with all the unexampled grandeur and magnificence of Hadrian's Villa one felt—everywhere—its classic charm and restraint. . . .

Hadrian was the most sophisticated of all Roman Emperors. Well-informed on almost every subject, he prided himself upon his judgment and intelligence in matters of statecraft, economics, military matters and art.

He did not over-rate his ability in these subjects. In statecraft, he was the first to see that Rome was in danger of being over-extended militarily; so he shortened the Empire's frontiers, which had reached their greatest extent under Trajan. The new frontiers were chosen with an eye to defence. The move marked the end of Roman expansion, which had lasted for five hundred years.

Rome reached full maturity during Hadrian's reign. A student of economics and political science, he relieved Rome from the burden of war. Taxes were equalized, trade was stimulated through wise legislation and economic and just administration. He believed in seeing things with his own eyes, and although ancient travel was uncomfortable—even for an Emperor—he spent half of the eighteen years of his reign in travel.

The greatest builder who ever lived, Hadrian was a capable architect and took an active part in laying out cities and designing buildings. As an art collector he has never had an equal before or since. Worshipping at the shrine of Greek art, he devoted much time and vast sums of money in trying to encourage a Greek revival, both economically and artistically.

In spite of all his efforts, however, Hadrian was unable to rekindle the Grecian spark. Greece remained poor; industry and commerce failed to flourish; Greek sculptors and painters of his day were unable to rise above the artistic level of their own generation, which was by then far advanced in the period of Greek decadence.

The best Greek sculptors of Hadrian's time were capable of making good facsimiles of works of the Golden or Silver Period of Greek art when ordered to do so—as is shown by the wonderful copy of the "Hermes of Praxiteles" at Olympia. This copy is so good that opinion is divided as to whether or not it is the work of Praxiteles. But it is probably an exact copy made by order of Hadrian to replace the original, which presumably found its way to Rome probably in the time of Nero, since Nero had a house at Olympia and was a great admirer of the works of Praxiteles.

Hadrian's own taste in sculpture was inseparably part of the taste of cultivated men of his own generation. He admired the powerful works of Greek sculptors of the fifth century B.C.—the Golden Age, and of the fourth century B.C.—the Silver Age. He liked the work of Hellenistic sculptors extending from the death of Alexander in 323 B.C. to his own day.

All first-class sculptors were Greek or pupils of Greeks. It was taken as a matter of course that Romans possessed no outstanding gifts in the fine arts.

The statue of Herakles proved itself a great favourite of Hadrian's. Had he lived some five hundred years earlier he might have been less enthusiastic about this work. Doubtless he would have objected to the weakness of the face. But he was a child of the late Hellenistic, and this disturbed him not at all.

. . . The young Herakles was destined to remain at Hadrian's Villa near Tivoli for a long time. During its first two centuries this palatial residence was well maintained. Later on, however, the Emperors were not rich enough to keep it up.

Four hundred years after Hadrian's reign the famous edifice was partly destroyed by a barbarian army. The Dark Ages had set in and such a villa was of no use or interest to anyone. Dust of the centuries gradually covered most of it—in some places to a depth of thirty feet.

The Dark Ages were finally succeeded by the Middle Ages and these in turn by the Renaissance. Mankind was again enlightened. For the first time in a thousand years the remains of Hadrian's Villa, which were still visible above the ground, attracted attention.

A certain amount of digging for buried art treasures took place. Some were found, but the villa and its grounds were so vast and extensive that most of the works of art remained undiscovered.

In the latter half of the eighteenth century, however, excavations were again resumed. More treasures were unearthed, among them the statue of the young Herakles. This sculpture, fortunately, was relatively undamaged.

. . . The Herakles came into the possession of an aristocratic Italian family. Later it changed hands again, eventually to be sold in 1792 for six hundred pounds to an English nobleman— the Marquis of Lansdowne, who was then acquiring an important collection of ancient marble statuary for his London home, Lansdowne House in Berkeley Square.

He considered this Pentelic marble statue one of the gems of his collection, in which it remained for one hundred and sixty years.

Then, like many other choice works of art, the young Herakles from Corinth, silent witness to the courtship of Daphne and Glaucus, to worlds long since gone, and to man's age-old struggles, followed the sun westward to the New World.

· II ·

A Stroll along Minerva Street

IN August of the year *Ab Urbe Condita*, 810, Nero Aheno-barbus, or "Red Beard", had been Emperor for two years and eight months.

For centuries his character has been severely mauled by the historians. His name became a synonym for ruthless cruelty; he was charged with the persecution of Christians, evil government and outrageous personal behaviour. He has, however, some apologists. Suetonius and Tacitus, the two foremost anti-Neronians, were sympathizers with the political party which opposed Nero. Their treatment of the Emperor indicates a lack of objectivity and balanced judgment.

It is no doubt true that Nero's personal conduct was bad; it is also true that he had no interest in good government. Like many other rulers, he did not realize the responsibilities of his office, nor understand that rank and power were given him to protect the people he ruled.

For the defence it may be said that his cruelty, when compared with the organized horror of the modern world, involved few people. His seizure of property is also modest when compared with the deeds of contemporary confiscators. The charge of buffoonery levied against him because he associated with actors and actresses and took part in the theatre and ballet is relatively unimportant. He was accused—no doubt justly—of gross personal extravagance.

To Nero's credit, however, is the fact that he loved peace and loathed war; in other words, he was a pacifist. His personal expenditure, excessive though it was, meant less to

330

Rome than the cost of even a minor war. Much of this wealth was spent on fine buildings, works of art and public festivals to be enjoyed by the Roman people.

His taste in art—or that of his advisers—was discriminating. Every work of art found and traced back to Nero has been of excellent quality and taste. The Empire was well administered during his reign. And, above all, Nero was both intelligent and magnanimous in his gift of Roman citizenship to the Greeks.

. . . The Vicus Minerva in Neapolis was lined with dealers in antiques and works of art. The Emperor strolled down this narrow street accompanied by friends. An enthusiastic and critical collector, he seldom missed an opportunity to visit the art dealers in any cities through which he travelled.

He was a rather stout young man of medium height, with a fair complexion, blue eyes and reddish blonde hair. Born on December 15th, A.D. 37, he was at the time of this incident twenty years of age.

. . . A marble statue of a deer attacked by hounds displayed in the show-room of Possildo—perhaps the leading art dealer on Minerva Street—attracted his eye. As Nero paused to look Possildo ventured to speak to his Cæsar.

After offering his humble respects and devotion he volunteered the information that this marble group was the master work of Dikretes, a Greek sculptor from Alexandria.

The Emperor examined the work carefully, while his friends and the dealer anxiously awaited his verdict. It soon came. "Nothing to rave about," he proclaimed. "The work is a little too stiff—it lacks artistic balance. The proportion between deer and dogs is wrong. It was a waste of time and money to ship such a statue all the way from Alexandria. I am sure there must be many a local stone-cutter who wouldn't have done worse."

Having thus disposed of the work of Dikretes, Nero now

331

turned an observant eye on other works of art displayed in the show-room. Seeing nothing which excited his enthusiasm, he asked whether Possildo had any real collectors' items at hand. Perhaps something in his back room, something the art dealer might be saving for an important collector! Or maybe something being held back as an investment?

Possildo regretted that his collection contained no work of art worthy of such a discriminating collector as the Emperor; unfortunately, his little shop had nothing else of importance.

"Well," said Nero, "you probably know what the other art dealers in Neapolis have. Is there anything of quality I can see anywhere in these parts?"

Possildo thought for a moment and then replied: "I can take Cæsar to someone who has a small marble Venus which might be of interest."

Nero said he would like to see this statue, so the dealer led the way to a neighbouring shop.

The Venus was a Pentelic marble statue, seven-eighths life-size, representing the goddess stepping out of the sea, wringing sea-water from her hair.

Again there was an anxious wait while the Cæsar closely examined the sculpture. He soon gave his verdict. "A rather good work, pleasing rather than great, but good enough for me to ask its price."

"The price is seven thousand sesterces, Exalted Cæsar," the dealer, Trimalchio, told him.

Nero pretended to fan himself, as though in need of air. Caustically he remarked that this statue was doubtless of Pentelic marble, but he wondered if there was any gold hidden anywhere in it to justify such a price!

Trimalchio thereupon launched into a eulogy of the work. It was an important piece of antique Greek art, he insisted.

Nero questioned this statement, maintaining that the statue did not appear to be more than a hundred years old; which would hardly qualify it as being antique. Trimalchio admitted, diplomatically, that his Emperor must assuredly be right, although he himself would have judged this work to be quite two hundred years old.

"Well, Trimalchio, I will compromise with you and agree it is probably a hundred and fifty years old. But, mind you, I do not think this adds anything to its commercial value."

Realizing that the Cæsar enjoyed bargaining, the dealer replied: "I have a reputation for fair prices, and would not reduce my price for anyone save such a discriminating collector as the Cæsar. It will indeed be an honour for me to add a work of art to your fine collection! I therefore offer you the Venus for precisely the sum I paid for it—four thousand sesterces."

"Done," said Nero. "My secretary here will pay you your money. Please take the statue to an address he gives you. . . . I would like you two dealers to keep your eyes open for any really important work of Greek sculpture. Such works are becoming extremely scarce. Here, however, in a centre of the old Greek civilization, there are no doubt a few great sculptures still hidden away in country villas. They might, perhaps, be bought if a high price were offered. Do you know of anything that is of top quality? Mind you, I don't want rubbish."

Neither dealer knew of anything good enough for their Emperor, but promised to keep their eyes open. They asked for details of what period and which artist their Cæsar was most interested in; whether he preferred bronze or marble; or if a painting would suit his taste as well as statues.

Their questions gave Nero an opportunity to expound his views, theories and opinions on statuary and paintings.

Other art dealers on the Vicus Minerva had heard news that their Emperor was visiting Trimalchio's, and by this time a small, inquisitive group gathered outside the little shop, and were privileged to hear their Cæsar speak.

"I do not follow the views of any particular authority on

333

this subject," the Emperor declared. "I am young, so naturally have not studied sculpture or painting over a long period of years. I have, all the same, had time and opportunity enough to form my own opinions, and get good advice from many teachers and authorities. But do not hold them responsible for my theories.

"I like sculpture better than painting. This may seem a radical preference to you. Nevertheless, there are good grounds for my belief. To me, even the best of our paintings—works by Apelles and Polygnotus—do not attain the excellence of the best sculptures. There is a certain lack of freedom and power in paintings as compared with works in bronze or marble. Of course, paintings have an advantage in being profound studies in colour, light and shade. Even then, I prefer the finest statue to the finest painting.

"I like best the statues made by Pythagoras; and next to him, those of Phidias. Next to Phidias I like those of Myron. In my opinion, this period was the peak of Greek art. Ever since then the Greeks have gone downhill—very slowly at first, and then more rapidly. Scopas, Praxiteles and Lysippos are somewhat freer and more realistic in their working of marble. But they have lost some of that marvellous simplicity and majesty which ennobles the works of Pythagoras and his contemporaries.

"In the last three hundred years, I do not think Greek sculptors have produced a single statue of really first-rate artistic quality. It is true that both on the Greek mainland, and on the islands, there have been many well-known and successful sculptors whose work has found a ready acceptance among all collectors. This, however, was more from necessity than from choice.

"If a collector limited himself to the works of Pythagoras, he would have no collection—for such works are unobtainable. The people of Athens would rather their city was burnt down than lose the statue by Pythagoras in their market-place!

Our sculptors today—and even our dealers in sculpture—are all Greek. Any artist or dealer who is not Greek would have to change his name and call himself a Greek in order to obtain clients. Dancing girls must be Syrian or pretend to be Syrian; sculptors likewise must be Greek or pretend to be so.

"Today, there are probably twenty sculptors for one such artist in the time of Pythagoras and Phidias. They all compete with each other for the prize of excellence; yet none of their work is comparable with that of Pythagoras, Phidias or Myron. Why is this? I offer you my humble opinion. Periods occur, in the development of every art. There is always a Primitive Period, a Golden Age, a Silver Age and a Period of Decadence.

"No man can control the date of his birth; therefore an artist born in the Primitive Period cannot be compared with one born in the Golden Period. Nor with another who was born in the Period of Decadence. I repeat that an artist born in our age—which is an Age of Decadence—can never equal in quality the work of an artist of the Golden Age. I do not know the reasons for this; nevertheless, we all recognize it to be the truth, even though most of our modern artists do not like to believe it.

"I have spoken much about Greek art and made no mention of the art of my own people. I am as fond of Greek sculpture as any man, yet I freely admit never having seen a Greek portrait-bust which surpassed a good Roman one in life-like representation. This is the one branch of sculpture in which we Romans have nothing to fear from anyone. I am speaking now of statues and paintings: not of architecture.

"There are many fine buildings in Greece, yet I do not consider there is anything in that country which surpasses—or even equals—some of our Roman buildings. We Romans can claim equality with the Greeks in architecture.

"I prefer Greek marble for sculptures. Statues worked in Greek marble appear more life-like than those worked in our

335

Italian marble. The Parian variety rather than the Pentelic is my personal choice, although it is claimed there is but little to choose between them.

"Do not ever try to sell me any sculpture as being Greek if I can see that the marble is Italian! I consider any statue made in Italy during the last century Roman—no matter if its sculptor was of the Greek race or not. A Greek statue is made in Greece, of Greek marble, always."

The art dealers and the small crowd of people who had gathered outside Trimalchio's little shop respectfully applauded their Cæsar's eloquence. Then they stepped aside as, accompanied by his friends, Nero continued his stroll along Minerva Street towards the beach.

. . . The Pentelic marble statue of Venus was placed in the peristyle of Nero's great villa at Antium, where it was destined to remain for nearly nineteen centuries. During this period of time the Emperor's villa was invaded by both barbarians and the sea, and eventually buried beneath many feet of water. What was left of the structure and its contents rested there.

About a century ago, a row-boat, which had gone out after a storm, drew near to the shore and its occupant, a keen-eyed fisherman, noticed a glint of white in the depths of the water. His curiosity aroused, the man was not satisfied until he recovered the object. It proved to be the marble torso of a woman. He took the statue to a local dealer in antiques, who purchased it at once.

In the dealer's opinion, which was supported by experts, it was an exquisite torso of a statue of Venus; and an ancient marble. The absence of head, arms and lower limbs was doubtless due to the zeal of early Iconoclasts, who considered it their bounden duty to destroy—or mutilate—all statues of pagan divinities.

. . . In the years that followed "Venus with the Looking

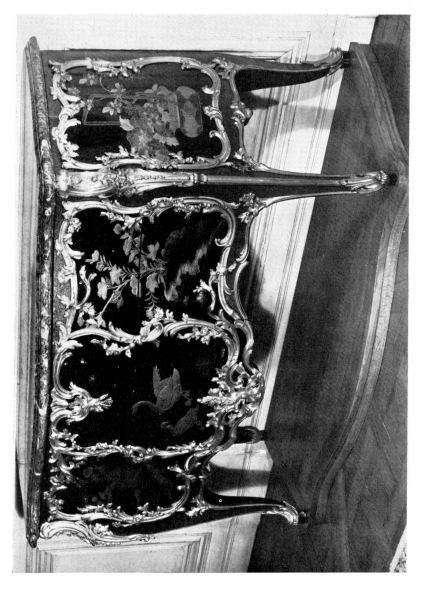

BLACK LACQUER COMMODE, LOUIS XV PERIOD,
FORMERLY IN THE SIR A. CHESTER BEATTY
COLLECTION, LONDON

(*Acquired 1955*)

LOUIS XV BUREAU PLAT—DATED ABOUT 1730—FORMERLY THE PROPERTY OF A COL-
LECTOR IN ST. PETERSBURG, LATER IN THE SIR A. CHESTER BEATTY COLLECTION

(Acquired 1955)

Glass", or "Aphrodite" as she is perhaps better known, found her way to Barsanti's Galleria in Rome, and thereafter to the American's ranch museum in Santa Monica, California.

Is it too far removed from the realm of possibility to suggest that this torso of a small and delicately formed woman might be the remains of a seven-eighths life-sized statue of Venus, bought by the Emperor Nero from the dealer Trimalchio of Neapolis, nineteen centuries ago?

After all, she *was* found in the sea. And on the exact site where Nero's great villa, which time and the elements have since destroyed, once stood.

· III ·

The Emperor's Birthday

IT was the tenth hour of the day, two hours before sunset. A group of citizens of Nola, a small town some twenty miles from Neapolis, gathered together near the statue of Demeter, in the Forum, to discuss the choice of a suitable birthday gift for their Emperor, Augustus. The discussion proved lively—in keeping with the meridional temperament of Nola's inhabitants. Augustus was revered, and the choice of a gift was far from easy. He was fond of works of art—any first-rate collector's item would be sure to please him, they knew. Such items, however, were difficult to find in the market, and still more difficult to buy, since the price of an important work would doubtless be far beyond their means.

All classes of society were represented at the meeting, even to a senator with a Greek slave as his secretary. There were two or three knights, but the majority of those assembled were men of the professional and tradesman classes. As was usual at such gatherings, a scattering of what might be termed ne'er-do-wells joined in the discussion: although they could subscribe nothing but their time. The senator and knights were distinguished from the lower ranks by their clothes: a broad stripe on the tunic for a senator; a narrow stripe for a knight.

"A tapestry would be acceptable," proposed a knight who praised the excellent workmanship and artistic design of tapestries woven at Alexandria in Egypt. Such works of art were fashionable, and Augustus would be sure to appreciate a first-class example, he maintained. Its price would probably be in the region of ten thousand sesterces. His sister had bought

338

such a tapestry for this amount not long ago—a panel ten feet by sixteen feet in size, representing the Calydonian boar-hunt. The Mayor of Nola said that there were many available tapestries, but only one Empress. A fine portrait-bust of his wife would assuredly give more pleasure to Augustus than any other work of art. This suggestion found favour, and a subscription of ten thousand sesterces for such purpose was opened.

After some further discussion as to the procedure to be followed, a committee was appointed to select a sculptor—preferably a local artist—and to arrange his fee, the cost of the marble, transportation of the finished work, and, finally, its presentation to their Emperor.

Three of the assembled citizens, M. Porcius Elvitor, F. Marcus Lahunal and J. Claudius Feron, were nominated and approved as members of the committee. They were charged with carrying out this work at a total cost not exceeding ten thousand sesterces within the time-limit imposed by the Emperor's birthday—which was about six weeks hence.

The crowd dispersed while the committee conferred. There was only one local sculptor of repute. Their choice therefore lay between him and other artists of equal or greater repute living in neighbouring cities. Finally, they decided to employ the local sculptor, Leochares, provided he could undertake the work for a price within their budget. They decided to call upon him immediately.

It was a few minutes past the eleventh hour, and the sun was already low in the horizon. The western end of the Forum was shaded from the sun's rays by the magnificent and recently built baths of Augustus. Its eastern end was still in sunlight, and this combination of light and shade lent interest and beauty to the many works of art and fine buildings which, with three acres of marble flooring, constituted the principal public square, or forum of Nola. Statues, fountains, porticos, all richly supplied, were mostly the work of contemporary artists:

339

or at least of artists living within the preceding century. The statue of Demeter was the one exception, being of Greek origin and some two hundred and fifty years old.

The finest statue in Nola—a gift from Augustus—stood in the Shrine of Diana, where it was protected from the elements and also from public view. Only on ten days of each year was this shrine open to the public and the statue of the goddess on view.

Life-sized, in Pentelic marble, Diana was depicted fitting an arrow to her bow, with an eager hound at her feet. The face of the goddess was that of a beautiful woman, yet such was the mastery and faith of the sculptor that even the most insensitive observer could feel that here was indeed the countenance of a divinity.

The sculptor was Kalamis. During the four centuries which had elapsed since the work was completed, it had commanded universal praise and admiration. That such a great and priceless example of the Golden Age of Greek sculpture was to be found in a small town like Nola was proof—even more so than its magnificent baths—of the affection in which Augustus held his birthplace and family home. It was often said that many a great city would celebrate a three days' public holiday if this statue of the goddess ever came into its possession.

The committee were deep in discussion of statuary as they approached the Shrine of Diana. Feron remarked that their task would be easier if Kalamis were still alive, and still living in Nola. They would then be assured of a great work of art as well as a good likeness.

Elvitor replied that he had never heard of Kalamis creating any living portraits. For a good likeness, he preferred contemporary artists with their realism to the old Greeks with their idealism.

Lahunal did not speak. His mind was preoccupied with the distribution of the ten thousand sesterces set as a budget: so much for the marble block, so much for the sculptor. And then

340

there was freight and handling! He must find out how much the freight to Rome would be; and how long it would take to ship the portrait-bust there. Should they transport the completed work direct to Puteoli, take it with them on the boat from there to Ostia, and then cart it to Rome? Or should they drive straight along the Via Appia and take the marble portrait with them? It all had to be planned very carefully indeed.

In a few minutes they had reached the workshop of Leochares and were enquiring for the master. Soon a short, stocky, middle-aged Greek stood before them. He was well-known to the committee, who lost no time in disclosing the nature of their mission. They impressed upon the sculptor that their budget must include not only his services, but, in addition, the marble and delivery of his completed work in Rome within six weeks.

Leochares was delighted to be entrusted with such an important assignment. It was a tribute to his character and skill.

His workshop was small, since he did most of the work himself, his only help being two young apprentices. Three or four marble statues, examples of his art, were displayed for prospective clients. Copies of Greek works of the third and fourth centuries B.C., they lacked some of the grace and simplicity of the originals. But they were nevertheless fine examples of sculpture.

Leochares, himself, preferred statuary of the fifth and sixth centuries B.C. Most of his clients, however, preferred work of the third and fourth centuries B.C., because it was more realistic and dramatic. It was a sophisticated age, and the extreme simplicity of Greek sculptors of the fifth and sixth centuries B.C. was rather too severe for Leochares' clientele.

Feron was the committee-man best versed in sculpture. He now entered into an animated discussion with Leochares as to the type of portrait-bust they required. It must be life-size, or seven-eighths life-size: a striking likeness and a work of art at the same time.

341

This was always difficult to accomplish, the sculptor declared. A faithful likeness was seldom a great work of art. A sculptor must put something into his subject in order to transform it from a mere representation into a work of art.

Accepting this commission gladly, Leochares said that he would do his utmost to satisfy both them and their beloved Emperor. There was, however, one difficulty to overcome. In order to secure a life-like portrait, it would be necessary to have at least one two-hours' sitting from the Empress herself. How could it be arranged?

This presented an unexpected problem. After some discussion, the committee decided to write to their Empress, explain the situation, and crave her indulgence in order to make such a birthday gift to their Emperor possible. No time was lost in dispatching this letter.

After three days had elapsed, a reply arrived indicating that the Empress Livia would receive her subject, the sculptor from Nola, upon his arrival in Rome.

. . . The Via Appia, leading straight from Nola to Rome, carried a heavy traffic in travellers and goods. Mounted men walked and trotted their horses to or from Rome, while the occasional messenger or post-carrier proceeded at a gallop, with frequent changes of horses available at post stations located every five miles along the road. Great two-wheeled carts with wheels six feet in diameter, drawn by two to four oxen, carrying freight of all descriptions, were a common sight. Some of the country folk used wagons drawn by oxen to take their farm produce to the nearest market town.

The Via Appia was only sixteen feet wide; just sufficient room for two big carts to pass each other. Carriages drawn by one or two horses were in common use; but a modern observer would have been astonished by the large number of pedestrians.

Leochares was familiar with this scene, having made the

journey on several previous occasions. Inns were frequent along the road, travel was easy, and after a pleasant ride of four days he arrived in Rome.

. . . The House of the Empress Livia on the Palatine was a commodious villa such as any well-to-do Roman patrician might have lived in, with none of the pomp and grandeur of an Imperial residence.

Livia preferred life in the villa to life in their palace on the Palatine Hill, for it was quieter and more to her personal taste. Augustus spent as much time as was possible with his wife. They tried to live as normally as any ordinary married couple.

At the main entrance of the villa a *guardia*—or doorkeeper— was in attendance. Leochares showed his credentials—the letter he had received from Livia's personal secretary. Could the man find out when it would be convenient for the wife of Cæsar to give him a sitting? he asked. The *guardia* directed him to wait. Within a few minutes he returned with the information that the Empress would receive the sculptor at noon on the following day.

At the stated hour Leocharis was ushered into a comfortable but not ornate sitting-room. The sculptor from Nola presented himself to his Empress, who had been engaged in dictating letters to her secretary.

Livia at thirty-five years of age was a typical Roman patrician, giving the impression of energy and distinction. Of medium height and slender figure, her features were regular, her eyes dark and penetrating. If it had not been for a certain expression of ruthlessness in her face, she might have been called beautiful.

She smiled pleasantly, extending her hand in welcome to Leochares, who immediately felt at ease. He had brought with him a wooden board and a small sack of clay—enough to model head, neck and shoulders. The Empress asked whether

343

she could continue to dictate while he made his model. Leochares replied that it would be no handicap whatever, providing she could spare him an occasional minute or two of motionless sitting.

Under the magic of the artist's fingers the shapeless lump of clay soon began to take on a likeness of the Empress. In less than two hours the rough clay model was finished.

Livia became increasingly interested as she saw this likeness to herself emerging from the clay. As Leochares prepared to depart she complimented his talent, and said she was eagerly looking forward to seeing the completed work.

After covering the bust with a damp cloth in order to keep the clay moist, the sculptor carefully carried it out to the waiting carriage which was to drive him to a friend's workshop, where he had arranged to make a plaster cast from the bust. It would have been impracticable to transport a clay model from Rome to Nola.

. . . Gerontes, the Roman sculptor, examined the bust with professional interest when it was brought into his workshop. "You have secured a good likeness of our Empress," he said, greeting his friend warmly. "Leave it with me, and tomorrow morning you shall have your plaster cast."

He was as good as his word. Next day Leochares and the plaster cast were both on the Via Appia, headed for Nola.

Back in his little workshop, Leochares began the actual work of cutting the marble. A suitable block of Carrara marble of statuary quality had been selected, so, using the plaster cast for reference, his senior apprentice commenced to chip the stone.

Within a few days a rough outline of the portrait-bust was achieved. Leochares then took over the work, which now required the skilled hand of a master of the sculptor's art.

Day after day, chipping and drilling continually, and using a great variety of tools, the sculptor worked. Ten days after the

"THE NATIVITY" BY BENVENUTO DI GIOVANNI, A
FIFTEENTH-CENTURY SIENESE MASTER

(*Acquired 1955*)

"THE DEATH OF DIDO, QUEEN OF CYPRUS" BY
RUBENS

(Acquired 1955)

ANCIENT GREEK BRONZE STATUETTE (490–480
B.C.) OF ZEUS

(*Acquired 1955*)

LOUIS XV ORDERED THIS COMMODE AS A GIFT
FOR HIS DAUGHTER LOUISE. IT WAS MADE IN
1769 BY JOUBERT, THE ROYAL CABINET-MAKER.
FORMERLY IN THE SIR A. CHESTER BEATTY
COLLECTION

(Acquired 1955)

plaster model had reached his workshop the marble version was completed.

Leochares studied the work carefully, anxious to observe if in the translation from plaster to stone any of the life-like quality and artistry of his clay model had not been transferred to the marble. Noting a few places, he proceeded to model the marble until satisfied that he could do no better.

. . . The committee, when informed that the work was now finished and awaiting their inspection, arrived without loss of time.

Almost a month had passed, and the Emperor's birthday was now only two weeks' distant. They wanted to have Livia's portrait-bust safely in Rome several days ahead of the date, in order to run no risk of delay.

"Well, gentlemen, what do you think of it?" asked Leochares with pride.

The three men inspected the marble silently for several minutes. Feron, as always, was the spokesman. "I have seen our Empress only two or three times, and then only from a distance. As far as I can tell, this seems to be a good likeness."

The other members agreed. Discussion then began as to whether the portrait was a work of art in addition to being a good likeness. The sculptor listened anxiously. He was relieved when, after some reservation by Feron as to the treatment of Livia's hair, all unanimously agreed that in so far as they were concerned, Leochares' portrait was a work of art of satisfactory quality and good enough for presentation to their beloved Emperor.

The sculptor beamed. "Gentlemen, I have done many portrait-busts, and I honestly do not think I have ever done a better one."

. . . The committee of three men from Nola arrived at the Intendent's office in Rome fifteen minutes before the time set

Y   345 for their appointment with Augustus. The portrait-bust of Livia was with them, carefully wrapped to prevent any damage.

The Intendent greeted them courteously, directing that they wait for a couple of minutes. Then a Palace functionary accompanied by two slaves appeared, and asked the visitors to follow him.

They passed through a doorway into a corridor leading into a guard-room some twenty by thirty feet in size. Here a group of soldiers were posted. The three men from Nola were searched for concealed weapons: a package carried by the two slaves was also inspected. The group then followed their guide into a large waiting-room filled with people who sought interviews with their Emperor. Several clerks were busily engaged in processing their requests. A loud hum of conversation filled the air.

The Palace functionary made his way through this room to a door at its far end, which, at a word from him, was opened by a guard. The committee then found themselves in a second waiting-room, similar in size to the first one, only with fewer people present and a secretary's desk in one corner. They passed directly through this room into a hallway. At a word from the Palace functionary, a huge Nubian slave opened a door. The three men from Nola entered a fairly small, simply furnished room. This, they were told, was the private library and study of the Emperor Augustus.

The room was empty, so the visitors took this opportunity of observing its furnishings. An Egyptian carpet of attractive but subdued design covered the floor. A representation of the Gardens of the Academy of Athens, and portraits of the Seven Sages of Greece hung on the walls. Below each portrait was a favourite quotation of the Sage. Hardly had they finished their brief inspection when a curtain was drawn aside and the Master of the World entered.

. . . Augustus at the age of forty-three was quite a handsome

346

man, tall and athletic in figure. He was dressed in the simple tunic worn by most men of his time for everyday wear; only the band of royal purple proclaimed its wearer to be the Emperor. The committee were introduced. They then proceeded to inform him that his citizens of Nola, holding him in high esteem and affection and deeply conscious of the many favours shown to them in the past, had, at a public meeting, voted to make this presentation on his birthday. It was but a slight token of their gratitude, respectful loyalty and devotion. They earnestly hoped their humble gift might find favour in their Emperor's eyes.

At a word from the Palace functionary Livia's portrait-bust was revealed.

Augustus studied the work of Leochares' with keen interest. After a few minutes he said: "It is indeed a good likeness of my dear wife, Livia. I sincerely thank you and Leochares, who is an artist Nola can be proud of. Please tell my people of Nola that I am deeply touched by their remembrance of me, and that I hold them, as always, in my sincere affection."

. . . The three men were escorted out of the Palace by the same route as they had entered. As they left the Palace precincts behind them, Feron, most imaginative member of the committee, exclaimed: "What an experience it's been! Face to face with Augustus Cæsar! What a great man he is; so kind, so simple and unpretentious. He seemed to be genuinely touched by our gift. And by the thought that his people of Nola hold him in such veneration."

His two companions nodded their agreement as Feron continued: "It's been fortunate for Nola that he has so taken it under his favour! I was present when our Emperor—by divine intercession—escaped death in a great storm. Many around him were killed by the lightning bolts, but he escaped with no harm. Since that occasion, it has been said Augustus felt his life was spared in Nola.

347

"Have you ever thought how fortunate we are to live in these times when all men are united under our wise and beneficent ruler?" he asked his companions. "We know from history that in the old days the world was divided politically. There were city-states and nation-states, each one jealous of its political authority. States were allied with and against each other, and twenty armies stood ready to spring at each other. No man was secure from aggression—either his life or his property.

"We Romans cannot hope to claim equality with the Greeks —or some of the other races—in artistic achievement. But at least we can claim that Rome has brought world peace and political union. And no one today has any fear of losing life or property by aggression, unless he ventures into wild and distant regions beyond the reach of our law.

"It's true there are barbarian tribes in thick forests beyond the Rhine and in the distant north, outside our union. They are as uncivilized as the desert tribesmen far to the south, in Africa; they are also beyond our borders. The distant Orient, with its Persians, Indians, and Chinese, is outside our union. But there is no risk of their ever threatening our territories. No one within a thousand miles of us is not part of the same state!

"In the old days nearly every river marked a political frontier, with soldiers keeping watch. And any traveller who crossed was searched and questioned. Goods and merchandise taken over the frontier were subject in most cases to heavy Customs duties, often causing delay and vexation. How could trade be expected to prosper and flourish under such handicaps? I'm glad we are living now, instead of in the old days. I only hope our successors continue in the same happy condition of peace and political unity that we now enjoy," Feron concluded his oration to his understanding audience.

The committee reached their inn, packed their luggage, paid

their bill, mounted their horses and headed cheerfully for Nola. As they jogged along they sang in unison a well-known travel song of robbers and Customs' agents which had come down to them from the bad old days.

. . . Leochares' portrait bust of Livia remained in the villa of Augustus on the Palatine Hill in Rome. After Augustus joined his ancestors and his ashes had been placed in the great mausoleum in the Campus Martius, his home and its contents were maintained as a museum. As long as Roman power endured, this home of the founder of the Roman Empire was kept as a memorial. Its small size and lack of ostentation contrasted forcibly with the magnificent palaces of some of his successors.

After the fall of Rome the Dark Ages began. The Classical world, with its heritage of five thousand years of civilization, was replaced by a world of barbarians. The villa of Augustus was of no use to them, and dust of the centuries gradually covered it to a depth of twenty feet. Since it had been built into a hillside, so that its rooms would be warm in winter and cool in summer, none of it remained above ground after a few centuries.

As the chapters of history succeeded each other, gradually the barbarians were civilized. After a lapse of a thousand years mankind again became interested in the life of Augustus, who did so much for the Roman Empire, and of whom it is said that: "He found Rome brick and left it marble." The patron of Virgil and Horace and inspirer of the glories of the Augustan Age became a revered memory. But several centuries were still to pass before his villa was excavated.

During these excavations a few marble sculptures were found, including a portrait bust of Livia.

Epilogue

By Ethel Le Vane

"MINE is one of the very few portrait-busts of the Empress Livia now extant which show her as a young woman," Getty broke the somewhat lengthy silence.

The hot sun of Greece had bronzed his face, his eyes were never bluer, his serious expression was lightened by anticipation as he went on: "Back at the ranch in Santa Monica, Mueller, I told you how I had acquired the Livia—together with the little torso of Venus. Both came from my usual dealer, Barsanti of Rome."

Cured of his sciatica attack and slimmer in girth after a course of stringent treatment at Ischia, the Dutchman looked up at the American. They were sitting on a stone step at the entrance to Pompeii's impressive House of the Fawn in Via della Fortuna, whose original occupants had been swept into oblivion when Vesuvius erupted almost two thousand years ago.

Pompeii, by day a hive of sightseeing activity, at dusk again became a deserted city. The *guardia*, on his patrol, stared with unconcealed curiosity at the two men on their improvised seat, absorbed in a sheaf of papers. "Crazy Americans!" He shrugged his shoulders, as if to ask who else could be crazy enough to spend hours in such discomfort and with no protection from the strong afternoon sun.

Mueller's eyes began to blink as he handed the many pages of typewritten manuscript back to his companion. "I'm sorry," he apologized, "I didn't hear what you just said. These stories transported me into other realms. I shall always envy you that visit to Greece. What an adventure! And how much ground you covered in that short spell. No wonder you were inspired to write! To satisfy my curiosity, how did you find the time to write, as well as to research all the factual data in your stories? You were sightseeing all day. You must have worked every night and far into the night. . . ."

What would this man have been in life, what would he have achieved—as an individual—had he not inherited a vast business empire and the responsibilities great wealth carries with it? thought the Dutchman.

Getty seemed to read his companion's mind. "The translation of thought into the written word has always fascinated me. Had I had the time and opportunity necessary to harness my meagre talent and my imagination, I might have developed into a professional writer." He went on: "I'll share my secret with you, Mueller. I was always avid for learning—fired with an ambition to gain knowledge and have the authority to relay it. In other words, in my youth I dreamed of becoming a worthy, perhaps even a renowned, college professor." An expression of regret clouded his face. His voice dropped into such low pitch that the Dutch art dealer was compelled to strain his ears in order to pick up the American's concluding sentence:

"Even with the magic wand of great resources at one's disposal, Mueller, one's dreams rarely come true."

Index